Dalmatian
P·R·E·S·S
an imprint of dalmatian publishing group

LEGENDS OF POP

Published by Dalmatian Press, an imprint of Dalmatian Publishing Group.
Copyright © 2007 by Dalmatian Publishing Group, LLC

Produced by Hylas Publishing, 129 Main Street, Irvington, NY 10533.

Publisher: Sean Moore
Publishing Director: Karen Prince
Art Directors: Gus Yoo, Brian MacMullen
Editorial Director: Aaron Murray
Senior Editor: Ward Calhoun
Project Editor: Sylke Jackson
Editors: Suzanne Lander, Rachael Lanicci, Lisa Purcell
Designer: Eunho Lee
Proofreader: Gabrielle Kappes

ISBN: 1-40373-720-7
16561-0607

07 08 09 10 SFO 10 9 8 7 6 5 4 3 2 1

LEGENDS
of POP

DEREK CANEY

CONTENTS

INTRODUCTION

Early one Tuesday morning, in a quiet Philadelphia suburb, two kindergarten children coincidentally brought records to school for show and tell. One toted ABBA's "Dancing Queen," the favorite from her collection. And the other presented Elton John's "Philadelphia Freedom." Although it's fair to say that their classmates were more familiar with the Mickey Mouse Club theme song, both of these songs had everyone in the class up and dancing. The kids responded physically and emotionally to the music

Or maybe it was the animal crackers.

Whatever it was, for the class full of 6-year-old children, there was no cool music, hip music, lame music, or commercial music. It was all just pop music—music that came on the radio that, in some divine act of democracy, was liked by everyone.

One definition of a pop legend is an artist who fundamentally changes the vocabulary of not only music, but culture. So when you introduce an equation like popular culture + Stevie Wonder, you don't merely get the symmetrical result of Stevie Wonder + popular culture. In effect, you get a whole new culture, one in which the old ways of describing and defining seem inadequate. Elvis Presley, the Beatles, Ray Charles, James Brown, and Michael Jackson all fall into this category.

Many of these stories are still being told. Ten years from now, we're likely to be viewing the careers of Gwen Stefani, Eminem, the Dixie Chicks, and Jay-Z with the same reverence that we now pay Madonna, the Beastie Boys, Garth Brooks, and Run-DMC.

Some stories were over much too soon but lasted long enough to create a new language. Clyde McPhatter's hit-making string lasted only about six years. But in that time, he would usher in a new era of harmony singing with the Drifters that took its cues from gospel group singing of the '40s. In eight years, Sam Cooke took the language of gospel, turned it into soul music, and set the benchmark against which all rhythm and blues would be measured.

A few artists may not have made their mark on the sales charts, but contributed in ways that pure numbers don't recognize. Jackson Browne and Carole King represented the zenith of the singer-songwriter movement of the '70s. Many would follow in their footsteps, but few would match the quality of their finest work. And Moby added the cult of personality to the relatively anonymous world of techno. His skill and talent opened up the genre to pop audiences.

Some bands were more influential than successful. Sly and the Family Stone had three #1 hits between 1968 and 1971, but that doesn't even begin to explain the scope of their influence on pop music. The O'Jays and their conspirators at Philadelphia International picked up the torch from Sly and became the standard bearer for dance music in the '70s, helping to usher in the disco era. Curtis Mayfield seized on Sly's darkest messages and turned them into social commentary with a beat that wouldn't quit.

Some are legends simply because their star power was undeniable even if their music wasn't necessarily influential. At his peak, Rod Stewart was one of the most talented white rhythm and blues singers, but this wasn't the only skill that made him one of the biggest stars of the '70s. His star power was equally the result of his larger-than-life image and the songs he sang. In this sense, he was the perfect prototype for the Spice Girls and Britney Spears.

Image and sex appeal have proven vitally important elements in the careers of pop stars. Madonna, Janet Jackson, and even the Monkees presented personas that had a powerful effect on their audiences. Some groups like Duran Duran capitalized on music videos, and others like ABBA and Elton John used performance stunts or wild costumes in their live concerts. By whatever means, many pop legends know how to get attention and speak to the masses.

The public's connection to pop music is often evocative of a specific time period. Some artists represented a moment so powerful that, even though they didn't have long careers, their music defined an era. Donna Summer is synonymous with disco. You can't even think about the '80s without conjuring up images of Boy George, Annie Lennox, or George Michael. And En Vogue, Mary J. Blige, and TLC provide a virtual soundtrack for the '90s.

Supporting characters show up in these pages as well. People behind the scenes sometimes have a significant influence on an artist's work. An understanding of this influence can illuminate gradual shifts or decisive turning points in a performer's development. In some instances, visionary moguls shaped the music as much as the artists themselves, whether it's Ahmet Ertegun and Jerry Wexler, the architects of Atlantic Records, or David Geffen, one of the most powerful figures in music. Producers like Quincy Jones or singers like Darlene Love are legends unto themselves.

The artists included in this book have shaped pop music as we know it today. Each band can be seen as one of 100 stories or as a ripple in the oncoming tide. Pop music is a snapshot in time. In 10 years, the picture will be completely different. But, hopefully, the kindergartners will still be dancing.

Janet Jackson took creative control of her career and became a pop legend in her own right.

ABBA

ABBA was a defining force in the pop culture of the '70s. Shimmering costumes and lavish concerts, were always part of the package. From the opening notes of their debut single "Waterloo," they established a treasure trove of infectious melodies, charming vocal turns, and clever arrangements. With two dramatic singers up front and crafty songsmiths behind, they would have 18 straight Top 10 hits in the U.K. and become one of the most beloved bands of the decade.

Guitarist Bjorn Ulvaeus and keyboardist Benny Andersson were a songwriting team in Stockholm in the late '60s when they met Agnetha Faltskog and Anni-Frid "Frida" Lyngstad. They collaborated with one another by contributing songs, musical backing, production or vocals to their respective projects. Faltskog and Ulvaeus would get married in 1971.

Under the name Bjorn & Benny, Agnetha & Anni-Frid, they had a modest hit in Sweden in 1972 called "People Need Love." After finishing third in the annual Eurovision Song Contest (a sort of *American Idol* of its time) in 1973 with "Ring Ring," they changed their name to ABBA and won the competition the following year with "Waterloo." The song topped the charts in the U.K. and went to #6 in the U.S.

After eight years of marriage, Ulvaeus and Faltskog grew apart and would divorce in 1979. But since the split was amicable, ABBA would still crank out blockbuster hits including "The Winner Takes It All." Andersson and Lyngstad were married in 1978, but divorced in 1981 and the band broke up a year later.

Since the breakup ABBA's popularity has only grown, helped by cult films like

FROM LEFT: BJORN ULVAEUS (GUITAR, VOCALS), AGNETHA FALTSKOG (VOCALS), ANNI-FRID LYNGSTAD (VOCALS), BENNY ANDERSSON (KEYBOARDS, VOCALS). ABBA PERFORMS AT THE MIKE YARWOOD CHRISTMAS SHOW IN LONDON IN 1978.

The Adventures of Priscilla, Queen of the Desert, and *Muriel's Wedding*. ABBA would become hip again in the '90s and '00s (and downright revered in gay circles) with tribute bands like Bjorn Again and the massively successful Broadway musical *Mamma Mia*, which is set to ABBA's greatest hits.

Thank You for the Music

After ABBA split, Ulvaeus and Andersson would cowrite the concept album *Chess* with lyricist Tim Rice in 1984, which yielded the Top 10 single "One Night in Bangkok" by Murray Head in 1985. They adapted the album into a musical that opened in the West End of London in 1986 and ran for three years. It was a flop, however, on Broadway when it opened in the U.S. in 1988. The two collaborated on a Swedish musical in 1995, which ran for three and a half years in Sweden.

Frida made the Top 20 in the U.S. in 1982 with the single "I Know There's Something Going On," which was produced by Phil Collins and got a fair amount of play on MTV.

Faltskog would have a minor hit with "Can't Shake Loose" in 1983.

GREATEST HITS

YEAR	SONG
1974	"Waterloo"
1975	"S.O.S."
	"Mamma Mia"
1976	"Fernando"
	"Dancing Queen"
	"Money Money Money"
1977	"Knowing Me Knowing You"
	"The Name of the Game"
1978	"Take a Chance on Me"
1979	"Does Your Mother Know"
1980	"The Winner Takes It All"
1981	"One of Us"

CHRISTINA AGUILERA

December 18, 1980–

"I'm the one who can sing," Christina Aguilera once boasted, distinguishing herself from the new crop of pop stars to arrive in the late '90s. And indeed, Aguilera has a strong voice, capable of impressive vocal gymnastics. She cites such influences as Aretha Franklin, Billie Holiday, and Etta James, though some think her sound resembles the more recent generations of R&B singers, like Mariah Carey and Whitney Houston, rather than the gospel and R&B sources that influenced them.

Aguilera got her start at the age of 8 on *Star Search* a talent contest in the mold of today's *American Idol* without the hype. She garnered a role as one of the younger cast members of the Mickey Mouse Club in 1992 and 1993, along with Britney Spears, Justin Timberlake, J. C. Chasez, and actress Keri Russell. In 1998, she contributed the song "Reflection" to the Walt Disney movie *Mulan*, which she parlayed into a contract with RCA Records.

Riding the crest of a teen pop wave, Aguilera topped the charts four times in two years, beginning with "Genie in a Bottle" and "What a Girl Wants." She would also land on the Top 10 with a cover of Labelle's "Lady Marmalade" from the *Moulin Rouge* soundtrack, performing with Lil' Kim, Mya, and Pink.

Like many female pop singers of the '80s and '90s, Aguilera offered a contradiction between her ambitions to be taken seriously as singer and an artist, and her image on stage and on magazine covers as a sex kitten. Will she follow in the footsteps of powerhouses like Madonna and Janet Jackson to create a career of lasting achievement? Stay tuned.

"Women should feel empowered in their sexuality, not want to cower down or hide themselves because of what men have put onto us throughout the years"—Christina Aguilera

CHRISTINA AGUILERA IS ONE OF THE MORE TALENTED SINGERS OF THE NEW CROP OF YOUNG STARS.

Awards:
1999 Grammy Award, Best New Artist
2001 Grammy Award, Best Pop Collaboration with vocals, "Lady Marmalade"
2001 Latin Grammy Award, Best Female Pop Vocal Album, *Mi Reflejo*
2001 MTV Video Music Award, Best Video of the Year, "Lady Marmalade"
2003 Grammy Award, Female Pop Vocal Performance, "Beautiful"
2007 Grammy Award, Best Female Pop Vocal Performance, "Ain't No Other Man"

GREATEST HITS	
YEAR	SONG
1999	"Genie in a Bottle"
	"What a Girl Wants"
2000	"I Turn to You"
	"Come on over Baby"
2001	"Lady Marmalade"
2002	"Beautiful"
2003	"Can't Hold Us Down"
2006	"Ain't No Other Man"

BEACH BOYS

1974–

FROM LEFT: CARL WILSON, DENNIS WILSON, BRIAN WILSON, MIKE LOVE, AND AL JARDINE PICTURED HERE IN LONDON, IN 1964. THE BEACH BOYS PEDDLED IDYLLIC IMAGES OF WHITE MIDDLE-CLASS SURBURBAN LIFE.

It starts with a dream world—a world where your biggest worry is your father taking away your car keys—and your biggest ambition is a tasty wave to ride to shore. But as you get older, your dreams become more modest: "hold each other close the whole night through." And then comes desperation: "God only knows what I'd be without you."

GREATEST HITS

YEAR	SONG
1963	"Surfin' U.S.A"
	"Surfer Girl"
1964	"Fun, Fun, Fun"
	"I Get Around"
	"Dance Dance Dance"
1965	"Help Me Rhonda"
	"California Girls"
1966	"Wouldn't It Be Nice"
	"Good Vibrations"

Such is the story of Brian Wilson.

Like the Brill Building songwriters who preceded him, Wilson purveyed homilies of teen life. But rather than the urban stories rooted in the black experience peddled by Jerry Lieber and Mike Stoller, Wilson was selling a white middle-class suburban experience of surfing, cruising, and finding romance. And few were better at telling those stories than Wilson. Luckily for Wilson, his two brothers, Carl and Dennis, cousin Mike Love, and family friend Al Jardine were also up to the task.

Carl Wilson was one of Chuck Berry's greatest guitar disciples this side of Keith Richards. Although he possessed a limited range, lead singer Love would give Brian Wilson's words a conversational tone. The beat was held down by one of Los Angeles' best session drummers, Hal Blaine. Brian's soaring falsetto would seal the deal, making the Beach Boys one of the top-selling acts of all time.

Between 1963 and 1966, they would have 15 Top 10 hits. But in 1967, in the wake of their early success, Brian Wilson had a breakdown that prohibited him from touring. He would instead become the main creative force in the studio. Inspired by the Beatles' *Rubber Soul*, his productions became more layered and ornate, reaching a peak with the landmark *Pet Sounds* album.

The album would bid farewell to Wilson's idyllic images of youth and betray a more fearful view of the world, like "Wouldn't It Be Nice," "God Only Knows," and "I Just Wasn't Made for These Times."

The Beatles' *Sgt. Pepper's Lonely Hearts Club Band* would one-up *Pet Sounds* and in turn inspire Wilson to up the ante with an elaborate production called *SMiLE*, which eventually collapsed along with Wilson's mental health.

With the help of a controversial therapist, Eugene Landy, Wilson reunited with the Beach Boys for *15 Big Ones* in 1976, which featured mostly cover songs. He would appear in a somewhat embarrassing television special produced by *Saturday Night Live*'s Lorne Michaels, but after the *Love You* album in 1977, he retreated from the limelight. He would not be productive again until his 1988 solo album *Brian Wilson*.

In the meantime, the rest of the Beach Boys weren't faring any better. In 1983, Dennis Wilson drowned after diving off a boat in a drunken stupor. Fifteen years later, Carl Wilson died of lung cancer.

Mike Love still tours under the name of the Beach Boys with a rotating cast of sidemen. Love parted ways with the only other surviving founding member, Al Jardine, in 2005. Wilson has made a number of solo albums of varying degrees of quality.

The three surviving members do perform together on occasion, including the 40th anniversary of *Pet Sounds*. Nevertheless Mike Love and Brian Wilson seem to be in a constant state of litigation against one another over songwriting credits, promotional rights, and what one another had for breakfast on any given day.

The Landy Years

After *SMiLE* imploded, Brian Wilson gradually withdrew from the band and into his own world of drugs, junk food, and mental illness. The family called upon controversial therapist Eugene Landy, who, depending on whom you believe, was either a life saver or a hustler.

BRIAN WILSON WAS THE DISTURBED GENIUS BEHIND THE BEACH BOYS' BEST MUSIC.

Landy engineered Wilson's first recovery in 1976, which led to a reunion with the Beach Boys and an accompanying album *15 Big Ones* and tour. By 1982, Wilson had ballooned to nearly 300 pounds. His increasing cocaine habit led Landy to put him on a regimented plan to recovery. He eventually got healthier and began a solo career.

Landy's methods were thought to be unorthodox as they included high dosages of psychotropic drugs. He also went beyond the boundaries of traditional therapy to include co-songwriting credits and management of his client. Wilson sued Landy to regain the rights to those songs. Landy lost his license to practice psychology in California. He died of lung cancer in 2006.

DENNIS WILSON, AL JARDINE (TOP), MIKE LOVE, BRUCE JOHNSTON (MIDDLE), CARL WILSON, AND BRIAN WILSON (BOTTOM) LOUNGE IN 1966, AT THE TIME OF THE HIT "GOOD VIBRATIONS."

SMiLE

SMiLE was a collaboration with Van Dyke Parks that was supposed to trump the Beatles' *Sgt. Pepper's* and become a pop masterpiece. It was intended to be composed of small fragments of sound, painstakingly layered and edited together to create a unified work with recurring themes of American life throughout history.

The project began to fall apart in late 1966, as Wilson began to show symptoms of depression and paranoia. It's also been said that he was taking increasing amounts of drugs. Parks and Mike Love got into a heated dispute over the direction the record was taking, and Capitol Records was also said to be opposed to the project. Parks ultimately abandoned the project in March 1967.

Some of the songs would be salvaged on the *Smiley Smile* album released in September 1967, but the album was the band's weakest-selling album to date. And Wilson would gradually withdraw from the band and, well, reality.

But in 2004, Wilson and Parks would resurrect the project with new recordings of the original material. The album was released to wildly positive reviews and was followed by a nationwide tour by Wilson accompanied by an expanded band to perform the elaborate compositions.

BEASTIE BOYS

1981–

The Beastie Boys were white punk rock fans from New York City who became infatuated with black culture and hip-hop. Mike D (Mike Diamond), MCA (Adam Yauch), and Ad-Rock (Adam Horovitz) fused this love for hip-hop with heavy metal sensibility and punk rock attitude. In the process of becoming the most important and most talented white hip-hop act in history, they got criticism from all sides.

Called decadent, sexist, culture thieves by their critics, to their fans they were the latest in a rich tradition of taking the innovations of black musicians, improving upon them and selling them to a wider audience. Instead of undercutting the auteurs of the original art form, they called attention to them. And ultimately they advanced the form with songs and innovations of their own.

Rick Rubin, a founder of Def Jam records, produced the Beasties' first album, *Licensed to Ill*, which featured relatively sparse beats, but very cleverly and strategically placed samples from classic rock acts like Led Zeppelin and Creedence Clearwater Revival. The jokes and rhymes ultimately proved irresistible to fans and critics alike, and the album gave the Beasties their only Top 10 pop hit, "(You Gotta) Fight for Your Right (to Party)."

Their sophomore effort, *Paul's Boutique*, was a commercial disappointment when it was first released. But what listeners initially missed was layer upon layer of samples and noise that yielded something different to focus on every time the songs played. The album would eventually become a key touchstone in hip-hop.

The 2004 album *To the 5 Boroughs* was something of a "back to basics" tribute to New York after September 11, 2001. With the innovative brilliance that this group has shown, there's no telling how they'll address the changes that other artists have brought to the form.

THE BEASTIE BOYS COMBINED ELEMENTS OF HIP-HOP, HEAVY METAL, AND PUNK ROCK TO BECOME ONE OF THE MOST IMPORTANT WHITE HIP-HOP ACTS.

GREATEST HITS

YEAR	SONG
1986	"(You Gotta) Fight for Your Right (to Party)"
1987	"Brass Monkey"
1989	"Hey Ladies"
1992	"So What'cha Want"
1994	"Get It Together"
	"Sure Shot"
1998	"Intergalactic"
2004	"Ch-Check It Out"

"Actually, it wasn't inflatable, it was hydraulic. It was in a box, the lid opened and it sort of . . . grew about 30 or 40 feet. Someone stole it in New Jersey." —Ad-Rock, 1994, on a prop phallic symbol used on the *Licensed to Ill* tour.

Rick Rubin

If you go to your record shelf and pick out a handful of your favorite records from the last 20 years, there's a better-than-even chance that the "producer" listed on the back of at least one of them is Rick Rubin. He's worked in every genre there is: pop (Dixie Chicks), country (Johnny Cash), adult contemporary (Neil Diamond), heavy metal (Slayer), alternative rock (Red Hot Chili Peppers), classic rock (Tom Petty), and hip-hop (Beastie Boys).

THE BEATLES

1962–1970

THE BEATLES GAB WITH REPORTERS AT A PRESS CONFERENCE IN GERMANY IN 1966.

The Beatles were the best students of '50s rock and roll. George Harrison reproduced Chuck Berry's riffs flawlessly. Paul McCartney adopted Little Richard's scream. John Lennon internalized the best of the blues singers. And Ringo Starr melded it all together with a steady unadorned hand. They filtered this combination through the skiffle sounds of their youth (skiffle was something of a hybrid of jug band music, jazz, folk, and blues) and then stacked harmonies on top of one another—harmonies reminiscent not only of the Everly Brothers and the Coasters, but barber shop quartets and show tunes.

And then, when they mastered all that, they blew it up and changed the vocabulary of pop music forever.

Compositionally, nothing the Beatles did after 1963 was straightforward. They transformed simple I-IV-V modes into modal music, borrowing from classical and jazz forms, but still maintaining their roots in rhythm and blues. They were reliant on their own compositions, ending the dominance of the Brill Building publishing companies over pop music. They changed the emphasis of pop music from singles to albums. Their experimentation in the studio with tape loops, orchestrations, and instrumentation was matched only by Brian Wilson. Along with Dylan, they changed the balance of power in pop music from label/producer/manager to artist. After the Beatles, pop music became something of a wild frontier in which anything was possible.

And they did all this in just eight years.

> **NUGGET:** Like many pop stars, it was only natural for the Beatles to seek an outlet in film. They acquitted themselves well in their debut, *A Hard Day's Night*, which has aged surprisingly well in the last 40-odd years. The "Can't Buy Me Love" sequence remains hilarious to this day and is now often thought of as the first music video. Publishing mogul Don Kirshner would model the Monkees and their television series after *A Hard Day's Night*.

THE BEATLES PERFORM ON THE "THANK YOUR LUCKY STARS" TELEVISION SHOW IN 1963.

JOHN LENNON, PAUL MCCARTNEY (TOP) RINGO STARR, AND GEORGE HARRISON (BOTTOM) BACKSTAGE AT THE FINSBURY PARK ASTORIA IN 1963.

John Lennon, Paul McCartney, and George Harrison were members of a skiffle group called the Quarry Men. After the group broke up, the three added bass player Stu Sutcliffe and drummer Pete Best, and toiled for a year in the clubs of Hamburg (see sidebar). When they returned they were the best band in Liverpool. They headlined in larger places like the now-legendary Cavern Club, where

they attracted the attention of Brian Epstein, who ran a local record store. He soon became their manager.

Parlophone Producer George Martin liked the group, but didn't like the drummer Pete Best. So the Beatles sacked him and sought the best drummer they knew in Liverpool, Ringo Starr, who was then playing with Rory Storm & the Hurricanes. The Beatles' first single, "Love Me Do," peaked at #17 on the U.K. charts. Their follow-up in 1963, "Please Please Me," became their first #1 hit in the U.K. Depending on which British sales chart you look at, it would be their first of 12 consecutive #1 hits in the U.K. through 1966.

In the U.S., only Elvis Presley sold more records in pop music during the rock era. No band would have more #1 hits. And once the Beatles found their way into the U.S. market, the American hegemony on pop music ended. Beatlemania was the mode of the day.

With albums like *Rubber Soul* and *Revolver*, the Beatles began to texture their songs with new and different instrumentation and to use the studio itself as an additional instrument. Vocals and guitar solos would be recorded

Birth of the Beatles

When McCartney was 15 years old, he went with some friends to Woolton Village Fete in their hometown of Liverpool. The band that was playing that summer afternoon in 1957 was a skiffle group called the Quarry Men, led by John Lennon. Lennon was impressed by McCartney's repertoire of Jerry Lee Lewis and Little Richard, and the fact that McCartney knew Eddie Cochran's "Twenty Flight Rock" made him a shoo-in for the band.

Harrison was a schoolmate of McCartney's who shared a passion for rock and roll, rhythm and blues, and guitars. Harrison wowed McCartney with a note-for-note version of the 1957 Bill Justis hit "Raunchy." Upon demonstrating this ability to the rest of the Quarry Men, Harrison was asked to join.

When the rest of the group left to go to college or get jobs, the three guitar players stayed together to hustle gigs around Liverpool. They added bass player Stu Sutcliffe, who couldn't play bass but had money, looked good, and was a friend of Lennon's from art college. Drummer Pete Best was hired on the recommendation of his mother, who owned a coffee bar where they hung out.

Lennon and Sutcliffe came up with the name Beatles, as a play on beat music. They were also fans of Buddy Holly, whose backup duo, the Crickets, was another inspiration for the name.

One of the local Liverpool club owners was known for sending local bands to

FROM LEFT: JOHN LENNON, GEORGE HARRISON, PAUL MCCARTNEY, PETE BEST. THE BEATLES POSE IN THEIR LEATHER GEAR IN THE DAYS BEFORE RINGO STARR AND SUITS.

Hamburg. The Beatles would do three tours of duty playing in Hamburg nightclubs, honing their stage act. On their third tour, in 1961, a German record producer noticed their act and hired them to back up a budding singer named Tony Sheridan on a rock version of the old shanty "My Bonnie." This became the first professional record made by the Beatles (worth $15,000, if you have one).

They returned to Liverpool in the summer of 1961, without Sutcliffe, who remained in Hamburg to get married and start a career as a painter. He died of a brain hemorrhage in 1962 at age 21.

backwards, nonsensical tape loops would be thrown into the mix, and sound effects would be used—anything that added to the dynamics of the record would be considered.

When the Beatles returned to the studio in 1967, their priorities had shifted. They assembled tracks meticulously and methodically, often adding producer George Martin's elaborate arrangements and orchestrations to the mix. The opening salvo was the single "Strawberry Fields Forever," with Mellotron keyboard and distorted vocals.

In *Sgt. Pepper's Lonely Hearts Club Band*, the Beatles went on to rewrite all the rules of pop music. The sophistication of its recording, the layers of instrumentation, the distortion of the guitars, and the merging of the '20s and '30s British music hall tradition with rock spelled a whole new language for pop music.

That album was the Beatles' last shot at really working together as a unit. By 1968, they were recording in the studio separately, on songs they'd largely written individually, on a collection that came to be called *The White Album*. The music was still brilliant, but it reflected the fragmenting of a group that no longer had much in common personally.

They wanted to rehearse and record a "back-to-basics" album in 1969 that would accentuate their rock and roll roots, with all the proceedings filmed. The finale was to be a concert at an unspecified location. They got their film. But rather than a document of a band returning to its roots, *Let It Be* showed four men who no longer enjoyed making music together, each pulling in separate directions.

Despite the misery of *Let It Be*, the Beatles reassembled for one last album, *Abbey Road*, arguably their finest hour, in which they consolidated everything they learned over the previous seven years and laid it all out with precision and passion.

After the Beatles broke up, each assumed solo careers, with varying degrees of success. Rumors were persistent that the band would consider reuniting. While none of them were particularly enthusiastic about such a prospect, they wouldn't explicitly rule it out while John Lennon was alive. But in fact, the four members were never even in the same room together at the same time after 1970.

NUGGET: *Saturday Night Live* did a wonderful gag in 1976 featuring producer Lorne Michaels offering $3,000 for the Beatles to reunite on the show. The story goes that Lennon and McCartney were together that evening watching the program. They momentarily considered participating in the show as part of the gag, but eventually decided against it. Some time later, Harrison (who was the scheduled musical guest) tried to claim a fourth of the money, only to be told that the offer was only good if all four Beatles appeared.

FROM LEFT: RINGO STARR, PAUL MCCARTNEY, AND GEORGE HARRISON REUNITED IN 1995 TO RECORD NEW MUSIC OVER JOHN LENNON'S REHEARSAL TAPES.

Reunited

The three surviving Beatles sang on "All Those Years Ago," a tribute to Lennon written by George Harrison following Lennon's murder in 1980. Starr would play sessions with Harrison and McCartney individually from time to time. But the three would not reunite until 1995, when they dubbed their instruments and voices over two demos made by Lennon in the '70s, "Free as a Bird" and "Real Love." Even better, on the nine-volume DVD set of *Anthology*, the documentary makers record a jam session of the three surviving Beatles singing "Blue Moon of Kentucky." After 25 years, the harmonies of McCartney and Harrison were as gorgeous as ever.

GREATEST HITS	
YEAR	SONG
1962	"Love Me Do"
1963	"Please Please Me"
	"She Loves You"
	"I Want to Hold Your Hand"
1964	"A Hard Day's Night"
	"Can't Buy Me Love"
1965	"Help"
1966	"Paperback Writer"
1967	"Strawberry Fields Forever"
1968	"Hey Jude"
1969	"Something"
1970	"Let It Be"

BEE GEES

FROM LEFT: BARRY GIBB, MAURICE GIBB, AND ROBIN GIBB. ALTHOUGH THE BEE GEES' BIGGEST HITS WERE IN THE DISCO VEIN, THEY WERE AGILE SONGWRITERS IN THE SOUL, POP, AND PROGRESSIVE ROCK GENRES.

The most enduring image of the Bee Gees is of the three brothers, smiling broadly, teeth shining as white as their suits, chirping about staying alive or night fever to a disco beat. This image only tells part of the story. They've purveyed versions of richly orchestrated pop rock, progressive rock, soul music, and disco, making them one of the more versatile and successful bands of the '70s. The sound that unites all of their music is their tight three-part harmony that ranks with the very best the rock era has to offer.

The Gibb brothers' (Barry, Robin, and Maurice) first U.S. hit "New York Mining Disaster 1941" drew on the Beatles' harmonies and a surreal narrative that recalled Bob Dylan's work. In addition the song was buoyed by a skillful orchestral arrangement.

After splitting up for a brief period in 1969, they would score their first #1 hit in 1971 with "How Do You Mend a Broken Heart," which would be covered by Al Green. But the next four years would yield no big hits. They brought in Arif

Saturday Night Fever

The film *Saturday Night Fever* was adapted from a *New York* magazine article by music critic Nik Cohn called "Tribal Rites of the New Saturday Night," which profiled the night life around Brooklyn discos. The working title of the script was *Saturday Night* when the film's producer Robert Stigwood approached the Bee Gees, whom he managed, for songs for the soundtrack.

The original director of the film, John Avildsen, didn't like the Bee Gees' songs. Stigwood eventually replaced Avildsen with John Badham. The soundtrack went on to sell more than 40 million copies worldwide.

Mardin, an extraordinary arranger who orchestrated some successful hits in the '70s for Aretha Franklin. Mardin steered the group first towards R&B and eventually to full-on disco in 1975. The result was three Top 10 hits, including the chart-topping "Jive Talkin'" and "You Should Be Dancing," which featured Barry Gibb's trademark falsetto.

The Bee Gees were enlisted to contribute to the *Saturday Night Fever* soundtrack, which pushed disco into the mainstream. And they didn't just perform great disco. They wrote and produced great disco, too.

The group continued to record and tour until Maurice died in 2003 of heart failure. While they remain defined by their disco hits, their palate was broader than many people appreciate.

"We're not a pop group that falls out of fashion and comes back again—we're a songwriting team." —Barry Gibb

GREATEST HITS	
YEAR	SONG
1967	"New York Mining Disaster 1941"
	"To Love Somebody"
	"(The Lights Went out in) Massachusetts"
1971	"How Do You Mend a Broken Heart"
1975	"Jive Talkin'"
	"Nights on Broadway"
1976	"You Should Be Dancing"
1977	"How Deep Is Your Love"
	"Stayin' Alive"
1978	"Night Fever"
	"Too Much Heaven"
1979	"Tragedy"

BOBBY BLAND

JANUARY 27, 1930–

BOBBY "BLUE" BLAND, PICTURED HERE IN A PUBLICITY SHOT FROM THE '50S, COMBINED THE POP OF FRANK SINATRA WITH THE SOUL OF SAM COOKE.

Imagine a combination of Frank Sinatra and Sam Cooke and you'll have an idea of what Bobby "Blue" Bland sounds like. Bland and his arranger Joe Scott constructed a fusion of pop and big band arrangements with blasts of brass, saxophones, and occasionally strings. At the same time, there was no doubt that these were blues songs, anchored by the brilliant guitar playing of Wayne Bennett and Mel Brown.

Soaring above the guitars was Bland's majestic voice, hovering between gospel and pop. When he was making his most passionate emphasis, Bland had a resonant growl that sounded like the wrath of God. That he never hit higher than #20 on the pop charts is a mystery (he had 25 Top 10 R&B hits), because few people would use the arrangements of pop music in blues songs better than Bobby "Blue" Bland.

Bland cut his first sides in 1950, but none made a dent in the charts. After returning to Memphis from the army in 1955, he joined Junior Parker's tour as an opening act and served as Parker's valet. He would also valet and chauffeur for B. B. King. Such jobs were considered apprenticeships in those days, until singers had hits of their own.

Around this time, Bland was inspired by the recorded sermons of the Rev. C. L. Franklin, a nationally known minister who was also Aretha Franklin's father. Bland modeled his voice after the timbre of the minister's voice to create the sonorous "squall" that would eventually become Bland's trademark.

Bland was one of the top-selling R&B acts between 1957 and 1961, with hits that included "Farther up the Road" and "I Pity the Fool." During the '60s, however, he descended into alcoholism and depression. He sobered up in 1971, went back on the road, and has been on it ever since. After his triple bypass surgery in 1995 Bland cut his workload down to 100 from 300 nights a year.

Still, he remains influential. Eric Clapton, the Allman Brothers, and offshoots of the Grateful Dead, to name a few, still play his hits in concert, and the vocals of Van Morrison and Boz Scaggs betray his influence. Bland was inducted into the Rock and Roll Hall Of Fame in 1992.

GREATEST HITS

YEAR	SONG
1957	"Farther up the Road"
1958	"Little Boy Blue"
1959	"I'll Take Care of You"
1960	"Lead Me On"
1961	"I Pity the Fool"
	"Don't Cry No More"
	"Turn on Your Lovelight"
1962	"Stormy Monday"

Don Robey

Bobby Bland had his greatest success at a black-owned, Houston-based label called Duke. Although not nearly as widely known as Motown or Stax, the label's roster included Clarence "Gatemouth" Brown ("Mary Is Fine," #8, R&B 1949), Johnny Ace ("Pledging My Love," #1, R&B, 1955) and Junior Parker ("Driving Wheel," #5, R&B, 1961). And it was headed by a colorful character named Don Robey.

Robey, who was rarely separated from his .45, was the owner of the Bronze Peacock Dinner Club, which was believed to have a gambling and a numbers operation in its back room. Robey would go on to form a talent agency, a record store, and eventually a gospel label called Peacock. He bought a stake in Duke Records in 1952 and "encouraged" his partners out of the business. Under his name or pen name "Deadric Malone," he would be credited with writing many songs by Duke artists, even though many claimed he never wrote a note.

MARY J. BLIGE

JANUARY 11, 1971–

If there's a place where singer-songwriter confession, R&B, and hip-hop meet, there's a good chance that Mary J. Blige will be standing at the crossroads. Citing Aretha Franklin as an influence, she is one of the few singers who manages to pull off fragile and tough gal at the same time. Not for nothing is she called the queen of hip-hop soul.

Blige was raised by a single mother in a housing project in the Bronx. When she was 5 years old, she was molested by a family friend. She dropped out of school in the 11th grade. Many of these experiences, as well other personal issues,

> *"You might not want to do what I've done, because you might not come out of it like I did."* —Mary J. Blige

would become an integral part of her lyrics and her world view. Shortly after leaving school, she recorded an Anita Baker song, "Caught Up in the Rapture," at a karaoke booth at the mall. The tape wound up in the hands of Andre Harrell, president of Uptown Records, who signed her.

> **NUGGET:** Mary J. Blige was a directory assistance operator before starting her singing career.

Her first album, *What's the 411*, was a success out of the gate with a Top 10 pop single "Real Love," and a #1 R&B single "You Remind Me." But she was unprepared for the scrutiny that came with fame and she took to drugs, alcohol, and diva fits. She was in a romantic relationship with Jodeci front man Cedric "K-Ci" Hailey for six years that has been described as emotionally abusive. The relationship ended in 1997.

Much of this angst was poured into the 1994 album *My Life*, which featured the medley, "I'll Be There For You/You're All I Need to Get By," a duet with Method Man. In 1996, she reached the Top 10 again with "Not Gon' Cry," a Babyface song from the soundtrack of the film *Waiting To Exhale*.

By 2001, she'd kicked drugs and found herself in a stable relationship with record exec Kendu Isaacs. The stability in her life was reflected in the appropriately titled *No More Drama*, which yielded her first #1 pop hit "Family Affair," produced by Dr. Dre. *Love & Life* in 2003 marked her reunion with Puffy/P. Diddy, but the collaboration did nothing for sales, which were her weakest yet.

Her most recent album of new material, *Breakthrough*, marked a thorough rebound, including "Be Without You," which went Top 10 and earned her a Grammy.

> **NUGGET:** Blige has recorded raps under the pseudonym Brook Lynn.

MARY J. BLIGE PERFORMS IN 2004, AROUND THE TIME OF HER *LOVE & LIFE* ALBUM.

GREATEST HITS	
YEAR	SONG
1992	"You Remind Me"
	"Real Love"
1995	"I'll Be There for You/You're All I Need to Get By" (with Method Man)
1996	"Not Gon' Cry"
2001	"Family Affair"
	"No More Drama"
2005	"Be Without You"
2007	"Runaway Love" (with Ludacris)

MICHAEL BOLTON

February 26, 1954–

Michael Bolton was one of the top-selling acts of the '90s. He sang soul ballads, in a style similar to Joe Cocker, but with more technical proficiency and with updated arrangements for the adult contemporary market.

Bolton, originally Michael Bolotin, got his first record contract at age 15. He recorded several albums in the mid '70s that hinted at his current style of pop-soul. But back then, his sound never found an audience. Later in the decade, he formed a heavy metal band called Blackjack, which had a minor hit in 1979 called "Love Me Tonight."

He went back to a solo career in 1983, this time as Michael Bolton, in a slick arena-rock mode. By 1988, he moved back to the pop-soul hybrid and broke through with a cover of Otis Redding's "(Sittin' On) The Dock of the Bay." Whether it was hubris or a preemptive strike, the promotional copies of the record distributed to radio and critics came with an endorsement from Redding's widow.

> **NUGGET:** In addition to his singing career, Bolton has written or cowritten songs for Kiss, Barbra Streisand, Kenny Rogers, Cher, Joe Cocker, and Patti LaBelle.

GREATEST HITS

Year	Song
1988	"(Sittin' On) The Dock of the Bay"
1989	"How Am I Supposed to Live Without You"
1990	"How Can We Be Lovers"
	"When I'm Back on My Feet Again"
1991	"Love Is a Wonderful Thing"
	"Time Love and Tenderness"
	"When a Man Loves a Woman"
1993	"Said I Loved You . . . But I Lied"
2002	"Only a Woman Like You"

Michael Bolton, pictured here at the World Music Awards in Monte Carlo in 2002, purveyed rhythm and blues ballads for the adult contemporary set.

After that, *le deluge*. The 1989 smash *Soul Provider* yielded three Top 10 singles, including his first #1, "How Am I Supposed to Live Without You," which he had written for Laura Branigan in 1983. The streak continued with 1991's *Time, Love & Tenderness*, which included a Grammy-winning, chart-topping version of Percy Sledge's "When a Man Loves a Woman," which won a Grammy.

In 1994, Bolton was found to have plagiarized his Top 10 hit "Love Is a Wonderful Thing," from a 1966 Isley Brothers tune of the same name. He was ordered to pay nearly $1 million, even though Bolton insisted he'd never heard the Isley Brothers' song and never owned an Isley Brothers record.

After being initially defensive about his successful career, Bolton has acquired something of a sense of humor about it, including droll send-ups of himself on *The Larry Sanders Show*. His response to his critics has always been the same: Millions of people enjoy what he does.

BON JOVI

1983–

Bon Jovi was the premier hair metal band of the '80s.

It Started All with Glam Rock . . .

The lineage of hair metal can be drawn back to glam rock in the '70s, when bands like Mott the Hoople, T-Rex, Aerosmith, and Thin Lizzy, added a quasi-androgynous look that managed not to undercut their machismo. Alice Cooper and Kiss would mint money by exaggerating the look and, in the case of the latter, streamlining the sound further. (A case could be made for Kiss' "Beth" being the first heavy metal power ballad). By the '80s, with the advent of MTV, image would become as important as musical ability, and bands like Ratt and Motley Crüe raced up the charts.

Bon Jovi epitomized the look of hair metal in the '80s, with a streamlined hard rock sound and booming production that had the subtlety of a sledgehammer. The result was eight Top 10 hits in just two years, including four #1's and a sound that resonates today with repeated sold-out victory laps around the globe.

John Bongiovi was a gofer at the Power Station, a legendary New York recording studio built by his cousin, Tony Bongiovi. In his off-hours he would record his own songs with a pick-up band of musicians. One of these songs, "Runaway," found its way to a Long Island disc jockey who was assembling an album of

"Our band has lasted so long because we are friends first and foremost and we truly do like each other's company."—Bon Jovi

unsigned acts. The song became a local hit and eventually earned him a record contract with Mercury Records in 1983. He then changed his name to Jon Bon Jovi and his band's name to Bon Jovi. With the help of song-doctor-for-hire Desmond Child, the band's third album, 1986's *Slippery When Wet,* was a massive success, with two #1 hits: "You Give Love a Bad Name" and "Livin' on a Prayer." Bon Jovi would also be one of the first to perfect the heavy metal ballad with "Wanted Dead or Alive." The follow-up, *New Jersey,* yielded five Top 10 singles and two #1's.

When the band regrouped in 1992, the music environment had completely changed. The breakthrough of Nirvana, with its punk influences, and the rise of alternative rock made hair metal a nostalgia fetish. Bon Jovi's return to the Top 10 in 1993 with "Bed of Roses" was therefore even more impressive.

The band has proved amazingly resilient. The 1999 hit album *Crush,* a blockbuster sold-out arena and stadium tour, and Bon Jovi's #1 country music single "Who Says You Can't Go Home" in 2006, all attest to Bon Jovi's staying power. They continue to issue slick hard-rock albums that sell well worldwide, and every summer, they're guaranteed to be one of the stronger concert attractions.

GREATEST HITS	
Year	Song
1986	"You Give Love a Bad Name"
	"Livin' on a Prayer"
1987	"Wanted Dead or Alive"
1988	"Bad Medicine"
	"Born to Be My Baby"
1989	"I'll Be There for You"
	"Lay Your Hands on Me"
	"Living in Sin"
1993	"Bed of Roses"
1994	"Always"

BOOKER T. & THE MGS

1962–

Along with Motown, Stax Records would be the most important R&B label of the '60s. Although Memphis was deeply segregated in the '60s, black kids and white kids would gather at Stax's studios in the heart of West Memphis. Four of those kids formed the backbone of the most important rhythm and blues hits of '60s, Booker T. & The MGs.

During a jam session, they came up with a blues riff around Jones' organ and the off-beat rhythm stabs of Cropper's guitar. The song was "Green Onions," which peaked at #3 on the pop charts in 1962, when the band adopted the name Booker T. & The MGs (MG stood for Memphis Group). In 1964, Steinberg would be permanently replaced by Donald "Duck" Dunn, a friend of Cropper's from the Mar-Keys.

> *"I never thought it would last. I always wondered if I was doing good enough. I kept waiting for them to get someone else."* —Duck Dunn

The MGs played on virtually every hit by Otis Redding, Sam & Dave, and many others. The group would stay together until the Stax label began to collapse. Jones eventually became a popular record producer. Cropper and Dunn would join the backup band for Dan Aykroyd and John Belushi's *Blues Brothers*. Al Jackson remained in Memphis and became an integral part of Al Green's backup band until he was murdered in 1975 at age 39.

The surviving three members still tour from time to time. Jones and Dunn have also intermittently played with Neil Young.

FROM LEFT: BOOKER T. JONES (KEYBOARDS), DONALD "DUCK" DUNN (BASS), AL JACKSON JR. (DRUMS), STEVE CROPPER (GUITAR). BOOKER T. & THE MGS PLAYED ON THE GREATEST RHYTHM AND BLUES HITS OF THE '60S, INCLUDING SONGS BY OTIS REDDING, SAM & DAVE, AND WILSON PICKETT.

A 16-year-old Booker T. Jones used to sneak into the clubs and sit in on bass with the local R&B acts. In one such band, he met drummer Al Jackson Jr., whom he brought down to hang out at Stax. Jones would eventually learn organ; that organ's swirling sounds would define most Stax hits.

The MG's guitarist Steve Cropper played in the Mar-Keys, a white R&B group that had a Top 10 hit with the instrumental "Last Night." MG's Lewis Steinberg was an in-demand bassist around town. Together the four musicians became the house band for Stax Records.

GREATEST HITS

YEAR	SONG
1962	"Green Onions"
1965	"Boot-Leg"
1966	"My Sweet Potato"
1967	"Hip Hug Her"
	"Groovin'"
1968	"Soul-Limbo"
	"Hang 'Em High"
1969	"Time Is Tight"

PAT BOONE

JUNE 1, 1934–

With the emergence of "race records" in the '40s and '50s, white artists would record sanitized versions of R&B songs to be played on white radio stations and sold to white audiences. Pat Boone would benefit from this dynamic more than virtually any other performer. In so doing, Pat Boone became the second-biggest-selling artist of the '50s after Elvis Presley and the 11th-top-selling artist of all time, according to Joel Whitburn's Record Research.

Boone, for his part, has dismissed accusations of racism. The artists whose music he covered "forget that they were thrilled when I did their songs in the mid-'50s," he told Montreal's *The Gazette* in 2005. "It introduced these R&B songs to a wide, mainly white, pop audience. Within a very short space of time, people knew who Little Richard was, they knew who Fats Domino was, and their careers flourished. I sometimes call myself a midwife in the birth of rock 'n' roll."

Boone was born in 1934, a descendent of frontier hero Daniel Boone. He won a local Nashville talent contest that put him on the national stage on the television show *Ted Mack's Original Amateur Hour,* an *American Idol* of its time, and he was also a regular on *The Arthur Godfey Show.*

His first assault on the pop charts came in 1955, when he took Fats Domino's "Ain't That a Shame" to #1. He also scored hits with the Flamingoes' "I'll Be Home," Big Joe Turner's "Chains of Love," and Little Richard's "Tutti Frutti" and "Long Tall Sally."

Never beyond a touch of irony, Boone lent credibility to heavy metal groups like Led Zeppelin, Judas Priest, and Black Sabbath on his album *In a Metal Mood: No More Mr. Nice Guy.*

GREATEST HITS

YEAR	SONG
1955	"Ain't That a Shame"
1956	"I'll Be Home"
	"Long Tall Sally"
	"Tutti Frutti"
	"I Almost Lost My Mind"
	"Chains of Love"
	"Don't Forbid Me"
1957	"Love Letters in the Sand"
	"April Love"
1958	"A Wonderful Time Up There"
	"It's Too Soon to Know"

BY COVERING VERSIONS OF R&B SONGS, PAT BOONE BECAME THE SECOND BEST-SELLING ARTIST IN THE '50S AFTER ELVIS PRESLEY.

BOYZ II MEN

1991–

BOYZ II MEN'S "END OF THE ROAD" IN 1992 BROKE ELVIS PRESLEY'S 36-YEAR-OLD RECORD FOR THE SONG THAT SPENT THE MOST TIME AT THE #1 POSITION.

NUGGET: When Boyz II Men were starting out, they used to practice in Philadelphia's subways because of the great acoustics.

New Jack Swing

"Mentally, hip-hop, smoothed out on the R&B tip with a pop feel appeal to it." This is how Bell Biv DeVoe described New Jack Swing, a hybrid of contemporary R&B and hip-hop. New Jack can be traced to the split of New Edition into two acts: Bobby Brown and Bell Biv Devoe. On an album produced by New Jack forefather Teddy Riley, Brown would have nine consecutive Top 10 hits with the new style, including five from the 1988 landmark album *Don't Be Cruel*. Bell Biv DeVoe would score two Top 10 hits from the album *Poison*, aided by top producers Terry Lewis and Jimmy Jam, and Public Enemy's production team the Bomb Squad. The sound would influence a number of new producers and artists in the late '90s, including R. Kelly and Sean "Puffy" Combs.

Boyz II Men became one of the top-selling acts of the '90s by combining the tight harmonies of '70s R&B with a touch of hip-hop beats and stylings. They started out as devotees of the Jackson 5-inspired harmonies of New Edition. But at the peak of their career, they owed a huge portion of their sound to the vocal pyrotechnics of Mariah Carey. With a string of successful ballads, only three acts would rank higher in the '90s according to *Record Research*—Carey, Janet Jackson, and Madonna.

Michael McCary, Nathan Morris, Wanya Morris, and Shawn Stockman were all voice students at the Philadelphia High School for Creative and Performing Arts when they formed a singing group in 1988. They snuck backstage at a concert hosted by Michael Bivins, a member of early '80s R&B sensation New Edition and then a current member of New Jack Swing pioneer Bell Biv DeVoe. They requested an audition and sang a note-perfect version of New Edition's hit "Can You Stand The Rain." Bivins allegedly signed the group to his production company on the spot, and soon after they were signed to Motown.

In 1991, they scored their first hit "Motownphilly," which was in the New Jack style of combining slick R&B with hip-hop, in this case with a rap provided by Bivins. But their bigger success would come with ballads, first with "It's So Hard To Say Goodbye to Yesterday." A year later, they would score one of the biggest hits of all time, "End of the Road." Their 1994 hit "I'll Make Love to You," outperformed "End of the Road," locking down the #1 slot for 14 weeks.

They continued to score Top 10 hits through 1997. After that, they issued two more albums. Both were commercial disappointments, but their sound became an important influence on the boy band craze of the late '90s, which included groups like *NSYNC and the Backstreet Boys. McCary left the group in 2003, due to back problems stemming from scoliosis. The group continues to tour and record as a trio.

GREATEST HITS	
YEAR	SONG
1991	"Motownphilly"
	"It's So Hard to Say Goodbye to Yesterday"
1992	"End of the Road"
	"In the Still of the Nite (I'll Remember)"
1994	"I'll Make Love to You"
	"On Bended Knee"
1995	"Water Runs Dry"
	"One Sweet Day"
1997	"4 Seasons of Loneliness"
	"A Song for Mama"

GARTH BROOKS

February 7, 1962–

Garth Brooks was the biggest country crossover artist since Johnny Cash. His combination of soft rock with the Bakersfield sound of country essentially obliterated the barrier between popular and country music. His lyrics were interspersed with vivid details and clever rhymes that showed that he was as much about substance as style. His arena rock antics, some of them straight out of the Kiss playbook, made him one of the most popular touring acts of the '90s.

Brooks grew up in Oklahoma listening to George Strait. He went to Nashville in 1985 with dreams of becoming a country star, and went home to Oklahoma 23 hours later, already disillusioned with the business. He gave it another try in 1987, and

GARTH BROOKS, PICTURED HERE IN 1997, ROCKS THE ARENA.

this time made it stick. Two years later, his debut album, *Garth Brooks*, which included the hit "If Tomorrow Never Comes," peaked at #2 on the country music charts.

The follow-up, *No Fences*, broke down the barrier between pop and country music, selling over 16 million copies, while the next album, *Ropin' the Wind*, sold 10 million copies in its first two years, making him one of the best-selling artists of the '90s in any genre.

The Death of Chris Gaines

In 1999, Garth Brooks was slated to co-produce a movie called *The Lamb*, in which he was to play a rock star named Chris Gaines. To prepare for the role, he assumed the personality of Chris Gaines as an alter ego, which included wearing leather pants, eyeliner, and a soul patch. He issued an album of rock songs called In *The Life of Chris Gaines*, which was a huge sales disappointment, and the movie was never released.

"The fact that Aerosmith and Kiss and Billy Joel can look me in the eyes and don't make jokes about me to my face, that respect is awful nice and very appreciated." —Garth Brooks

The backlash began in 1992 when *The Chase* was released, and sold "only" 5 million copies in the following year. Each of Brooks' albums, while still huge sellers, began to sell less than the previous one. After releasing *Scarecrow* in 2001, he announced his retirement to spend more time with his children. He has performed several shows, such as the 80th birthday of the Grand Ole Opry in 2005.

In 2005, he cut a deal with Wal-Mart, making the world's largest retailer the exclusive seller of Garth Brooks' back catalog. Later that year, Wal-Mart offered an exclusive 5-CD box set at a budget price. And in 2006, he issued an album, *The Lost Sessions*, exclusively through the retailer, making him a groundbreaker in the way that music is sold.

But mostly Brooks will be known for the trails he's blazed, trails that allowed Shania Twain, Faith Hill, and other country stars to cross over into the pop market.

GREATEST HITS	
YEAR	SONG
1989	"If Tomorrow Never Comes"
1990	"Friends in Low Places"
	"The Dance"
1991	"The Thunder Rolls"
1992	"Somewhere Other Than the Night"
1993	"American Honky-Tonk Bar Association"
1995	"The Fever"
1996	"The Beaches of Cheyenne"
1997	"Longneck Bottle"
1999	"Lost in You"

JAMES BROWN

May 3, 1933–December 25, 2006

Almost every rhythmic innovation in popular music from 1965 through 1971 came from James Brown. And when James Brown no longer set the pace for dance music, his progeny inherited the cause. His music spawned Sly & the Family Stone in San Francisco and the Meters in New Orleans. Alumni from his band would join George Clinton's Funkadelic as well as Parliament in 1971 and lead the charge into funk, which later begat disco. One of the greatest innovators in jazz, Miles Davis, would credit Brown for changing the direction of his music in the '70s. And hip-hoppers would come to rely on "Funky Drummer" and "Give It Up or Turnit a Loose" the way rock and rollers would rely on Chuck Berry's signature "Roll Over Beethoven" riff.

"I taught them everything they know, but not everything I know." —James Brown

While most popular music would focus on melody and harmony, Brown put the emphasis on rhythm. His accents were completely different from the music of Motown or Phil Spector. His lyrics had no narrative. By 1967, he would barely have any tunes or chord changes to speak of. Every instrument from the horn section to the guitar to the piano became a rhythm instrument. He relied on no community, such as Motown, for his success. No producer defined his sound. He became a symbol of self-sufficiency and self-respect as "Say It Loud, I'm Black and I'm Proud" exemplifies.

James Brown's 1956 debut single, "Please Please Please," for the Cincinnati-based King Records gave no hint of what was to come. It was a basic R&B ballad set to triplet chords with gospel-derived call-and-response vocals courtesy of Bobby Byrd and the Flames, the group that Brown would eventually co-opt as his own. The record made Top 10 on the R&B charts.

"Papa's Got A Brand New Bag," broke through with a totally new sound. It begins with a horn explosion, Brown sings "Come in, sister!" and the band is off.

JAMES BROWN USED ALMOST EVERY INSTRUMENT, INCLUDING VOCALS, TO CREATE RHYTHM IN HIS MUSIC.

Make My Funk the P-Funk

One of the most important disciples of James Brown was George Clinton and his Funkadelic and Parliament collectives. They would inherit from Brown the notion that groove was all. But like Sly & the Family Stone, they would also add elements of psychedelic music. They were known to jam for hours in concert, and nobody could make you dance like George Clinton could.

Clinton began his career leading a harmony group in New Jersey called the Parliaments, which had a Top 10 R&B hit in 1967 with "I Wanna Testify." By 1971, he'd drop the plural and begin experimenting with extended jams in the mode of James Brown, only with more focus on virtuosic playing. Simultaneously, he would form a separate group, Funkadelic, which would have more explicitly political songs and focus on the explosive guitar work of Eddie Hazel.

Their zenith would come in 1976 with the *Mothership Connection* album, which yielded the Top 10 R&B hit "Tear the Roof Off the Sucker."

Legal problems would force Clinton to drop the names Funkadelic and Parliament in the late '70s, but he continued to play with the same musicians under the P-Funk All Stars moniker. Their 1982 song "Atomic Dog" became one of the most sampled songs in hip-hop.

Clinton continues to tour to this day, carrying the torch for James Brown.

The gospel call and response is replaced by a horn section, punctuating each line. And after Brown exhorts, "Papa's got a brand new bag," the guitar scratches out a riff and the horns blow again. It is possibly the most exciting two minutes of music ever recorded.

You can point to 1967's "Cold Sweat" as the beginning of funk. With barely any chord changes, the whole song is essentially owned by drummer Clyde Stubblefield, who puts everything he has on the downbeat. The horns and guitars stab rather than play. All of the instruments, including the voice, serve the rhythm.

No one would have more Top 10 R&B hits and only three would have more #1 R&B hits (Aretha Franklin, Stevie Wonder, and Louis Jordan). According to Joel Whitburn's *Top Pop Singles*, only Elvis Presley and the Beatles rank higher on his top 200 artists, based on Billboard chart positions.

Brown was omnipresent on the R&B charts until 1975. He would later be upstaged by musical forms that he invented. There were drugs, arrests (a three-year prison sentence in 1988), financial problems, and marital problems. He toured regularly until he died at age 73, on Christmas Day in 2006, a week before he was to have played a New Year's Eve gig in New York.

JAMES BROWN INFLUENCED GENERATIONS OF MUSICIANS.

Famous Flames

A stint as a member of the Flames, James Brown's backup band, was a prelude to future success for many of Brown's musicians.

Maceo Parker: Maceo Parker formed Maceo & All the King's Men in 1970 after quitting Brown's band. He would also sit in with George Clinton's Parliament and Funkadelic collectives. He is one of the most in-demand horn men in popular music, playing with everyone from Keith Richards to Prince. His own band continues to tour regularly.

Bootsy Collins: After Parker quit in 1970, Brown hired a group of local Cincinnati teenagers called the Pacesetters, and renamed them the JBs. Among these players were bassist William "Bootsy" Collins and his brother Phelps "Catfish" Collins on guitar. They would leave in 1971 to become integral members of Parliament. Boosty would go on to form Bootsy's Rubber Band. He remains one of pop's most innovative bass players and hilarious entertainers.

GREATEST HITS	
YEAR	SONG
1956	"Please, Please, Please"
1958	"Try Me"
1960	"Think"
1965	"Papa's Got a Brand New Bag"
	"I Got You (I Feel Good)"
1966	"It's a Man's Man's Man's World"
1967	"Cold Sweat"
1968	"I Got the Feelin'"
	"Say It Loud—I'm Black and I'm Proud"
1969	"Give It Up or Turnit a Loose"
1970	"Get Up (I Feel Like Being a) Sex Machine"
1985	"Living in America"

JACKSON BROWNE

October 9, 1948–

Jackson Browne was the poster child for the '70s singer-songwriter: earnest, literary, and confessional. But he never forgot how to rock, as exemplified by "Running on Empty," a Top 20 hit in 1977. He could still knock off a good joke like in the 1983 hit "Lawyers in Love." And he chronicled the transition from '60s altruism to '70s cynicism with a suspicious eye.

Even before the '80s, when he explicitly wrote about politics, one constant theme in his songs was the pursuit of ideals in an inherently corrupt world. Browne explored these themes without being naïve or mawkish, because he understood the cost of cynicism—he documented that cost in songs like "The Pretender" and "For Everyman." As philosophical as Browne's lyrics were his guitarist, David Lindley, could always keep the party going.

"Who you choose as role models, as your personal heroes, has a lot to do with who you are. And for that reason I sort of dismiss people who pick me as one. What could they possibly know?"—Jackson Browne

Browne's musical pedigree begins in 1966, when he joined an early incarnation of the Nitty Gritty Dirt Band. He later played in a backup band for folk singer-songwriter Tim Buckley. Under a publishing contract with Nina Music, Browne would have his songs recorded by Tom Rush and Nico, who was Browne's girlfriend for a time. By the age of 16, he had penned the song "These Days," which was recorded by Gregg Allman.

In the early '70s he fell in with a group of California musicians who played at the L.A. club The Troubadour, which was ground zero for the L.A. singer-songwriter movement. Some of these musicians would back up Linda Ronstadt,

JACKSON BROWNE WAS ONE OF THE FEW SINGER-SONGWRITERS TO HOLD FAST TO '60S IDEALS EVEN AFTER THE WORLD TURNED MORE CYNICAL IN THE '70S.

JACKSON BROWNE IS AN EARNEST, CONFESSIONAL SONGWRITER WHO HAS NEVER FORGOTTEN HOW TO ROCK.

GREATEST HITS

YEAR	SONG
1972	"Doctor My Eyes"
	"Rock Me on the Water"
1977	"The Pretender"
1978	"Running on Empty"
1980	"Boulevard"
1982	"Somebody's Baby"
1983	"Lawyers in Love"
1986	"For America"

who had a hit in 1967 with "Different Drum" and held court at the club. One such performer, Glenn Frey, would add a verse to one of Browne's songs—one that Browne wasn't particularly fond of. Frey and his band, the Eagles, would score a hit with the song "Take It Easy" in 1972. Browne would score a Top 10 hit of his own later that year with "Doctor My Eyes."

Browne didn't reach the Top 10 again until 1982 with "Somebody's Baby," from the soundtrack of *Fast Times at Ridgemont High*. But he was a mainstay on classic rock radio throughout the '70s and '80s. He participated in a number of benefits opposing nuclear power, U.S. military involvement in Central America, and anti-apartheid movements in South Africa. He was also one of the headline performers on the unsuccessful "Vote For Change" concerts in 2004 to elect John Kerry (he would be more successful on a smaller scale when he stumped for Orleans ("Still the One") guitarist John Hall who was elected to Congress in 2006 representing New York. Browne's political commitment and his ability to look outside himself for inspiration separate him from his peers.

NUGGET: Jackson Browne helped the late songwriter Warren Zevon get a record contract with Asylum Records. He would go on to produce Zevon's first two albums, including *Excitable Boy* which climbed to the Top 10.

The Mogul

The story of Jackson Browne's discoverer, David Geffen, is the stuff of such legend, that it has become almost cliché in the media business. Infatuated with the entertainment business since he was a child, Geffen arrived in New York seeking an apprenticeship at the powerful William Morris Talent Agency. Such trainees were not required to have college degrees. But despite never having graduated, Geffen claimed he had attained a degree from UCLA. When he learned that his employers checked transcripts, he made sure that he was the first one in the mail room every morning to intercept the transcript.

His first big gamble was with an odd New York songwriter named Laura Nyro. He became her manager and soon got her songs placed with the likes of Barbra Streisand ("Stoney End"—#6 Pop, 1971), the Fifth Dimension ("Wedding Bell Blues"—#1 Pop, 1969) and Three Dog Night ("Eli's Coming"—#10 Pop, 1969).

One of his first management clients was Jackson Browne. When Geffen couldn't get Atlantic Records to ink a deal with the earnest young songwriter, he decided to start his own record company, Asylum Records, which would eventually become a home to Browne, the Eagles, Joni Mitchell, Linda Ronstadt, and even, briefly, Bob Dylan.

Geffen sold Asylum to Warner Brothers for $7 million in 1972 and left the company in 1976. Three years later, Warner Brothers would bankroll Geffen Records. But his first batch of signings proved to be unsuccessful. John Lennon was murdered after recording two albums' worth of material. Elton John, Joni Mitchell, Donna Summer, and Neil Young would enter the most commercially fallow eras of their careers. But the record label would later get a boost from Guns N' Roses' massively successful *Appetite for Destruction* in 1987.

He sold Geffen Records to MCA Records for around $550 million in stock in 1990. When the consumer electronics firm Matsushita bought MCA in 1991, Geffen's previous stake in the company was reportedly worth $710 million.

In 1994, Geffen formed Dreamworks SKG with Steven Spielberg and Jeffrey Katzenberg, after the latter was ousted from the Walt Disney Company.

MARIAH CAREY

March 27, 1970–

Mariah Carey is the best-selling female artist in pop history. Picking up the torch from Whitney Houston, she changed the field of R&B so that technical proficiency became as important as emotion. That said, few of her contemporaries could match her five octave range. And none were married to Sony Music president Tommy Mottola.

Mariah Carey's mother sang with the New York City Opera. And after Mariah finished high school in Long Island, she came to New York City to seek a career in music. She got a gig singing backup with fledgling pop singer Brenda K. Starr, who passed Carey's audition tape onto Sony Music president Tommy Mottola. By age 20, she had a record contract. She debuted with five consecutive #1 hits and 11 straight Top 10 hits. Only the Beatles and Elvis Presley have had more #1's.

Her third studio album, *Music Box*, sold 30 million copies worldwide and yielded two more #1 hits. Her collaboration in 1995 with Boyz II Men, "One Sweet Day," stayed at the #1 slot for 16 weeks. She separated from Mottola in 1997 and issued *Butterfly*, which added some hip-hop colorings to her palette.

Her reign as queen of the pop charts lasted until 2001, when she signed a record-setting, four-album, $80-million contract with Virgin Records. Shortly thereafter, she was hospitalized for "extreme exhaustion." When the albums *Glitter* and *Charmbracelet* stiffed, the industry wrote her off.

MARIAH CAREY HAS ONE OF THE MOST DYNAMIC VOCAL RANGES IN POP MUSIC.

She returned in 2005 with a successful album called *The Emancipation of Mimi* that focused on her R&B roots and yielded two Top 10 hits, her first in five years. While the album sales never reached the peak of Mariah mania in the early '90s, they seem to indicate that the show's not over yet.

Glitter Fades

In July 2001, after spending months working on the movie and soundtrack to *Glitter*, Mariah showed up on MTV wearing little more than a T-shirt. She also left two rambling messages on her Web site that suggested that she was having a nervous breakdown. She checked into a hospital shortly thereafter. The *Glitter* soundtrack album was released to mixed reviews and poor sales on September 11, 2001, the day that terrorists attacked the World Trade Center. The accompanying movie was a critical and commercial bomb. Virgin bought out her contract in early 2002 for $28 million. She eventually signed with Def Jam records and after a disappointing 2002 release, *Charmbracelet*, she clawed her way back up to the Top 10 in 2005 with *The Emancipation of Mimi*.

GREATEST HITS

Year	Song
1990	"Vision of Love"
	"Love Takes Time"
1991	"Someday"
	"I Don't Wanna Cry"
	"Emotions"
1992	"I'll Be There"
1993	"Dreamlover"
	"Hero"
1995	"Fantasy"
	"One Sweet Day" (with Boyz II Men)
2001	"Loverboy"
2005	"We Belong Together"

CARPENTERS

1968–1983

Carpenters were one of the best-selling acts of the '70s, and one of the only acts of the era to draw on music that had nothing to do with rock, rhythm and blues, or country. Their sound harkened back to an earlier era of pop, with ornate and intricate orchestral arrangements and smooth crooning vocals. Had Karen Carpenter lived, she may very well have felt at home singing at a house gig in Las Vegas, like Barry Manilow and Celine Dion do today.

Richard Carpenter was weaned on pre-rock pop crooners like Perry Como and Nat King Cole. By age 15, he was the pianist in a trio that played around his hometown of New Haven, Connecticut. His younger sister, Karen, played glockenspiel in the high school marching band, and soon became proficient at the drums and formed a group with Richard. After several false starts in different incarnations, their audition tape got the attention of Herb Alpert in 1969. Alpert was the co-owner of A&M Records and a pop musician in his own right.

Burt Bacharach, one of Carpenters' labelmates, was intrigued by Richard's arrangements, as well he should have been, since Richard was heavily

KAREN AND RICHARD CARPENTER DEFINED THE ADULT CONTEMPORARY GENRE IN THE '70S.

GREATEST HITS	
YEAR	SONG
1970	"(They Long to Be) Close to You"
	"We've Only Just Begun"
1971	"For All We Know"
	"Rainy Days and Mondays"
	"Superstar"
1972	"Hurting Each Other"
	"Goodbye to Love"
1973	"Sing"
	"Yesterday Once More"
	"Top of the World"
1974	"Please Mr. Postman"
1975	"Only Yesterday"

influenced by the sound of Bacharach and lyricist Hal David's productions. And in 1970, Carpenters would score their first #1 hit with a Bacharach-David song, "(They Long to Be) Close to You."

"Close to You" was the first of 12 Top 10 hits from 1970 to 1975, three of which would top the charts. Only Elton John, Paul McCartney, and the Bee Gees would sell more records than Carpenters in the '70s.

After 1975, sales began to dip, although Carpenters' live act was very much in demand outside the U.S. But trouble was brewing. Richard Carpenter had become addicted to Quaaludes and would go into rehab in 1978. And Karen Carpenter began a battle with anorexia nervosa that would eventually kill her in 1983.

Interestingly, Carpenters music continues to sell well today, even to jaded hipsters. In 1994, a tribute album *If I Was A Carpenter* was assembled featuring a number of alternative rock acts such as Sonic Youth, American Music Club, and Matthew Sweet. The high point of the record was a blistering punk rock cover of "Top of the World" by the Japanese trio Shonen Knife. Even in these drastically different contexts, the songs hold up as excellent examples of pop craft.

LEGENDS OF POP • 31

RAY CHARLES

September 23, 1930–June 10, 2004

THE GENIUS ADDRESSES THE FAITHFUL AT THE NORTH SEA JAZZ FESTIVAL IN 1997.

When Ray Charles set secular words to "Jesus Is All the World to Me" and released "I Got a Woman" in 1955, he effectively invented soul music. If that was all he did, he would be assured a place in this book. But listen to his Atlantic records with Milt Jackson in 1958 and 1961, and you'll hear a man who had a delicate and refined touch in be-bop jazz. (In addition to piano, he more than held his own on alto saxophone). Or listen to his pre-R&B recordings for the Swing Time label from 1949 to 1952. Here he sounds like blues piano pioneer Charles Brown mixed with Nat King Cole.

In the landmark album *Modern Sounds in Country & Western Music* he adds lush strings and pop arrangements to Hank Williams and Buck Owens numbers. Paul Simon's "Still Crazy After All These Years" never sounded better than when Charles sang it in 1993. He even made Pepsi commercials sound good.

At the age of 5, Charles would witness his younger brother drown in a bathtub. Not long afterwards, he contracted glaucoma and would be blind by age 7. By the time he was 23, he had recorded more than 40 sides for Swing Time Records in Seattle. One such single, "Baby Let Me Hold Your Hand," would attract the attention of Miriam Bienstock, one of the founders of Atlantic Records, which would buy Charles' Swing Time contract in 1952 for $2,500. That's akin to buying Manhattan for trinkets.

With Atlantic, Charles would rule the R&B charts from 1955 to 1959 with songs like "I Got A Woman," "A Fool for You," and "Drown in My Own Tears," among others. His first pop success was "What'd I Say" in 1959.

He left Atlantic in 1960 for ABC records, where a string of hits awaited him including "Georgia on My Mind," "Hit the Road Jack," and "I Can't Stop Lovin' You." His last Top 10 pop hit was "Crying Time" in 1965, although he would top the country singles chart in 1984 with "Seven Spanish Angels."

"It was not a question of mixing gospel with the blues. It was a question of singin' the only way I knew how to sing."—Ray Charles

Charles never stopped recording even after he contracted liver cancer in 2003. His album of duets, *Genius Loves Company*, featuring contemporary artists such as Norah Jones and Diana Krall, as well as uber-stars like Elton John, Bonnie Raitt, and Willie Nelson, would win seven Grammy awards in 2005, a year after he died.

In short, few performers have changed the vocabulary of popular music like Ray Charles did. You could simply call him a "Genius."

GREATEST HITS

Year	Song
1959	"What'd I Say"
1960	"Georgia on My Mind"
1961	"One Mint Julep"
	"Hit the Road, Jack"
	"Unchain My Heart"
1962	"I Can't Stop Loving You"
	"You Don't Know Me"
	"You Are My Sunshine"
1963	"Take These Chains from My Heart"
	"Busted"
1965	"Crying Time"

BY 1964, RAY CHARLES HAD DEMONSTRATED HIS TALENT IN R&B, JAZZ, POP, AND COUNTRY.

Atlantic Records

Atlantic Records was started in 1947 by Ahmet Ertegun, the son of a Turkish ambassador and a fanatic of black culture. Upon his arrival in the U.S. as a child, he was said to empathize with black Americans because the discrimination against them reminded him of the treatment of Muslim Turks in Europe. He borrowed $10,000 from a family dentist, and started Atlantic Records with Herb Abramson. The goal at first was an independent label that would specialize in what were then called "race records."

They began recording jump blues with little national success until Stick McGhee scored a #2 R&B hit with "Drinking Wine Spo-Dee-O-Dee" in 1949. On a recommendation by a local DJ, Abramson signed Ruth Brown, who would have 19 Top 10 R&B hits between 1949 and 1958.

In 1952, Ertegun bought Ray Charles' contract from Swing Time Records. Charles was not the first Atlantic artist to reach the Top 10 on the pop charts. But Charles was the artist that made Atlantic a force to be reckoned with in the world of R&B.

With the help of new partner Jerry Wexler, Atlantic would continue to be the dominant player in R&B in the '60s, along with Motown. It struck distribution deals with Stax Records and sent Otis Redding and Sam & Dave to record there. The Drifters and Solomon Burke also delivered regular hits. In Alabama, they would cut deals with smaller labels, giving them distribution rights for Joe Tex and Clarence Carter. And 1967 saw the signing of Aretha Franklin.

Ertegun, meanwhile, was attracting a number of top-shelf rock and pop acts, such as Buffalo Springfield, Crosby Stills and Nash, Eric Clapton's Derek & the Dominoes, and Led Zeppelin. Ertegun's brother and partner, Nesuhi, would establish the label as a home to jazz artists, anchored by John Coltrane and Charlie Mingus. Ahmet Ertegun would also prove instrumental in signing the Rolling Stones in 1971.

By the '70s, Atlantic would no longer be known as the pre-eminent R&B label; Atlantic would instead garner most of its hits in the rock and pop world. By the '80s, it would be just another cog in wheel of the giant Time Warner empire. But Ertegun remained chairman of Atlantic throughout. He helped found the Rock and Roll Hall Of Fame, and would be inducted in 1987. Ertegun died in 2006 from injuries sustained from a fall backstage at a Rolling Stones concert. To the music industry, his death marked the end of an era.

CHER.

May 20, 1946–

Long before there was MTV, Cher learned that presentation, image, and a popular television variety show go a long way. That's not to say she didn't have some great songs, such as "Gypsys, Tramps & Thieves." But she was equally known for the Bob Mackie costumes, the attitude, and her personality. Plus, there aren't many performers who've had Top 10 hits in four decades.

Cherilyn Sarkasian LaPier was the wife of Sonny Bono, a denizen of Phil Spector's Gold Star Studios. In 1965, Sonny & Cher topped the charts with "I Got You Babe." Cher had a solo hit shortly thereafter with "Bang Bang (My Baby Shot Me Down)."

"I'm rich. I'm famous. Maybe it's too much to ask to be talented, too."—Cher

The popularity of the *Sonny & Cher Comedy Hour* on CBS would earn the couple two more Top 10 hits in 1971 and 1972, and would vault Cher's single "Gypsys, Tramps and Thieves" to the top of the charts. After divorcing Bono in 1975, Cher took up a tumultuous marriage with Gregg Allman, the keyboardist of the Allman Brothers Band, a union that lasted less than two weeks. She scored a disco hit in 1979 with "Take Me Home." And after a failed bid in a rock band, Black Rose, it seemed that she was done.

But in the '80s, she re-emerged as a talented actor with excellent performances in *Silkwood* and *Mask,* and eventually won an Oscar in 1987 for her role in *Moonstruck.* She parlayed that success into another run of pop hits in the late '80s, including the Michael Bolton-penned "I Found Someone." By the '90s, she was hawking artificial sweeteners, fitness videos, and hair products. So it was nothing less than shocking when she returned to the Top 10 in 1998 with "Believe." Cher launched a so-called farewell tour in 2002, but given her ability to rise like Rasputin every 10 years or so, the smart money says, there's more to come.

Sonny Bono

Sonny Bono (née Salvatore Bono) was a self-described flunky for Phil Spector in the early '60s, getting him coffee and telling him what he wanted to hear. In return, he would play tambourine and sing backup on some of the best-known songs of the era. He cowrote the single "Needles and Pins," which became a hit for the Searchers in 1964.

In the late '70s, after *The Sonny and Cher Show* went off the air, Sonny opened a restaurant in Palm Springs, California. Frustrated with the local bureaucracy, he successfully ran for mayor of Palm Springs in 1988. He was elected to the House of Representatives in the Republican sweep of Congress in 1994. He died in a skiing accident in 1998.

CHER HAS HAD TOP 10 HITS IN FOUR DECADES.

GREATEST HITS	
YEAR	SONG
1966	"Bang Bang (My Baby Shot Me Down)"
1967	"You Better Sit Down Kids"
1971	"Gypsys, Tramps and Thieves"
1972	"The Way of Love"
1973	"Half-Breed"
1974	"Dark Lady"
1979	"Take Me Home"
1987	"I Found Someone"
1989	"After All" (with Peter Cetera)
	"If I Could Turn Back Time"
	"Just Like Jesse James"
1998	"Believe"

CHICAGO

1967–

I n the late '60s, sometimes it seemed like it wasn't enough to be a rock and roll band. Progressive rock purveyors like the Nice and Yes were mixing classical music concepts into rock. Elsewhere, Al Kooper decided that rock needed a big band jazz element. So he concocted Blood Sweat And Tears.

It was in all these categories that Chicago Transit Authority (later just Chicago after Chicago's public transportation system threatened to sue) plied their wares. Their debut album featured jazz-rock hippie-babble hits like the Latin-tinged "Beginnings," and "Does Anybody Really Know What Time It Is."

The follow-up, *Chicago II* featured "25 or 6 to 4," which demonstrated not only a slick horn section but the prowess of guitarist Terry Kath. It also struck paydirt with "Colour My World," the first of a string of successful pop ballads.

Chicago ultimately became one of the best-selling acts of all time by abandoning experimentation and focusing on the vocals of bassist Peter Cetera. Behind him, the band ratcheted no fewer than 12 Top 10 hits between 1970 and 1977 including "If You Leave Me Now" and "Saturday in the Park."

After Kath died in 1978, the band wouldn't have another Top 10 hit until 1982. Cetera brought the band back to earn three Top 10 hits: "Hard To Say I'm Sorry," followed by "Hard Habit to Break," and "You're the Inspiration" in 1984. A year later, Cetera left the band.

CHICAGO (WITH PETER CETERA AT FAR RIGHT) PERFORMED SOME OF THE GREATEST PROM THEMES OF THE '80s.

GREATEST HITS	
YEAR	SONG
1970	"Make Me Smile"
	"25 or 6 to 4"
	"Does Anybody Really Know What Time It Is"
1971	"Beginnings"
1972	"Saturday in the Park"
1973	"Just You N Me"
1976	"If You Leave Me Now"
1982	"Hard to Say I'm Sorry"
1988	"Look Away"

Without Cetera, Chicago would score five more Top 10 hits between 1986 and 1989: "Will You Still Love Me," "I Don't Wanna Live without Your Love," "Look Away," "What Kind of Man Would I Be," and "You're Not Alone."

You can still find them summer after summer playing amphitheatres, with four original members, to nothing less than adoring fans. Can you dig it? Yes I can.

NUGGET: The first chapter Chicago's career came to an abrupt end in 1978 in one of the more tragic deaths in pop history. In a drunken state, guitarist Terry Kath, 31, was cleaning a pistol that he believed to be unloaded. When a friend warned him to be careful, he put the pistol to his head and pulled the trigger to prove the gun had no bullets. He was wrong. He was replaced by Donnie Dacus.

Ex-Cetera

Cetera went solo in 1985 and had a pair of chart-topping hits the following year: "Glory of Love (Theme from *Karate Kid II*)" and "The Next Time I Fall," a duet with Amy Grant.

THE COASTERS

1955–1964

THE COASTERS WOVE HUMOROUS AND SOMETIMES SOCIALLY CONSCIOUS NARRATIVES INTO THEIR IMPECCABLE HARMONIES.

T he Coasters were far more than a doo-wop group. They could harmonize with the best of the rhythm and blues groups of their day, but their songs were dramatic, or more appropriately comedic narratives. That's not to say they were novelty songs. Novelty songs don't have the class struggles implicit in "Yakety Yak" and "Shopping For Clothes." And novelty songs don't have King Curtis, the finest saxophone sideman to put his lips on a rock and roll song.

The antecedent to the Coasters was a Los Angeles-based harmony group called the Robins that started in 1947 with Ty Terrell, Billy Richards, Roy Richards, and Bobby Nunn. The Robins signed to an independent label called Spark Records, which was run by songwriters Jerry Lieber and Mike Stoller. In 1954, they added two tenors, Carl Gardner and Grady Chapman, and recorded "Smokey Joe's Café," a hilarious tale about a patron who gets mixed up with the wrong girl.

Lieber and Stoller subsequently took jobs with Atlantic Records in New York and offered to have the Robins come east with them. Gardner and Nunn accepted the offer, leaving behind the other Robins, and formed the Coasters with Leon Hughes and Billy Guy.

With Atlantic, the Coasters would have six Top 10 pop hits, including the #1 hit "Yakety Yak," which would be one of the greatest and funniest demonstrations of irreverence in a rock song. Will "Dub" Jones replaced bass singer Nunn and would become infamous for his "roles" in the songs "Charlie Brown," "Along Came Jones," and "Shopping for Clothes."

The group's string of hits ended in 1961 and they splintered to form several groups that would perform as "The Coasters." But their main contribution to pop music is that they were one of the first R&B groups for whom the lyrics would be as important as the music.

GREATEST HITS

Year	Song
1957	"Searchin'"
	"Young Blood"
1958	"Yakety Yak"
1959	"Charlie Brown"
	"Along Came Jones"
	"Poison Ivy"
1960	"Shoppin' for Clothes"
1961	"Little Egypt"

Lieber & Stoller

Jerry Lieber and Mike Stoller were the most accomplished songwriters to emerge from the Brill Building. Their claim to fame was what they called "playlets in song." These three-minute narratives were usually funny stories, with a social message, that resonate to this day.

Their first hit was "Hard Times," recorded by blues piano legend Charles Brown in 1952, which went to #7 on the R&B charts. They would pen "Hound Dog" for Big Mama Thornton in 1953, although Elvis Presley would have the big hit with the song in 1956.

Having proven their value to Atlantic Records, Lieber and Stoller were given free reign to write and produce for the Coasters and the Drifters. The South American rhythm and the wild string arrangements on "Save the Last Dance for Me," for example, is the work of Lieber and Stoller.

By the late '60s they had retreated from the spotlight, while producing and writing for Peggy Lee. Their music was turned into a 1995 musical, *Smokey Joe's Café*.

SAM COOKE

JANUARY 22, 1931–DECEMBER 11, 1964

Sam Cooke is the fount from which just about all soul music flows. He was the first gospel singer to cross over to success in the secular market. He was able to tackle rhythm and blues, pop standards, and show tunes with equal aplomb. His own songwriting could be sentimental, funny, inspiring, and, in his final single, political. He would eventually become an entrepreneur, no small feat for a black man in the early '60s. And above all, he was, quite possibly, the greatest singer of all time.

Cooke was the son of a Chicago-based minister in whose church he sang with two sisters and two brothers in a group called the Singing Children. He would later join a teenage gospel group called the Highway QC's, who modeled themselves after the Soul Stirrers, one of the most popular gospel groups of the day. The Highway QC's, performed regularly on radio programs and caught the attention of J.W. Alexander, a talent scout for Los Angeles-based Specialty Records.

> *"My future lies more in creating music and records than being a nightclub performer."* —Sam Cooke, 1963

In 1950, when the Soul Stirrers' lead singer quit, Cooke was recommended to Alexander as a replacement By the time Cooke was 20 years old, he was singing with the preeminent gospel group of the '40s and '50s.

Cooke's melisma (a single syllable that is sung as a run of notes) that would become his trademark is evident from his first recordings with the group. His silken voice appears almost fully formed—confident and expressive, but never showy. With his leading-man good looks, Cooke became a sensation in the gospel world.

It was only a matter of time before Cooke and others in his circle saw the possibilities of turning pop. At the risk of trivializing, this was akin to the betrayal that folk purists felt when Bob Dylan went

SAM COOKE WAS NOT ONLY ONE OF THE GREATEST SINGERS IN THE HISTORY OF POP MUSIC, HE WAS ALSO ONE OF ITS MOST ACCOMPLISHED ENTREPRENEURS

A Change Is Gonna Come

Cooke, with his manager J. W. Alexander's help, took an almost unprecedented step for a black entertainer by establishing his own publishing company for the songs that he wrote (his biggest hits were all self-penned). Then in 1959, Cooke and Alexander established their own independent record label, SAR Records (Sam and Alex Records). The label put out records by the Soul Stirrers, Johnnie Taylor, the Sims Twins, who recorded the original version of Sam & Dave's greatest song "Soothe Me," and the Valentinos, whose Bobby Womack would go on to solo success (and infamy for marrying Cooke's widow).

Cooke also formed a music production company, a talent agency—Malloy Artist Management, and SAR Pictures, which bought the film rights for a movie in which Cooke would star. In so doing, he paved the way for other black entrepreneurs to operate their own businesses, namely Berry Gordy who would form Motown Records in 1960.

SAM COOKE'S INFLUENCE CAN BE HEARD IN THE WORK OF BRUCE SPRINGSTEEN, ROD STEWART, OTIS REDDING, AND BOYZ II MEN.

electric, only exponentially worse because some believed Cooke was turning his back on the Lord. Nevertheless, when Cooke released "You Send Me" in 1957, it stayed in the #1 spot for three weeks.

His next few singles, while not as successful, were important because they demonstrated his versatility. Cooke nailed "Summertime," the Gershwin classic from *Porgy And Bess* that was a hit for Billie Holiday in 1936. "(I Love You) For Sentimental Reasons," a #1 hit for Nat "King" Cole in 1946, reached #17 on the pop charts for Cooke in 1957.

Cooke also began to take more of an interest in record production and songwriting. "A Change Is Gonna Come" was his response to Bob Dylan's "Blowin' in the Wind." Musically, the song is a tour de force with swelling strings and a brass section that comments ominously on every line like fate breathing down the man's neck.

After his death in 1964, his singing would go on to inspire multiple generations of singers including Otis Redding, Rod Stewart, Bruce Springsteen, and Boyz II Men.

The Death of Sam Cooke

Peter Guralnick's biography, *Dream Boogie: The Triumph of Sam Cooke,* describes his death as follows: After having a late dinner with friends at a Los Angeles nightspot, Sam Cooke picked up a model and took her to a motel out by the airport. He was allegedly aggressive with her and when he excused himself to use the bathroom, the woman took his clothes and left the motel room. Wearing just a sports jacket and shoes he went looking for his date and broke into the manager's apartment. There was a scuffle, and the manager shot him in the chest.

Some would claim that the model was a professional con artist. Others would speculate that Cooke was eliminated because that's what happens when black men become too successful. That said, despite his public image, no one believed Cooke to be a saint. He was known to be a proud man with a fierce temper. Whatever the truth was, what was he left behind is a story that didn't seem to be half over in 1964 and a body of work that few singers could even hope to touch.

GREATEST HITS	
YEAR	SONG
1957	"You Send Me"
	"I'll Come Running Back to You"
1958	"Win Your Love for Me"
1959	"Everybody Loves to Cha Cha Cha"
1960	"Wonderful World"
	"Chain Gang"
1962	"Twistin' the Night Away"
	"Bring It on Home to Me"
1963	"Another Saturday Night"
1964	"Good Times"
1965	"Shake"
	"A Change Is Gonna Come"

CULTURE CLUB

1982–

Culture Club took the best of Motown, Philadelphia International, and even a touch of '60s soul music and reggae, and filtered it through the synth pop—the synthesizer influenced sound of the era.

Boy George (née George O'Dowd) was a denizen of the New Romantic club scene, which featured transvestites, androgynous scenesters, and models that haunted such London clubs as Blitz, where George was a cloakroom attendant.

George was recruited by punk impresario Malcolm McLaren to join Bow Wow Wow of "I Want Candy" fame. But he was kicked out of the band by McLaren. In part, as an act of revenge, George pledged to form his own band. And when he did, he scored six Top 10 songs in a row between 1982 and 1984, including the #1 "Karma Chameleon."

George's heroin addiction eventually destroyed Culture Club. He would have a #1 solo hit in the U.K. with "Everything I Own" in 1987, and a minor hit with the title song from *The Crying Game* (produced by Pet Shop Boys) in 1992. He continued to record a number of projects in the '90s, ranging from rock to electronica to an acoustic collection of songs. He mounted a musical, *Taboo*, in 2002, which was successful in London but flopped on Broadway.

In 2006, he was fined $1,000 and sentenced to community service for drug possession. When

FROM LEFT: BOY GEORGE (VOCALS), JON MOSS (DRUMS), ROY HAY (GUITAR), MIKEY CRAIG (BASS). CULTURE CLUB CRANKS UP THE NORTHERN SOUL.

reporting for service—garbage pickup— he was pursued by the media hordes and became fodder once again for the tabloids, a somewhat unfitting denouement for one of the strongest acts to emerge from the MTV era.

GREATEST HITS	
YEAR	SONG
1982	"Do You Really Want to Hurt Me"
1983	"Time (Clock of the Heart)"
	"I'll Tumble 4 Ya"
	"Church of the Poison Mind"
	"Karma Chameleon"
1984	"Miss Me Blind"
	"It's a Miracle"
	"The War Song"

I Want My MTV

When MTV was launched in 1981, American labels were suspicious of the new medium. Mostly they thought MTV should pay the labels to create music videos to fill the new channel's programming hours. MTV, for its part, reasoned it should be treated like a radio station, with the labels providing the programming for free. The payoff would come in the promotional value and exposure of their artists on the new channel.

Without the American labels on board, MTV was forced to seek programming outside the U.S., which led it to England where a number of bands were already making music videos and looking for exposure in the U.S. Out of this era came a number of flamboyant British acts, whose stock in trade was style, image, and personality—three qualities that would make for good television, especially on a 24-hour music channel. The result was the so-called Second British Invasion, which included Duran Duran, Eurythmics, Wham!, and Culture Club.

BOBBY DARIN

May 14, 1936–December 20,1973

Bobby Darin was one of pop music's most versatile singers. He was able to put over rock and roll songs like "Splish Splash" and "Queen of the Hop," but he was also known for his ability to work pop standards. "Mack the Knife," for example, was one of the biggest-selling hits of 1959. His crooning in "Beyond the Sea" showed that Darin could have been worthy of the many comparisons made between him and Frank Sinatra had he lived.

Darin lived the better part of his life in fear that a congenital heart defect would kill him before he turned 30. Consequently, he believed that he needed to cover a lot of ground before he died, and prided himself on his seemingly incongruous stylistic changes from rock to pop to folk to country (think of him as the '50s equivalent to Neil Young).

Don Kirshner, co-owner of the Brill Building publishing company Aldon Music, discovered Bobby Darin (née Robert Cassotto) working in a candy store in upper Manhattan. He got Darin a record deal at the major label Decca, but his singles there were not big sellers. Atlantic Records co-founder Herb Abramson saw potential and signed the 21-year-old in 1957. By the end of that year, he would have two Top 10 hits, "Splish Splash" and "Queen of the Hop." The beautiful ballad "Dream Lover" followed in 1959, as did a definitive version of "Mack the Knife."

"Mack the Knife" gave Darin credibility outside the rock world. But he wasn't through genre-hopping. In 1966, he would put away his toupee and his tuxedo —temporarily—and don an acoustic guitar and a pair of blue jeans to ply a hybrid of pop and folk music. His last Top 10 hit, "If I Were a Carpenter," was in this vein, alienating the nightclub audiences he'd won over the previous seven years.

The heart ailment he feared eventually killed him in 1973 during surgery. His successes in nearly every genre that he toyed with testify to his amazing range and prove that rock performers need not be hemmed in by any one style.

BOBBY DARIN WAS COMMERCIALLY SUCCESSFUL IN VIRTUALLY EVERY GENRE HE TRIED.

Line Forms on the Right

Atlantic Records' cofounder Ahmet Ertegun was lunching with Lotte Lenya, the widow of Kurt Weill. Over the course of lunch conversation, Lenya inquired about Ertegun's record label and wondered if any of Ertegun's artists would be willing to record her late husband's songs. Ertegun replied that while he admired Weill's work, his label recorded mostly blues and jazz and that Weill's songs might not be compatible. But he promised Lenya that he'd try.

Several days later, Ertegun ran into Bobby Darin, who had just seen a revival of Weill's *Threepenny Opera*. Darin was so enthusiastic about the production, he wanted to record "Mack the Knife." "Great idea," Ertegun said.

The song would top the charts in 1959 for nine weeks. And for Ertegun, it demonstrated that the label could have success outside the R&B market.

GREATEST HITS	
Year	Song
1958	"Splish Splash"
	"Queen of the Hop"
1959	"Dream Lover"
	"Mack the Knife"
1960	"Beyond the Sea"
1961	"You Must Have Been a Beautiful Baby"
1962	"Things"
1963	"You're the Reason I'm Living"
	"18 Yellow Roses"
1966	"If I Were a Carpenter"

DESTINY'S CHILD

1997–

Destiny's Child, led by Beyonce Knowles, combined smooth contemporary R&B with hip-hop, much in the way that En Vogue did earlier in the '90s. Fueled by Knowles' technical brilliance, the group would become one of the top-selling female acts of all time.

After making their debut on the soundtrack to *Men In Black* with "Killing Time," Beyonce, her cousin Kelly Rowland, LaTavia Roberson, and LeToya Luckett reached the Top 10 in 1997 with "No No No Part 2," which was produced by Wyclef Jean from the Fugees. They scored their first #1 hit 18 months later with "Bills Bills Bills." They would have four #1 hits over the next two years.

At the peak of their popularity, Roberson and Luckett were replaced by Michelle Williams and

DESTINY'S CHILD, LED BY BEYONCE KNOWLES (CENTER), IS ONE OF THE BEST-SELLING FEMALE GROUPS IN HISTORY.

Farrah Franklin, leading the two exiled members to sue Rowland, Beyonce, and Beyonce's father, Matthew Knowles, who managed the group, for breach of contract. None of which stopped the follow up single, "Jumpin' Jumpin'," from reaching the Top 10 in 2000.

Franklin would leave the group after five months. Later in 2000, Destiny's Child would take "Independent Woman," from the film *Charlie's Angels*, to the top of the charts for 11 weeks, making it one of the biggest hits of the year.

Beyonce raised her profile by starring alongside Mike Myers in *Austin Powers 3: Goldmember*, which included her first solo single, "Work It Out." An enormously popular solo album, *Dangerously in Love*, followed with four Top 10 hits, including two #1's, "Crazy in Love" and "Baby Boy."

Contradicting rumors that Destiny's Child was finished, the group reunited for *Destiny Fulfilled* in 2004, which sold well, although not as well as its predecessors. For all intents and purposes, Beyonce was effectively the star of the show, a fact that was reinforced by the success of her second solo album *B'Day* and her starring role in *Dreamgirls* in 2005.

NUGGET: The name Destiny's Child is taken from a passage from the Book Of Isaiah.

GREATEST HITS	
YEAR	SONG
1997	"No No No Part 2" (with Wyclef Jean)
1999	"Bills Bills Bills"
	"Say My Name"
2000	"Jumpin' Jumpin'"
	"Independent Women Part 1"
2001	"Survivor"
	"Bootylicious"
	"Emotion"
2004	"Lose My Breath"
	"Soldier"

"I still feel like I'm part of a group. I still have them to call and ask: "Did you like this song? Did you like this video?"—Beyonce Knowles

NEIL DIAMOND

January 24, 1941–

Neil Diamond 's "Girl You'll Be a Woman Soon" was used in the film *Pulp Fiction*.

GREATEST HITS	
Year	Song
1966	"Cherry Cherry"
1967	"Girl, You'll Be a Woman Soon"
1969	"Sweet Caroline (Good Times Never Seemed So Good)"
	"Holly Holy"
1970	"Cracklin' Rosie"
1971	"I Am . . . I Said"
1972	"Song Sung Blue"
1978	"You Don't Bring Me Flowers" (with Barbra Streisand)
1980	"Love on the Rocks"
1981	"Hello Again"
	"America"
1982	"Heartlight"

Neil Diamond walks the line between singer-songwriter and pure pop entertainer. He is one of the top-selling artists and one of the most popular live acts of the rock era. He has come to embrace more heavily orchestrated pop arrangements rather than the rock and roll that was his early bread and butter. But his voice, at once able to sound gruff and mellow, signifies intimacy and confession. That intimacy keeps fans lined up every time he hits the road.

Neil Diamond entered New York University as a chemistry major in the mid-'60s. But he spent more time writing songs than studying chemistry, so after flunking out in 1965, he was hired by Jerry Lieber and Mike Stoller's publishing company and record label, with budding hopes of becoming a performer.

He signed in 1966 with Bang Records, where he would have Top 10 hits with "Cherry Cherry" and "Girl, You'll Be a Woman Soon." Around the same time, publishing mogul Don Kirshner bought two of his songs for the Monkees—"I'm a Believer," their biggest hit, and "A Little Bit Me, a Little Bit You"—further establishing Diamond as a credible songwriter and performer.

A string of hits followed, including the introspective "I Am . . . I Said," "Cracklin' Rosie," "Sweet Caroline," and "Song Sung Blue." Even his albums without hit singles became wildly successful, such as *Jonathan Livingston Seagull* and the live album *Hot August Nights*. His biggest hit would be "You Don't Bring Me Flowers," a duet with Barbra Streisand.

The 1980 film soundtrack *The Jazz Singer* yielded three Top 10 singles, despite the movie's poor showing. His last major hit was "Heartlight," inspired by the film *ET*. While he continued to record throughout the '90s, Diamond's records failed to find an audience. But his tours still sell out in milliseconds. In 2005, he collaborated with uber-producer Rick Rubin for an album of unadorned rock songs, which reached #4 on the album charts.

Solitary Man

Producer Rick Rubin, who'd worked with everyone from the Beastie Boys to Johnny Cash to Slayer, began pursuing Neil Diamond in the early '90s to make a record with him. But Diamond didn't know anything about him and never returned his calls.

After finishing a tour in 2002, a flood of songs came to Diamond who, in the intervening years, had learned about Rubin's resume and reached out to the producer. The two met for months, just getting familiar with one another, before Diamond would play Rubin a note.

The result was as personal and intimate a record he'd ever made, with none of elaborate pop trappings that would sometimes get in the way of his songwriting. It was his highest charting album in 25 years.

DION

July 18, 1939–

D ion & The Belmonts were the best of the white harmony groups to come out of the early rock and roll era. Inspired by the Coasters and the Drifters, the group adopted a tight, four-part harmony. And after Dion left the Belmonts, he would expand into folk, pop, gospel, and blues, convincingly and adeptly.

Dion DiMucci grew up in the Bronx, running with Italian gangs and singing rhythm and blues songs on the stoops at night with his friends. Those friends—Fred Milano, Angelo D'Aleo, and Carlo Mastrangelo—became the Belmonts. They were known as the best of the neighborhood doo-wop groups, and soon signed to Laurie Records in 1958.

Dion Dodges Death

In the winter of 1959, Dion was invited on the legendary Winter Package Tour that included Buddy Holly, Eddie Cochran, Jackie Wilson, Ritchie Valens, and J.P. Richardson, better known as the Big Bopper. He was invited to board the chartered plane bound for Iowa, but he declined because he didn't want to pay $35 for the ticket. The plane took Holly, Valens, and Richardson to their deaths.

GREATEST HITS	
Year	Song
1958	"I Wonder Why"
1959	"Teenager in Love"
	"Where or When"
1960	"Lonely Teenager"
1961	"Runaround Sue"
	"The Wanderer"
1962	"Lovers Who Wander"
	"Little Diane"
	"Love Came to Me"
1963	"Ruby Baby"
	"Donna the Prima Donna"
1968	"Abraham, Martin and John"

DION REMAINED COMMITTED TO ROCK AND ROLL EVEN THOUGH HIS MANAGERS PUSHED HIM TOWARD POP.

Their debut, "I Wonder Why" hit the Top 40. Their first Top 10 hit would come a year later with "Teenager In Love."

The group scored its biggest hit in 1960 with "Where or When." Their next two singles were "When You Wish Upon a Star," the Disney staple, and "In the Still of the Night," the Cole Porter song. Neither sold particularly well, and Dion decided to go solo and move towards rock and roll. He scored the biggest hit of his career in 1961 with "Runaround Sue," and he would never rock harder than on the follow-up, "The Wanderer."

He had two more Top 10 singles in 1963. But he spent the next five years shooting heroin and drifting into obscurity. He had a religious epiphany in 1968 and cleaned up. Later that year he reached the Top 10 with the socially conscious "Abraham, Martin, and John," a tribute to Abraham Lincoln, Martin Luther King (who'd been assassinated six months before), and John and Robert Kennedy.

His phrasing has only improved after 39 years. When performing, he diverges from the original versions of his hits considerably, and sounds like a soul singer discovering his songs with each rendition. He recorded a blues album, *Bronx to Blue,* which was nominated for a Grammy in 2006.

CELINE DION

Celine Dion's classically trained voice and wide vocal range has made her one of the top-selling acts of the '90s. She didn't learn to speak English until her teens, but she has since become one of the biggest international stars in pop music. Despite a couple of flirtations with dance pop over the the years, her stardom comes largely on the strength of her ballads which take advantage of her full-bodied voice.

Dion is the youngest of 14 children, all of whom were musically inclined. Her parents operated a nightclub in Quebec, where she performed for the first time at age 5. When she was 12 years old, she compiled an audition tape for a local manager, René Angélil, who was so impressed with her voice that he mortgaged his house to finance her first two albums. The two would marry in 1994.

CELINE DION SMILES, AFTER RETURNING FROM HER SEMI-RETIREMENT IN 2002.

GREATEST HITS	
YEAR	SONG
1990	"Where Does My Heart Beat Now"
1991	"Beauty and the Beast" (with Peabo Bryson)
	"If You Asked Me To"
1993	"The Power of Love"
1996	"Because You Loved Me"
	"It's All Coming Back to Me Now"
1997	"All by Myself"
1998	"My Heart Will Go On" (Love Theme from *Titanic*)
	"I'm Your Angel" (with R. Kelly)
1999	"That's the Way It Is"

She was already a star in her local Quebec province when she released her first English language album in 1990. But the Top 10 song "Where Does My Heart Beat Now" set her on the path to international stardom. Next she scored a massive hit with the theme song to the Disney blockbuster *Beauty and the Beast*. The two songs would open up a run of 10 Top 10 hits, including four #1's. She took a temporary break from recording and performing in 1999.

In the late '90s, she faced some serious personal problems including her husband's throat cancer and the couple's thwarted efforts at having a child. She would eventually become a mother in 2001. When she returned in 2002 with *A New Day Has Come*, it was a huge seller internationally, although in the United States, the single, which was the title track, underperformed her hits of the '90s. In 2003, she landed a lucrative residency at Caesar's Palace in Las Vegas, which is expected to run through December 2007.

Awards:

992 Grammy Award, Best Pop Performance by a Duo or Group, Vocal, "Beauty and the Beast"

1992 Oscar, Best Song Written for a Motion Picture, *Beauty and the Beast*

1996 Grammy Award, Album of the Year, *Falling Into You*

1996 Grammy Award, Best Pop Vocal Album, *Falling Into You*

1998 Grammy Award, Female Pop Vocal Performance, "My Heart Will Go On" (Love Theme from *Titanic*)

1998 Golden Globe, Best Original Song, "My Heart Will Go On" (Love Theme from *Titanic*)

1998 Oscar, Best Original Song, "My Heart Will Go On" (Love Theme From *Titanic*)

1998 Golden Globe, Best Original Song from a Motion Picture, "The Prayer"

44 • LEGENDS OF POP

DIXIE CHICKS

1992–

When the Dixie Chicks broke through in 1998 with their gazillion-selling *Wide Open Spaces*, cynics underestimated them as another in a series of Nashville cookie-cutter products, purveying middle-of-the-road soft rock under the guise of country music. What the cynics missed was that Natalie Maines had pipes, fiddler Martie Maguire and banjo picker Emily Robison had chops, the three of them had gorgeous harmonies, and they surrounded themselves with top-notch Nashville sidemen.

Truth be told, their first two major label releases had more in common with the smooth California rock of the Eagles, James Taylor, and Bonnie Raitt (the Chicks themselves would cite the latter two as major inspirations) although a bit of down-home picking was layered in as well. Songs like "I Can Love You Better" and "Let 'Er Rip" were far more proud and assertive than contemporary country was used to hearing. This attitude would be taken to the extreme in "Goodbye Earl," in which our heroines poison an abusive husband and get away with it. The song would reach #19 on the pop charts.

They lost much of their country audience after Maines made critical remarks about President Bush. But for every country fan they lost, they picked up a pop fan. They abandoned most of their country colorings on *Taking the Long Way* in 2006, and lashed back at their critics in the single "Not Ready to Make Nice."

The media was filled with reports on how poorly the album sold relative to their previous records and how bad ticket sales were for the accompanying tour. In fact, it was one of the top-selling albums of the year in any genre. The album would top the country and pop charts and "Not Ready to Make Nice" would go to the Top 10. They won five Grammy awards in 2006 for Album of the Year, Record of the Year, Song of the Year, Best Country Album, and Best Country Performance by a duo or group.

FROM LEFT: EMILY ROBISON (BANJO, MANDOLIN, VOCALS), NATALIE MAINES (GUITAR, VOCALS), MARTIE MACGUIRE (FIDDLE, VOCALS). WHILE THE PRESS REPORTED ON HOW POORLY *TAKING THE LONG WAY* WAS FARING IN COUNTRY MARKETS, THE ALBUM WAS A HUGE SUCCESS ON THE POP CHARTS.

Shut Up and Sing

On the eve of the United States invasion of Iraq in March 2003, the Dixie Chicks were performing in London. The band's setlist included "Traveling Soldier," in which the protagonist befriends a soldier leaving for the battlefield and agrees to accept his letters from the front. She falls in love with him only to learn later that he's been killed. During the concert, lead singer Natalie Maines quipped, "Just so you know, we're ashamed the President of the United States is from Texas."

Maines would apologize for being "disrespectful." But she would not shy away from her stand and said, "I feel the President is ignoring the opinions of many in the U.S. and alienating the rest of the world. My comments were made in frustration, and one of the privileges of being an American is you are free to voice your own point of view."

Their songs were dropped from many country radio stations' playlists. In the age of radio consolidation, whole radio conglomerates were blackballing the group. Maines, Robison, and Maguire were also the subject of death threats. A documentary on the affair, *Shut Up And Sing*, was released in 2006.

GREATEST HITS	
YEAR	SONG
1998	"I Can Love You Better"
	"There's Your Trouble"
	"Wide Open Spaces"
1999	"Let 'Er Rip"
	"You Were Mine"
2000	"Goodbye Earl"
2002	"Long Time Gone"
	"Landslide"
	"Traveling Soldier"
2006	"Not Ready to Make Nice"

FATS DOMINO

February 26, 1928–

Fats Domino, born Antoine Dominique Domino, was the first and most popular rock and roller to emerge from New Orleans in the '50s. The loping rhythms, the cleaned-up Professor Longhair riffs, the horn arrangements of Dave Bartholomew, Lee Allen's saxophone, and Domino's cherubic countenance yielded 11 Top 10 hits in five years. But more importantly, Domino established the distinctive sound of New Orleans.

The story of Fats Domino begins with a local jazz trumpeter named Dave Bartholomew, who was building a reputation as one of the finest bandleaders in New Orleans. He played a mixture of jazz, big band, jump blues, and eventually rhythm and blues. Lew Chudd, founder of Imperial Records, took a liking to Bartholomew's band and in 1949, offered him a job as a talent scout.

At the time, Domino was one of the top draws at a popular Ninth Ward club called the Hideaway. Bartholomew took Chudd to see Domino play, and soon Fats was signed to Imperial. His debut single, "The Fat Man," in 1950, was the first national hit for Imperial, rising to #2 on the R&B charts. It would be cited by some as the first rock and roll song.

A string of Top 10 R&B hits followed, but he would break through on the pop charts in 1955 with "Ain't It a Shame," which went to #10. Some of the greatest songs in rock and roll history would follow, including "Blueberry Hill" and "I'm Walkin.'"

He left Imperial Records for a lucrative deal with ABC-Paramount Records in 1963, but would never again reach the upper rungs of the charts. He stopped touring in the '80s, but would make appearances at the annual New Orleans Jazz and Heritage Festival. He became a charter member of the Rock and Roll Hall of Fame in 1986. One of the most enduring images of Hurricane Katrina was a 77-year-old Domino being helped onto a Coast Guard helicopter.

Fats Domino brought the sound of New Orleans to the pop charts in the '50s.

Allen Toussaint

One cannot discuss New Orleans music without discussing Allen Toussaint and Minit Records. Minit yielded virtually every major New Orleans hit that wasn't recorded by Fats Domino.

Toussaint was the head talent scout, producer, arranger, and songwriter for Minit Records, where he worked with Irma Thomas, Lee Dorsey, and Aaron Neville. His songwriting credits include "Mother-In-Law" by Ernie K-Doe (#1, Pop, 1961) and "Working In The Coal Mine" by Lee Dorsey (#8, Pop, 1966).

After he returned from the draft in 1965, he established the Sansu production company with partner Marshall Sehorn. The company's house band was the Meters, who were pioneers of New Orleans funk. Toussaint opened Sea-saint Studios in the '70s, where everyone from Paul McCartney to LaBelle to Paul Simon would record.

As a songwriter, Toussaint's songs would be covered by Glen Campbell, Little Feat, and Boz Scaggs. More recently, he has assumed the role of ambassador for the recovering city of New Orleans, tirelessly campaigning for relief charities.

GREATEST HITS

Year	Song
1950	"The Fat Man"
1955	"Ain't It a Shame"
1956	"I'm in Love Again"
	"Blueberry Hill"
1957	"Blue Monday"
	"I'm Walkin'"
	"It's You I Love"
	"Valley of Tears"
1958	"Whole Lotta Lovin'"
1959	"I Want to Walk You Home"
	"Be My Guest"
1960	"Walking to New Orleans"

DR. DRE

FEBUARY 18,1965–

Dr. Dre is one of the most creative and influential DJs in rap music. A member of the hip-hop group N.W.A. (Niggaz With Attitude) in the late '80s, Dr. Dre helped pioneer the sound of "gangsta rap"—intricate and layered samples designed to be abrasive and reflective of the bleak lives of young black kids in South Central Los Angeles. When N.W.A. splintered, Dre became one of the most sought-after producers in rap. In the early '90s, he forged the so-called West Coast "G-Funk" style of rap that included melodic R&B, funk-based samples, and more laid-back and bass-heavy beats. Unlike the sound of the '80s and early '90s, in which the raps were as rhythmic as the beats, Dre's newer raps were looser. The blueprint was the massive hit *The Chronic*, which helped to launch the career of Snoop Doggy Dogg. He would also have huge success with his productions for Eminem and Busta Rhymes.

Dre was born Andre Young in Compton, California. He was raised by a single mother who loved music and allowed her 3-year-old son to DJ her card parties. By high school, he would be taken in by the radical sound of hip-hop and joined other South Central Los Angeles hip-hop fans in creating N.W.A.

In 1992, he formed Death Row Records with Marion "Suge" Knight. Dre's own *The Chronic* yielded two Top 10 hits, established West Coast rap in the pop mainstream, and introduced the world to Snoop Doggy Dogg.

DR. DRE IS ONE OF HIP-HOP'S MOST IMPORTANT PIONEERS AND MOST SUCCESSFUL PRODUCERS.

From 1992 to 1996, anything that came out of the rap world would feel the influence of Dr. Dre. He left Death Row in early 1996 and by 1997 the label was reeling from the murder of its most promising star, 2Pac, and the imprisonment of Knight for probation violation.

In 1996 Dre formed his own label, Aftermath Entertainment. Two years later, a tape from a white Detroit rapper named Marshall Mathers would find its way to Dre. Dre produced three songs for the rapper, nicknamed Eminem, which would help him on his way to becoming the most popular and critically acclaimed rapper of the new millennium. Dre hasn't released an album of his own since 1999, but he continues to focus on artists from his Aftermath label. Almost singlehandedly he turned gangsta rap into mainstream pop music without diluting the message or the music.

GREATEST HITS

YEAR	SONG
1992	"Deep Cover" (with Snoop Doggy Dogg)
1993	"Nuthin' But A 'G' Thang"
	"Dre Day" (with Snoop Doggy Dogg)
	"Let Me Ride" (with George Clinton)
1995	"Keep Their Heads Ringin'"
1996	"California Love" (with 2Pac and Roger Troutman)
1996	"No Diggity" (with BLACKstreet)
1999	"Still D.R.E." (with Snoop Doggy Dogg)
2000	"Forgot about Dre" (with Eminem)
	"The Next Episode" (with Snoop Doggy Dogg)

N.W.A.

Prior to N.W.A., rap was usually either good-natured boasting, storytelling, or in the case of Public Enemy and Boogie Down Productions, a political or social platform. N.W.A.—Ice Cube, Eazy-E, Dr. Dre, Yella, D.O.C., MC Ren, and the Arabian Prince—introduced what it called "gangsta rap," a reflection of life in South Central Los Angeles. Ice Cube's lyrics focused on visions and fantasies that were often violent but usually carried a cautionary and social message. Unfortunately, many people in the white mainstream were only familiar with the song title "F**k Tha Police," because an FBI agent said the song encouraged violence against policemen. The FBI would send thinly veiled threats to the group and their label, Ruthless Records. Ice Cube left the group in 1989 because of financial disagreements with management. Without Cube, N.W.A. lost whatever moral and political compass they had, and began focusing on Eazy E's puerile rants. Dre left in 1992, which effectively ended the group. Eazy E d ed of AIDs in 1995 and a posthumous album came out later that year.

THE DRIFTERS

1953–1966

THE DRIFTERS WERE INDUCTED INTO THE ROCK AND ROLL HALL OF FAME IN 1988.

GREATEST HITS	
YEAR	SONG
1953	"Money Honey"
1954	"Such a Night"
	"Honey Love"
1955	"Whatcha Gonna Do"
	"Adorable"
1959	"There Goes My Baby"
1960	"Save the Last Dance for Me"
1962	"Up on the Roof"
1963	"On Broadway"
1964	"Under the Boardwalk"

The Drifters were essentially two distinct groups, each of which made a huge but distinct contribution to pop music. The first, led by Clyde McPhatter, perfected the use of gospel stylings in secular subject matters, such as sex and money. They would have a string of R&B hits in 1953 and 1954, and were an essential piece of the pre-rock-and-roll story.

The second had the same name but different personnel and a different style. Led by Ben E. King, they would embrace more diverse influences, including Latin rhythms, intricate string arrangements, and wonderful narratives courtesy of the Brill Building songwriters.

Clyde McPhatter's first taste of success was with the Dominoes, a harmony group in the tradition of the Ink Spots and the Mills Brothers with gospel

stylings and phrasings. They applied those stylings to the bawdy "Sixty Minute Man," which reached the top of the R&B charts in 1951. Shortly thereafter, McPhatter left the Dominoes to form the Drifters, and had six straight Top 10 R&B hits.

The group disbanded in 1958 after a series of unsuccessful records. But they remained under contract to appear annually at the Apollo Theatre in New York. Their manager, George Treadwell, approached a harmony group called the Five Crowns, led by Ben E. King, and persuaded them to become the New Drifters.

This group became the best-known version of the Drifters in pop circles, with such hits as "There Goes My Baby" in 1959 and "Save The Last Dance For Me" in 1960. King would go solo in late 1960 and score two Top 10 hits with "Spanish Harlem," which was arranged by Phil Spector, and "Stand by Me."

Back in the Drifters camp, Rudy Lewis took over the lead singing duties and would score hits with "Some Kind of Wonderful," "Up on the Roof" and "On Broadway." Their last Top 10 hit, "Under the Boardwalk," featured Johnny Moore on lead vocals. They were inducted into the Rock and Roll Hall of Fame in 1988.

"I gave ['There Goes My Baby'] the back of my hand and refused to put it out for over a year. When it was finally released, it became one of the biggest hits in our history." —Jerry Wexler

DURAN DURAN

1978–

F ew bands would use the medium of music videos more effectively than Duran Duran. Their image doffed its chapeau to '70s glam rockers like David Bowie and Roxy Music, filtered through the British New Romantic movement of the early '80s. Their sound was Bowie mixed with Chic. And they came along at precisely the right moment, when MTV made image as important as music. The band had six Top 10 hits between 1982 and 1984 and was one of the top sellers of the '80s.

Bassist John Taylor was a student in art college in 1978 when he met keyboardist Nick Rhodes and formed Duran Duran, named after a character from the 1968 Jane Fonda sci-fi film *Barbarella*. The group had a number of members pass through their revolving door in the early days. One of the faces who stayed was drummer Roger Taylor. The three took a liking to modern postpunk sounds like Japan and Simple Minds.

After adding guitarist Andy Taylor and vocalist Simon LeBon, a local drama student, they got a contract with EMI in late 1980, and by mid 1981 they had their first U.K. Top 10 hit, "Girls on Film," powered by a racy video that would be censored on MTV.

But the formula was established synth pop textures set to a mildly funky beat and the good looks of

FROM LEFT: ANDY TAYLOR (GUITAR), NICK RHODES (KEYBOARDS), SIMON LEBON, (VOCALS), ROGER TAYLOR (DRUMS), JOHN TAYLOR (BASS). DURAN DURAN EXPLOITED THE POWER OF VIDEO MORE THAN ALMOST ANY OTHER BAND OF THE '80S.

Simon LeBon in front. The group's coup de grace was its videos. Rather than performance clips, almost every Duran Duran video had a concept. Whether it was an adventure film, a glorified travelogue, or a futuristic science fiction jaunt, the band made good television. Their second album, *Rio*, was a huge success on both sides of the Atlantic, fueled by hits like "Hungry Like the Wolf" and the title track.

The band went on a hiatus in 1985, from which it never really recovered. Duran Duran soldiered on in various incarnations throughout the '80s and '90s with an occasional Top 10 hit to remind the world that they were still around. In 2004, all original members reunited to release a new album, *Astronaut*, a simulation of their '80s sound that failed to garner much of an audience, although the accompanying tour was a huge success.

GREATEST HITS

YEAR	SONG
1981	"Girls on Film"
1982	"Hungry Like the Wolf"
1983	"Rio"
	"Is There Something I Should Know"
	"Union of the Snake"
1984	"The Reflex"
	"The Wild Boys"
1985	"A View to a Kill"
1986	"Notorious"
1993	"Ordinary World"

Duran's Offspring

Power Station featured bassist John and guitarist Andy Taylor. They added the rhythm section from Chic—drummer Tony Thompson and bassist Bernard Edwards—and front man Robert Palmer, who'd had a hit in the '70s with "Bad Case of Loving You (Doctor Doctor)" and would later storm the charts with "Addicted to Love" and "Simply Irresistible." Power Station scored two Top 10 hits with "Some Like It Hot" and a cover of T-Rex's "Bang a Gong."

Arcadia was formed by the remaining members of Duran Duran: Roger Taylor on drums, Nick Rhodes on keyboards, and Simon LeBon on vocals. Pink Floyd's Dave Gilmour, Sting, and jazz great Herbie Hancock would guest on the album, which spawned the Top 10 hit "Election Day."

EAGLES

1972–

The Eagles rose to prominence in the '70s with a smooth refined sound that combined the best of what California rock had to offer: the tight harmonies and country flavorings of the Byrds' *Sweetheart of the Rodeo* plus an ability to turn the guitars up to 11 à la Buffalo Springfield. But while there was a kind of chaos to much of this music, the Eagles added an element of craft to the proceedings. The lyrics, rather than reflecting the hippie optimism of the '60s, took a more cynical take on love. With this sound, they owned the pop charts from 1974 to 1980 with nine Top 10 hits, including six in a row from 1974 to 1977, and five chart-topping hits. Their first greatest hits collection is among the best-selling albums of all time.

"If we don't kill each other first."

—Don Henley on the prospects of a new Eagles album in 2007

Guitarist Glenn Frey and drummer Don Henley were part of the backup band for Linda Ronstadt in the early '70s, when Ronstadt was a regular at the legendary West Hollywood club The Troubadour. The club became a hotbed of local singer-songwriters. The scene included Jackson Browne, who would co-write the Eagles first hit, "Take It Easy" with Frey.

Frey and Henley were joined by bassist Randy Meisner, a member of the Buffalo Springfield-offshoot Poco, and Bernie Leadon, a guitarist and banjo

Flying Solo

Glenn Frey embarked on a career that reflected his love for Southern soul music and scored an occasional Top 10 soundtrack hit with "The Heat Is On" from *Beverly Hills Cop* in 1984 and "You Belong to the City," from the television show *Miami Vice* in 1985.

Henley would fare better commercially by departing from the Eagles' sound, favoring a harder edge both in sound and subject matter. "Dirty Laundry" was a scathing indictment of television news that made #3 in 1982. "The Boys of Summer," a collaboration with Tom Petty's guitarist Mike Campbell, reached #5 in 1984 and was one of the finest songs of the decade.

player from Gram Parsons' Flying Burrito Brothers. Originally conceived as a rock and roll band, producer Glyn Johns reorganized the Eagles, focusing on their tight harmonies to achieve a

FROM LEFT: BERNIE LEADON (BANJO, MANDOLIN, GUITAR), GLENN FREY (GUITAR, VOCALS), DON HENLEY (DRUMS, VOCALS), RANDY MEISNER (BASS, VOCALS), DON FELDER (GUITAR). THE EAGLES, PICTURED HERE CIRCA 1974–75, DOMINATED THE CHARTS THROUGHOUT THE '70S.

THE EAGLES PERFORM IN LONDON IN 2006 DURING A SERIES OF FAREWELL TOURS.

mellow country-rock flavor. The band scored hits with "Take It Easy," "Witchy Woman," and "Peaceful Easy Feeling."

They added second guitarist Don Felder in 1974, which toughened their sound somewhat, but their biggest successes were still in the country-rock vein with hits like "The Best of My Love," "Lyin' Eyes," and "Take It to the Limit."

When Joe Walsh arrived in 1976, replacing Leadon, most of the country was stripped out of the band ("New Kid in Town" was the notable exception), and in its place was a twin slide guitar attack that recalled the Allman Brothers. Nothing in the Eagles' formula was left to chance, and the pristine sound of songs like "Hotel California" and "Life in the Fast Lane" continues to influence classic rock radio to this day. Deciding they'd had enough of one another, they split in 1980. They would reconvene in 1994 for the *Hell Freezes Over* album and tour, so-called because up to that point, that was how they answered the inevitable question,

"When will the Eagles get back together?" They reunited again in 2003 for their ironically-titled "Farewell Tour I." At press time, they are putting the finishing touches on their first album of new material in nearly 30 years to add to their credentials as one of the best-selling acts in pop music.

NUGGET: The closing track of the Eagles 1975 album *One of These Nights*, "I Wish You Peace," was cowritten by Patti Davis, who may be better known as Patricia Ann Reagan, daughter of the former president.

The Flying Burrito Brothers

The roots of the Eagles' sound can be traced back to a band that had no singles to speak of but whose influence casts a long shadow over rock music: the Flying Burrito Brothers. The Burritos were a spin-off of the Byrds following the latter group's landmark country-rock fusion *Sweetheart of the Rodeo*. The Flying Burrito Brothers was the brainchild of a Georgia-born musician Gram Parsons, who aimed for a combination of the Rolling Stones and Buck Owens. He achieved this with their debut album *The Gilded Palace of Sin*, a sterling hybrid of psychedelia and down-home country. Multi-instrumentalist Bernie Leadon played with the Burritos in 1971 before joining the Eagles the following year. Parsons died in 1973 of a drug overdose after recording two fine albums with Emmylou Harris. Leadon wrote "My Man," from the Eagles' album *On the Border*, as a tribute to Parsons.

GREATEST HITS	
YEAR	SONG
1972	"Take It Easy"
	"Witchy Woman"
1974	"The Best of My Love"
1975	"One of These Nights"
	"Lyin' Eyes"
	"Take It to the Limit"
1976	"New Kid in Town"
	"Hotel California"
1979	"Heartache Tonight"

EARTH, WIND & FIRE

1969–

Earth, Wind & Fire fused early '70s funk, and a touch of big-band jazz with a mystical, almost prog-rock sensibility. It was slicker than the funk derived from Sly & the Family Stone or the R&B from Stax, but not quite mechanical enough to be disco. Their stage act was often an elaborate affair, with magic tricks and pyrotechnics that would eventually influence Michael Jackson's stage show in the '80s.

"Their music wasn't just music. It was therapy, food for the soul, with very conscious and self-motivating lyrical content." —Raheem DaVaughn on Earth, Wind and Fire

The group scored its first hit in 1975 with "Shining Star," which was a hit both in the discos and on the pop charts where it reached #1. From 1975 to 1981, they were one of the most popular R&B acts in the world, helped by their compelling live show. In 1978

> **NUGGET:** Earth, air, and fire are the elements that influence Sagittarius, which is Maurice White's astrological sign.

EARTH, WIND & FIRE (WITH MAURICE WHITE AT TOP) COMBINED ELEMENTS OF JAZZ, ROCK, RHYTHM AND BLUES, AND DISCO.

and 1979, they had four straight Top 10 hits, including the Bailey-driven ballad "After the Love Has Gone," which featured the soaring tenor of Philip Bailey.

The group took a break in 1983, and later, in 1984, point Bailey scored a Top 10 duet with Phil Collins, "Easy Lover." The Earth, Wind & Fire horn section toured with Collins and gave his music an R&B bent. They reunited in 1987 without making much of a dent in the sales charts. In 1994, the band's founder and guiding force, Maurice White, retired from touring as a result of complications from Parkinson's disease, although he continues to work with the group in the studio.

Legendary R&B production team Jimmy Jam and Terry Lewis produced Earth, Wind & Fire's most recent album, *Illumination*, which also included cameos from members of Black Eyed Peas.

In the Beginning

Earth, Wind & Fire was founded by Maurice White, who had been a session drummer for Chess Records from 1963 to 1967, playing with the likes of Etta James and Fontella Bass. He was briefly a member of the Ramsey Lewis Trio in 1969, four years after the group had its hit with "The 'In' Crowd." He then formed the Salty Peppers, which had a local hit in Chicago, but failed to follow up with anything significant. The Salty Peppers moved to Los Angeles in 1971 to reform as Earth, Wind & Fire, with White's brother Verdine on bass and eventually singer Philip Bailey who would provide the high harmonies.

GREATEST HITS

Year	Song
1975	"Shining Star"
	"Sing a Song"
1977	"Serpentine Fire"
1978	"Fantasy"
	"Got to Get You into My Life"
	"September"
1979	"Boogie Wonderland" (with the Emotions)
	"After The Love Has Gone"
1981	"Let's Groove"

ELECTRIC LIGHT ORCHESTRA

1971–2001

Although they were pooh-poohed by critics, John Lennon himself would give the Electric Light Orchestra his imprimatur as one of the better Beatles-influenced bands. One of several groups that fused classical music with rock and roll, ELO were more Beatles-influenced than any of them. And they were the only ones who approached the classical fusion with any sense of irony.

The band began as a side project of the Move, a British group heavily influenced by the Beatles that had seven Top 10 singles in the U.K. charts from 1967 to 1972. The Move would also garner attention for their Who-inspired act of destroying televisions on stage. Move members Roy Wood and Jeff Lynne were interested in adding a string section to a rock band. One of their first tries, a version of "Roll Over Beethoven," would run eight minutes long and include a musical quote from Beethoven's Fifth Symphony. U.K. record buyers pushed the song to #6.

Wood would leave ELO to form Wizzard. As ELO's new frontman, Jeff Lynne steered the band toward a more Beatles-influenced sound, although no less orchestrated than their previous material. Their breakthrough album (or "symphony," as they would call it) in the U.S., *Eldorado*, would include a 30-

ELECTRIC LIGHT ORCHESTRA AND THEIR BEATLESQUE POP EARNED APPROVAL FROM JOHN LENNON.

piece orchestra and spawned the Top 10 single "Can't Get It Out of My Head." By 1977, they had earned a reputation for their stage show, which featured a spaceship and elaborate lasers and lights. Their music would also begin to show the influence of disco in the Top 10 singles like "Turn to Stone" and "Shine a Little Love."

Although some of their music hasn't aged well (*Xanadu* soundtrack, anyone?), they approached their craft with enough tongue in cheek to create a body of work that endures. And if the John Lennon endorsement wasn't enough, Lynne would be tapped by George Harrison to produce his comeback album, *Cloud Nine*, and the surviving Beatles would call on him to produce their "reunion" singles, "Free as a Bird" and "Real Love."

GREATEST HITS	
YEAR	SONG
1974	"Can't Get It Out of My Head"
1975	"Evil Woman"
1977	"Telephone Line"
	"Turn to Stone"
1978	"Sweet Talkin' Woman"
1979	"Shine a Little Love"
	"Don't Bring Me Down"
1980	"Xanadu" (with Olivia Newton-John)
1981	"Hold on Tight"

Traveling Wilburys

While many supergroups start out with the best of intentions, the reality is that many sound contrived at best and exploitative at worst. The Traveling Wilburys is the exception. Rife with humor, spirited playing, and undeniable tunes, the off-the-cuff collaboration among Bob Dylan, George Harrison, Jeff Lynne, Roy Orbison, and Tom Petty would prove to be the best thing that any of the individual members had done in years.

Harrison said it gelled when he and Lynne, who was producing an album with Roy Orbison, were trying to come up with a B-side for a single from *Cloud Nine*, and they invited one-time touring mates Dylan and Petty to participate. The result was "Handle with Care." Harrison thought the song was too good to be relegated to a B-side, so the group decided to record a whole album.

MISSY ELLIOTT

July 1, 1971–

In a genre dominated either by men or by women eager to show skin and cleavage, Missy Elliott's career exploited her skills, not her body. Possibly the most popular female hip-hop star of all time, she was producer and songwriter before she ever recorded under her own name. When she did get her own record deal, she became not only commercially successful, but also one of the the most critically acclaimed acts in hip-hop. Her exuberance and her humor came as something of tonic in a world still reeling from the twin killings of Notorious B.I.G. and 2Pac.

Elliott began performing in the early '90s with a group called Sista. The group recorded an album in 1994 with DeVanté Swing, a member of and producer for popular R&B act Jodeci, who was establishing his own label Swing Mob. The label folded before the album was released. But the experience solidified her songwriting and production partnership with Tim "Timbaland" Mosley, who would later become one of hip-hop's most important producers.

Elliott and Timbaland went on to contribute songs for SWV, Destiny's Child, and most notably Aaliyah, for whom the duo wrote the hits "One in a Million" and "If Your Girl Only Knew." Elliot also appeared on Sean "Puffy" Combs' productions, which increased her stock further.

When she arrived with her debut album, *Supa Dupa Fly*, she became a darling of MTV because of the compelling video for "The Rain (Supa Dupa Fly)"

> "As much as I love Puffy and I know he makes stars, I didn't want to be under him, I wanted to be at the same table as him drinking the same champagne, I wanted to buy him drinks." —Missy Elliott

Missy Elliot performs in Amsterdam in 2004, at the time of *This Is Not a Test*.

that featured Elliot in an oversized spacesuit. She also notched two Top 10 hits with her appearances on "Make It Hot" by Nicole and "Trippin'" by Total. She's been a mainstay on the R&B charts throughout the '90s and early 2000s, hitting the Top 10 in 2002 with "Work It" and "Gossip Folks."

Timbaland

Timbaland (Timothy Mosley) has become something of a Phil Spector for the new century. His sounds are instantly recognizable: a heavy bass with understated drums, similar to '70s soul music, but his palette of sounds range from Cuban to African to avant garde to cartoon sound effects. He got his start as a popular DJ in and around his hometown of Norfolk, Virginia, where he began collaborating with Missy Elliott. The team began working with DeVanté Swing's Swing Mob label. He was discovered by an Atlantic Records executive, Craig Kallman, who paired him and his songwriting partner Missy Elliott with Aaliyah. In 1996, Elliott and Timbaland wrote seven songs for Aaliyah's *One in a Million*, three of which were hit singles, including "If Your Girl Only Knew." In 2002, Timbaland produced Justin Timberlake's massive hit "Cry Me a River." In 2006, he produced Nelly Furtado's *Loose* and Timberlake's *Future Sex/Love Sounds*, two of the best-selling albums of the year.

GREATEST HITS

Year	Singles
1997	"Sock It 2 Me" (with Da Brat)
	"The Rain (Supa Dupa Fly)"
1999	"She's a Bitch"
	"Hot Boyz" (with Nas, Eve, and Q-Tip)
2001	"Get Ur Freak On"
2002	"Work It"
	"Gossip Folks" (with Ludacris)

EMINEM

October 17, 1972–

"I don't give a f**k, God sent me to piss the world off," sang Eminem in his second single, "My Name Is." And as a statement of purpose, he succeeded pretty well. Hip-hop hating columnists and opportunistic politicians seized on lyrics in which the narrator rapes and murders his mother, sells drugs that lead to a fatal overdose, slits his ex-wife's throat, or baits homosexuals using impolite epithets.

Yet, throughout all of his most outrageous lyrics, there is almost always an internal dialogue, a context in which Eminem (or his id-obsessed alter-ego "Slim Shady") makes his choices. That dialogue makes his music more personal and more political than any rapper who preceded him. Not only do his critics ignore this internal dialogue, they miss the irony and humor in his lyrics.

Subject matter aside, Eminem (born Marshall Mathers) is also one of the most skilled rappers of his generation, using tension and release against the rhythm, shooting off blistering, rapid-fire invectives without ever losing the structure of the song. And underneath are Dr. Dre's supreme aural collages.

Upon hearing raps from his first two records, producer and hip-hop legend. Dr. Dre immediately offered Eminem a contract with his Aftermath label. Eminem's Aftermath debut, 1999's *The Slim Shady LP* was a huge success, yielding two Top 10 rap hits. The 2000 follow-up, *The Marshall Mathers LP*, did even better, scoring a Top 10 hit with "The Real Slim Shady." *The Eminem Show* in 2002 yielded two more Top 10 hits, "Without Me" and "Cleaning Out My Closet," which were about as confessional as hip-hop has ever gotten. That same year, Eminem starred in the hit movie *8 Mile*, which spawned another Top 10 single "Lose Yourself." The movie and the soundtrack earned him greater respect from critics and increased his adult fan base.

While each of his albums are autobiographical, he has relied less on character and fantasy to tell his story on recent albums. It remains to be seen if his more

EMINEM IS BETTER KNOWN FOR HIS CONTROVERSIAL LYRICS THAN HIS HUMOR AND IRONY. BOTH PLAY AN EQUAL ROLE IN HIS SUCCESS.

GREATEST HITS	
YEAR	**SONG**
1999	"Just Don't Give a F**k"
	"My Name Is"
2000	"The Real Slim Shady"
	"Stan"
2002	"Without Me"
	"Cleanin' Out My Closet"
	"Lose Yourself"
2003	"Superman"
2004	"Just Lose It"
2005	"Ass Like That"

confessional tone will resonate with hip-hop fans the way his early material did. Until then, we're left with a catalog that is as thought-provoking as any work in any genre.

50 Cent

Upon his success with Dre's Aftermath Records label, Eminem established his own label Shady Records, which scored a massive hit with 50 Cent, the latest in what has become a rich tradition of so-called "real gangstas" who gave up a life of crime to become rap stars. 50 Cent (Curtis Jackson) was born to a 15-year-old mother who left her child in the care of his grandmother. He began dealing drugs at age 11, was arrested several times over the next 10 years, and spent six months in a military-style boot camp. His raps caught the attention of Run-DMC's Jam Master Jay. He signed Jackson, who subsequently assumed the stage name 50 Cent, which was taken from the nickname of a murdered Brooklyn drug dealer. Shortly after his full-length debut came out in 2000, he was shot. While recuperating, he made raps and mixtapes, one of which found its way to Eminem, who signed him to a new deal. Since 2003, he has been one of the most popular artists in the genre, scoring chart-topping hits with "21 Questions," "In Da Club," and "Candy Shop."

EN VOGUE

1990–

En Vogue, along with TLC, laid the groundwork for contemporary R&B harmony groups by refusing to be pigeonholed into any one style. They separated themselves from other girl groups of the era— Exposé and Sweet Sensation, for example—by drawing on a broader palette that included pop, hip-hop, gospel, funk, soul, and rock. In addition to smooth harmonies, they were also capable of the vocal runs that helped divas like Mariah Carey find success. With their broad array of influences and stylish looks, they owned MTV and the pop charts in the early '90s.

Denzil Foster and Thomas McElroy, a production team who were once part of the R&B group Club Nouveau ("Lean On Me, #1, Pop, 1987), held auditions for a new girl group they were assembling. Dawn Robinson, Terry Ellis, Cindy Herron, and Maxine Jones were chosen for the group, but the catch was that no one singer was going to be named the frontwoman. All four members would have opportunities to shine both in lead and harmony roles. Their first single, "Hold On," peaked at #2 in 1990, but only hinted at what was to come.

With 1992's *Funky Divas*, they would score three Top 10 hits that demonstrated all of their talents. In 1994, the Top 10 song "Whatta Man," a collaboration with Salt 'N' Pepa, proved to be one of the best hybrids of soul and hip-hop ever.

En Vogue moved easily between R&B, hip-hop, funk, and rock.

"We don't want a Diana Ross and the Supremes type situation . . . with four solid singers, it's very easy for the public to pick up on one person."—Denzil Foster

En Vogue climbed to the Top 10 once more in 1996 with "Don't Let Go (Love)" from the Queen Latifah movie *Set It Off*. After that, the group began to splinter and they got dropped from their label in 2000. Although the roster of members keeps changing, they continue to perform.

GREATEST HITS

Year	Song
1990	"Hold On"
	"Lies"
	"You Don't Have to Worry"
1992	"My Lovin' (You're Never Gonna Get It)"
	"Giving Him Something He Can Feel"
	"Free Your Mind"
1994	"Whatta Man"
1996	"Don't Let Go (Love)"

Funky Divas

Funky Divas has sold more than 10 million copies worldwide and was one of the best R&B albums to emerge out of the '90s. "My Lovin' (You're Never Gonna Get It)" emphasized sultry contemporary R&B. "Giving Him Something He Can Feel" was a cover of a minor Aretha Franklin hit from 1976. In En Vogue's hands, it was a showstopper, demonstrating their vocal virtuosity without sacrificing any raw soul. And "Free Your Mind" was a great funk, rock, and soul tribute to George Clinton.

EURYTHMICS

1980–2005

Eurythmics was a study in contradictions. On one hand, Annie Lennox was able to internalize the gospel and soul of Aretha Franklin to become one of the greatest white female soul singers in pop music. But the underlying fabric of music was dehumanized synth pop with drum machines and few organic sounds. On top of that, you had the androgynous look of Lennox set against the acid casualty image of producer/instrumentalist Dave Stewart. The result is something of a synth soul combination that is one of the highlights of the MTV era.

Stewart began his career in the late '60s with a group called Longdancer, which would get picked up by Elton John's label Rocket Records, before they split up. He would join with paramour Lennox in a band called the Tourists, which had two U.K. Top 10 hits with a "So Good to Be Back Home Again" and a cover of Dusty Springfield's "I Only Want to Be with You."

Stewart and Lennox would form Eurythmics as a duo in 1981, but they wouldn't have their first U.S. hit until MTV latched on to "Sweet Dreams (Are Made of These)" and propelled the song to the top

EURYTHMICS' SOUND WAS A UNIQUE COMBINATION OF SOUL AND SYNTHESIZER.

of the charts in 1983. The follow-up "Here Comes the Rain Again" juxtaposed synth pop with the organic sound of strings. But their next Top 10 hit would leave synth pop behind and stand as a straight-forward R&B number. "Would I Lie to You" established Lennox as a top-notch singer.

Stewart would go on to have a successful career as a producer, working with such artists as Tom Petty, Bob Dylan, and Mick Jagger. Lennox would have a Top 10 hit in a duet with Al Green on a cover of the Jackie DeShannon song "Put a Little Love in Your Heart." She also recorded a number of successful solo albums.

Stewart and Lennox reunited in 1999 for the album *Peace*, a more organic affair that faded without a trace in the U.S., but did better in the U.K. In 2005, they recorded two new songs for the *Ultimate Collection* compilation.

GREATEST HITS

Year	Song
1982	"Love is a Stranger"
1983	"Sweet Dreams (Are Made of These)"
1984	"Here Comes the Rain Again"
	"Who's That Girl"
	"Right by Your Side"
	"Sexcrime (Nineteen Eighty Four)"
1985	"Would I Lie to You"
	"There Must Be an Angel (Playing with My Heart)"
	"Sisters Are Doin' It for Themselves" (with Aretha Franklin)
1986	"Missionary Man"

Annie on Her Own

While Eurythmics never really broke up, they took a seven-year break after the 1989 *We Too Are One*. Annie's first solo effort *Diva*, was a departure from the electronic sound of Eurythmics in favor of a warmer feel that centered on her soulful voice and confessional ruminations about fame and identity. It sold successfully on both sides of the Atlantic and yielded three Top 10 hits in the U.K., "Why," "Walking on Broken Glass," and "Little Bird."

EVERLY BROTHERS

1957–

The Everly Brothers set the standard for duo harmony singing in rock and roll by applying the styles of country and bluegrass singers such as the Stanley Brothers, the Monroe Brothers, and especially the Louvin Brothers. But the rhythms of the Everlys' best-known songs came from rhythm and blues, not Appalachia. In their lyrics, they articulated the teen angst of lost love through the compelling narratives of Boudleaux and Felice Bryant.

Phil, born in 1939, and Don Everly, born in 1937, were the sons of Ike and Margaret Everly, a popular traveling country act. From the ages of 7 and 9 the boys were often featured on their parents' radio program. In the mid-'50s, Phil and Don were signed as songwriters to the giant Nashville-based publishing firm of Acuff-Rose.

Archie Bleyer, the president of independent label Cadence Records, signed the Everlys in 1957. In addition, Wesley Rose, who ran the Acuff-Rose firm, introduced the Everlys to the husband-and-wife songwriting team Boudleaux and Felice Bryant. The Bryants, in turn, gave the Everlys "Bye Bye Love," which had already been rejected by 30 other performers. The Everlys rode the song to #2 on the pop charts, the first of 15 Top 10 hits they would have between 1957 and 1962.

In 1960, at the peak of their success, they signed with Warner Brothers. Their first single for the label, "Cathy's Clown," topped the charts and became their biggest hit. At this point their material took a turn toward sentimentality. Although their arrangements became more complicated, later songs never caught on with their fans like their earlier, simpler tunes.

In the mid '60s, Don Everly became addicted to amphetamines and even attempted suicide. As sales began to decline, the brothers began to fight more frequently. At a 1973 concert, Phil smashed his guitar and left the stage. Don was left to finish the concert alone. The brothers wouldn't perform together again until 1983.

FROM LEFT: DON AND PHIL EVERLY COMBINED RHYTHM AND BLUES WITH THE COUNTRY HARMONIES OF THE LOUVIN BROTHERS.

GREATEST HITS	
YEAR	SONG
1957	"Bye Bye Love"
	"Wake Up Little Susie"
1958	"All I Have to Do Is Dream"
	"Bird Dog"
	"Problems"
1959	"('Til) I Kissed You"
1960	"Cathy's Clown"
	"When Will I Be Loved"
1961	"Ebony Eyes"
1962	"Crying in the Rain"

But the Everlys' harmonies would echo in the vocals of the Beatles and Beach Boys. In a fitting coda, when Simon and Garfunkel reunited in 2003, they invited the Everly Brothers to tour with them.

Boudleaux and Felice Bryant

No Nashville songwriters had more success in the rock and roll field than Boudleaux and Felice Bryant. Like their counterparts in the Brill Building in New York, their specialty was crafting distillations of teen angst. Some were just declarations of love, requited or otherwise. At their best, like Jerry Lieber and Mike Stoller, they wove unique stories that unfolded over three minutes or less. "Wake Up Little Susie" is one famous example.

Matilda Genevieve Scaduto was a self-taught singer from Milwaukee who used to write her own song lyrics to traditional Italian tunes. During World War II, she sang and directed shows for the local USO. She met a traveling country and jazz fiddler from Georgia named Boudleaux Bryant in 1945. They eloped after two days and she became Felice Bryant.

The Bryants became songwriters for the legendary Nashville publishing firm Acuff-Rose, where they penned songs for such country artists as Little Jimmy Dickens, Eddy Arnold, and Jim Reeves.

FLEETWOOD MAC

1967–2005

When discussing Fleetwood Mac, you'll sometimes hear about the songwriting triple threat of Stevie Nicks, Lindsey Buckingham, and Christine McVie and the sexual tensions that leaked through into their passionate and evocative lyrics.

But Fleetwood Mac's secret sauce was in the rhythm section. Mick Fleetwood, one of the most underrated drummers in rock, applied his blues background to the singer-songwriter context of Fleetwood Mac perfectly, dragging the beat or turning it around to reflect the tension in the lyrics. Similarly, bassist John McVie's fluid playing kept pace and created the perfect bedrock for Nicks' ethereal ruminations, Buckingham's pop experiments, or Christine McVie's confessions. They also benefited from the skillful guitar playing of Buckingham, who could slide from blues to country to folk effortlessly.

After forming as a straight blues-rock outfit, the band slowly edged towards more polished pop during the early '70s. Mick Fleetwood invited a songwriting duo,

Lindsey Buckingham and Stevie Nicks, to join the band in 1975 With their arrival, the band took a hard turn toward more accessible folk rock. Their first album with Buckingham and Nicks, Fleetwood Mac, sold close to 5 million, helped along by three hit singles.

The long-awaited follow-up was recorded while the personal lives of all of the band members were shattering. John and Christine McVie divorced and were barely speaking. Buckingham and Nicks ended their romantic relationship and poured their angst into their lyrics. The result was Rumours, which would spawn four consecutive Top 10 singles, including the #1 hit "Dreams," and go on to sell more than 30 million copies.

The band reportedly spent more than $1 million recording their next record, Tusk. It would sell "only" 4 million copies, and "only" yield two Top 10 hits. After Tusk, Buckingham and Nicks would each score solo Top 10 hits. The band reconvened for Mirage, which yielded two hits in "Gypsy" and "Hold Me," before splitting up.

They've reunited in different configurations during the past 20 years, scoring a couple of Top 10 hits in 1987.

FROM LEFT: MICK FLEETWOOD (DRUMS), STEVIE NICKS (VOCALS), LINDSEY BUCKINGHAM (GUITAR, VOCALS), CHRISTINE MCVIE (KEYBOARDS, VOCALS), JOHN MCVIE (BASS). FLEETWOOD MAC TURNED THEIR PERSONAL ANGST INTO THE SOME OF THE BEST-SELLING POP SONGS OF THE '70S.

Stevie Nicks' Bella Donna

Laden with mysticism and a harder edge than Fleetwood Mac, Stevie Nicks' solo debut Bella Donna had three hit singles. The first was a duet with Tom Petty, "Stop Draggin' My Heart Around," which went to #3—making it Petty's biggest hit. Nicks would record "Leather and Lace" with Don Henley, which would feature more soulful and vulnerable singing than he ever allowed himself with the Eagles. The third hit was "Edge of Seventeen," propelled by the white funk of guitarist Waddy Wachtel.

GREATEST HITS	
YEAR	SONG
1975	"Over My Head"
1976	"Rhiannon (Will You Ever Win)"
	"Say You Love Me"
1977	"Go Your Own Way"
	"Dreams"
	"Don't Stop"
	"You Make Loving Fun"
1979	"Tusk"
	"Sara"
1982	"Hold Me"
1987	"Big Love"
	"Little Lies"

THE FOUR SEASONS

1961–

THE FOUR SEASONS WERE ONE OF THE MOST SUCCESSFUL GROUPS OF THE DOO-WOP ERA.

In the '60s, two groups would set the standard for harmony sounds. In California it was the Beach Boys. In New York it was the Four Seasons. No harmony group sold more records in the '60s than the Four Seasons. Propelled by the shrill falsetto of Frankie Valli and intricate, innovative harmonies and distinctive productions of Bob Crewe, the Four Seasons were one of the only groups that were able to hold on to their audience even after the Beatles swept the United States. Frankie Valli, Bob Gaudio, Tommy DeVito, and Nick Massi would call on street-corner doo-wop, Motown, and Phil Spector for inspiration. And in the same way that the Beach Boys reflected white middle-class living on the West Coast, the Four Seasons reflected the hopes and dreams of city-dwelling teenagers.

Frankie Valli (or Francis Castelluccio, as his mother called him) grew up in Newark, New Jersey, singing on street corners in doo-wop groups. One of these groups became the Four Lovers, which scored a minor pop hit in 1956 with "You're the Apple of My Eye." With the addition of keyboardist and songwriter

> *"I thought everybody sang in falsetto. If I sing in falsetto, everybody should be able to sing in falsetto."*—Frankie Valli

Jersey Boys

The Four Seasons are more popular than ever thanks to the hit musical *Jersey Boys*, which is based on the lives of the group and is a virtual greatest hits collection played eight times a week on Broadway. The story is based on interviews with the three surviving members and the unpublished autobiography of Nick Massi, who died in 2000 at age 73. It was directed by Des McAnuff, who also directed *The Who's Tommy*. *Jersey Boys* won the Tony for Best Musical in 2006.

NUGGET: Four Seasons keyboardist and songwriter Bob Gaudio was a member of the Royal Teens at age 15, when the group had their hit with "Short Shorts." Sessionman extraordinaire Al Kooper was also one of the Royal Teens.

Bob Gaudio, the group changed their name to the Four Seasons, a tribute to a nearby bowling alley. Gaudio went on to co-write the Four Seasons' biggest hits, including "Sherry," "Big Girls Don't Cry," and "Walk Like a Man." They would hit the Top 10 more than a dozen times between 1962 and 1967.

They split in 1970, but regrouped in 1975 to have two Top 10 hits that were influenced by the disco era, "Who Loves You" and "December, 1963 (Oh What a Night)." The latter would even rise to the Top 20 in 1994 in a dance remix version. Valli also had a successful solo career in the pop field, with four Top 10 hits. He continues to tour regularly as Frankie Valli and the Four Seasons, although none of the original members perform with him (one of them, Nick Massi, died in 2000). He also played "Rusty Millio," a recurring character on the HBO series *The Sopranos*.

ARETHA FRANKLIN

MARCH 25, 1942–

No singer in pop music has been better than Aretha Franklin at her best. Musically, she represents the evolution of black music from Ray Charles and Sam Cooke through Otis Redding into something more powerful. Besides her technical skill, which is formidable, she could transform the simplest of love ballads into a statement of purpose, a declaration for

"(Soul is) the ability to make other people feel what your feeling. It's hard to laugh when you want to cry. Some people can hide it. I can't, so when I sing, it doesn't come across as fake."—Aretha Franklin

GREATEST HITS	
YEAR	SONG
1960	"Today I Sing the Blues"
1961	"Rock-A-Bye Your Baby with a Dixie Melody"
1967	"I Never Loved a Man (The Way I Loved You)"
	"Respect"
	"Baby I Love You"
	"A Natural Woman (You Make Me Feel Like)"
	"Chain of Fools"
1968	"(Sweet Sweet Baby) Since You've Been Gone"
	"Think"
1985	"Freeway of Love"
	"Who's Zoomin' Who"
1987	"I Knew You Were Waiting (For Me)" (with George Michael)

gender equality or a metaphor for civil rights. Whitney Houston and Mariah Carey's careers, and by extension Alicia Keys, Beyonce, and Christina Aguilera's, would be unthinkable had Aretha not paved the way.

In 1960, John Hammond, the legendary talent scout who discovered Billie Holiday, and later Bob Dylan and Bruce Springsteen, signed Franklin to Columbia Records They never really knew what to do with Franklin. While she was capable of recording the most elegant blues in the mode of Billie Holiday and Sam Cooke, the label placed her in other contexts, as well, singing standards, show tunes, and popular songs, none of which found a large audience.

When her contract expired in 1966, Atlantic Records pounced and focused on Franklin's gospel roots, melding it with their successful R&B formula. The

ARETHA FRANKLIN PERFORMS ON THE BBC'S *TOP OF THE POPS* IN MARCH 1968.

"I Never Loved a Man"

When Atlantic vice president Jerry Wexler went looking for places for Aretha Franklin to record in 1967, his first thought was Stax Records, which is where Wexler brought Otis Redding, Sam & Dave, and Wilson Pickett for their hits. But he wanted Stax owner Jim Stewart to underwrite Atlantic's advance of $25,000, which Stax was unwilling to do.

So Wexler headed south to Fame Studios in Muscle Shoals, Alabama, where proprietor Rick Hall had cut successful hits with Pickett and Percy Sledge. To Wexler, it seemed like a perfect fit. And in fact, when she sang the first verse of "I've Never Loved a Man," the musicians were floored.

After the song was recorded, they started work on the B side "Do Right Woman–Do Right Man" but did not finish it. At the end of the session, celebratory drinks were poured. But later that night, Hall and Ted White, Aretha's husband and manager, got into a fistfight. Wexler tried to patch things up, but soon Franklin and White disappeared, Wexler wrote in his autobiography.

All the while, "Never Loved a Man" was becoming a radio hit. But without a B-side completed, Atlantic couldn't release the single to the public. When Franklin reappeared several weeks later, she finished the song in New York in one session. "Never Loved a Man" peaked at #9 on the pop charts, giving Franklin her first bona fide hit.

result was "I Never Loved A Man (The Way I Loved You)," which became her first Top 10 pop hit.

Her next hit topped the pop charts and became one of the most important songs in pop music. Aretha turned Otis Redding's R&B hit "Respect" into a call and response with her backup singers, a strategy that came straight out of church. Underneath were the Southern boys, in particular guitarist Jimmy Johnson, playing a similar call and response with the Memphis Horns. Not only was "Respect" a pop hit, but coming out a year before Martin Luther King Jr. would be assassinated, it would become a theme song for the civil rights movement.

A string of 12 Top 10 hits would follow "Respect" between 1967 and 1973. She continued to have success on the R&B charts throughout the '70s. In 1980, she would perform a hilarious cameo in the Dan Aykroyd and John Belushi comedy *The Blues Brothers*, reprising her 1968 hit "Think."

She left Atlantic for Arista Records in 1980, and had a pair of R&B hits produced by Luther Vandross. But her triumphant comeback was in 1985, when she returned to the Top 10 with "Freeway Of Love" and "Who's Zooming You."

Franklin continues to record albums from time to time without making much of an impact on the charts. But if there's anything that the past 47 years have proven, it is foolish to underestimate a talent as great as Aretha Franklin.

C.L. Franklin

A fiery and intellectual orator as well as a charming man, the Reverend Clarence LaVaughn Franklin rose through the ranks of rural churches before assuming the leadership of a church in Buffalo and then moving to New Bethel in Detroit in 1946. The minister soon became known nationally for his sermons, many of which had the theme of black pride. Rev. Franklin, along with Martin Luther King Jr., led a historic freedom march involving 125,000 people down Woodward Avenue in Detroit in 1963. The march would be the prototype for Dr. King's March on Washington later that year. Civil rights leaders of the day including Adam Clayton Powell and Dr. King were friends of Rev. Franklin, who also was adept at raising money for civil rights causes. He was affiliated with some of the greatest gospel singers of all time, including Mahalia Jackson, Marion Williams, and Clara Ward, all of whom tutored Aretha.

New Bethel Church became the crossroads for many black activist movements. While Rev. Franklin was a powerful voice in the Democratic Party and never affiliated himself with so-called Black Power movements, he understood the value of dialogue with black nationalist groups and would allow them to use the church for conferences. He remained a potent force throughout the '60s and '70s both in the community and in Aretha's life. He was shot in a burglary attempt in 1979, and slipped into a coma as a result. He never regained consciousness. Aretha visited her comatose father regularly and assumed responsibility for his care until he died in 1984 at age 69.

MARVIN GAYE

April 2, 1939–April 1, 1984

To call Marvin Gaye Motown's greatest singer is to sell him short. He was one of the three best singers of the rock era (along with Sam Cooke and Aretha Franklin) and among the greatest popular music singers of all time.

The son of a store-front preacher, Gaye grew up in a strict household. There was constant friction between him and his father. His solace came from the gospel singers in church and street corner doo-wop. Combine the two and you get a pretty good idea of what his earliest singles "Stubborn Kind of Fellow" and "Hitchhike" sounded like.

"I would like for my music to raise people's consciousness, to give people hope."

—Marvin Gaye

MOTOWN GRANTED MARVIN GAYE MORE CREATIVE CONTROL THAN ANY OTHER ARTIST ON THE LABEL AT THAT TIME.

GREATEST HITS

YEAR	SONG
1962	"Stubborn Kind of Fellow"
1963	"Pride and Joy"
1964	"How Sweet It Is (To Be Loved by You)"
1965	"Ain't That Peculiar"
1967	"Your Precious Love"
	"If I Could Build My Whole World around You" (with Tammi Terrell)
1968	"I Heard It through the Grapevine"
1971	"What's Going On"
	"Mercy Mercy Me (The Ecology)"
	"Inner City Blues (Make Me Wanna Holler)"
1973	"Let's Get It On"
1977	"Got to Give It Up (Pt. 1)"
1982	"Sexual Healing"

By mixing the silk of Sam Cooke and the grit of Ray Charles, Gaye would give Motown 17 Top 10 hits, including chart-toppers "I Heard It through the Grapevine," "Let's Get It On," and "Got to Give It Up."

Gaye had more depth than any Motown artist not named Stevie Wonder. He wanted the opportunity to croon Nat King Cole-like ballads. "Once upon a Time," a duet with Mary Wells, proved he would have been quite successful had he pursued that style further. But Motown founder Gordy, had a good formula of bright, upbeat R&B-based hits and was famous for sticking with it. Given his track record, few could blame him.

Brother, Brother

Against Motown founder Berry Gordy's advice, Marvin Gaye shed the character of the handsome leading man in 1971 and became part preacher and part activist on the album *What's Going On*. Although not every song has aged gracefully, the album was one of the most ambitious rhythm and blues albums ever made, and yielded three Top 10 hits: the title track, "Mercy Mercy Me (The Ecology)," and "Inner City Blues (Make Me Wanna Holler)."

It was among the first rhythm and blues collections conceived as an album rather than as a series of singles and assorted filler. It also centered on Gaye's new persona and his lyrics, rather than pop hits. *What's Going On*, along with Stevie Wonder's forthcoming albums, would change the balance of power within Motown to the artist from the production and songwriting teams.

Finally, by incorporating more layered instrumentations, including strings, percussion, and funk rhythms as well as more overt political themes, *What's Going On* would pave the way for the sound of the label Philadelphia International, which included such hitmakers as The O'Jays and Harold Melvin and the Blue Notes.

His duets with Tammi Terrell were a high watermark for soul duets, in particular "Ain't No Mountain High Enough" and "If I Could Build My Whole World around You." Terrell would collapse in Gaye's arms during a show in 1967. After being diagnosed with brain cancer, she died three years later at age 24.

Gaye's 1971 pièce de résistance, *What's Going On*, was an album-long suite about the lives of young black people in politically changing times. The album, two years in the making, would represent a turning point both for Gaye, Motown, and rhythm and blues overall.

After *What's Going On*, Gaye evolved into a sultry love man with gospel inflections, with the blockbuster "Let's Get It On" and "I Want You." Along with Al Green, Gaye would inhabit the compelling and contradictory world of God and sex.

As part of a painful divorce negotiation, he agreed to pay Anna Gordy the royalties from a forthcoming album. He originally planned to issue an album of subpar material to spite her. But in 1978 he reconsidered and released *Here, My Dear*, a double album of ruminations about his relationship and alimony. The result was alternately passionate, embarrassing, and bizarre. The level of honesty and confession on the album made Joni Mitchell sound like the Chiffons. But it didn't make the album an easy listen.

Despite his commercial success, over the last few years of his life, Gaye was a man tortured by drugs, two crumbling marriages, writer's block, and financial problems. He would have one more Top 10 hit with "Sexual Healing" in 1982. But a day before his 45th birthday, he was shot to death by his father during an argument.

Howling with the Moonglows

Gaye got his start in 1957 as a member of a doo-wop group called the Marquees, whose first record was produced by Bo Diddley. After that record flopped, he hooked up with doo-wop pioneer Harvey Fuqua, who scored hits with the Moonglows' "Sincerely" and "Ten Commandments of Love." Impressed with Marvin and the Marquees, Fuqua sacked the rest of his own group and hired Marvin's and dubbed them the Moonglows.

When the Moonglows petered out, Fuqua, who had become a surrogate father to Gaye, took his protégé to Detroit, where he was going to work for Anna Records, a label started by Gwen Gordy, who would eventually marry Fuqua, and Anna Gordy, who would eventually marry Gaye.

The Gordy sisters had a brother named Berry, who had written several of Jackie Wilson's early hits such as the Top 10 hit "Lonely Teardrops" and was starting a label of his own called Tamla, although most people are familiar with the sister label, Motown. Gordy eventually absorbed Anna records into the Motown family and made Fuqua one of his most prized executives. Fuqua, in turn, brought Gaye to Gordy's attention, thus giving Motown one of its brightest stars.

GENESIS

1967–

GENESIS WAS ONE OF THE MOST ACCLAIMED PROGRESSIVE ROCK BANDS OF THE '70s. IN 1987, THEY TRANSFORMED THEMSELVES INTO POP-ROCK HIT MAKERS.

One of the legacies of the British Invasion was the notion that in order for rock to "grow up," it needed to be imbued with more sophisticated concepts. This legacy begat progressive rock, and one of its most accomplished practitioners was Genesis.

Genesis was formed in 1967 by four students at the posh Charterhouse boarding school in England, including Peter Gabriel (vocals), Tony Banks (keyboards), Mike Rutherford (bass), and Anthony Phillips (guitar). After a number of personnel changes, the band gelled in 1970 around Gabriel, Banks, Rutherford, guitar virtuoso Steve Hackett, and former child actor and drummer Phil Collins. The band evolved into a high-concept act with elaborate stage shows and complicated song structures that earned them a loyal following, although they had little to show for it on the pop charts. But they would make a number of albums considered by many to be the high-water mark for the progressive rock genre.

> "We're all loaded enough not to worry about where the next million is coming from." —Phil Collins

When Collins replaced Gabriel as the band's front man, Genesis would leave behind the classical influences. Hackett left the band in 1977. Genesis had its first Top 40 hit the next year with "Follow You Follow Me." Each successive album would stray even further from progressive rock and begin to reflect Collins' infatuation with R&B.

Initially, Genesis was confined to classic rock radio. But a series of clever videos and an updated sound would eventually turn Genesis into a full-fledged pop band with virtually no correlation to its earlier career. The band landed five straight Top 10 hits from the *Invisible Touch* record. They recorded one more album, *We Can't Dance*, before Collins left to devote himself to his solo career. Banks and Rutherford would release one album with vocalist Ray Wilson in 1997.

Fifteen years after they last recorded together, Banks, Collins, and Rutherford announced a reunion tour of stadiums featuring the production staff of the Rolling Stones tours, which promises elaborate sets and lighting, and lots of nostalgia from the '80s.

The Solo Years

Peter Gabriel: Peter Gabriel experienced a personal epiphany after seeing Bruce Springsteen live in London in 1975 and left Genesis soon after. At first, his solo career seemed like an extension of his work with Genesis. But by his third album, he would begin writing more socially conscious lyrics and applying African rhythms and textures to his music. He broke through to the pop charts in 1986 with "Sledgehammer."

Phil Collins: In his solo career, Phil Collins turned his attention to his love for rhythm and blues. The horn section from Earth, Wind & Fire would be featured prominently on all of his solo records. He would become so proficient at pop-rock that he scored 13 consecutive Top 10 hits between 1984 and 1990, including seven #1 hits.

GREATEST HITS

YEAR	SONG
1978	"Follow You Follow Me"
1980	"Misunderstanding"
	"Turn It on Again"
1981	"No Reply at All"
	"Abacab"
1983	"That's All"
1986	"Invisible Touch"
	"Throwing It All Away"
	"Land of Confusion"
1987	"Tonight, Tonight, Tonight"
	"In Too Deep"
1992	"I Can't Dance"

GOO GOO DOLLS

1986–

The Goo Goo Dolls mix '70s styled power-pop with hard rock and a splash of post-punk indie rock. Their "overnight success" took eight years. The Dolls took the very best of post-punk indie rock, gave it a pretty face, and a finished sheen, and took it to the top of the pop charts.

Johnny Rzeznik, Robby Takac, and George Tutuska (replaced by Mike Malinin in 1995) got together in the mid-'80s in a Buffalo band called the Sex Maggots. But after a number of incidents made them unpopular among club owners, they changed their name to the Goo Goo Dolls. They quickly earned a reputation for explosive and sometimes unpredictable live shows.

"If you wanna be successful, it's construed by a lot of people as a sellout." —Johnny Rzeznik

While some would sneer and call them a poor man's Replacements, they never denied their influences—the Minneapolis trinity of the Replacements, Husker Du, and Soul Asylum. In fact, Paul Westerberg cowrote the single "We Are The Normal" for the Goos' major label debut. The originating album, *Superstar Car Wash*, is one of the underrated albums of the post-Nirvana era despite its similarities with the Mats' *Don't Tell a Soul*.

They would reach the teenybopper crowd in 1995 with *A Boy Named Goo*, which included the prom-theme "Name," but the album was far from a sell-out, as the band managed to maintain some of its punk rock attitude thanks to Takac's more tongue-in-cheek numbers.

By the time the ballad "Iris" was released from the *City of Angels* soundtrack, most of the punk attitude had been shed. The song would lodge itself at the top of the charts for 18 weeks, making it one of the top hits of the '90s and making the Goo Goo Dolls bona fide pop stars.

GOO GOO DOLLS' LEAD SINGER JOHNNY RZEZNIK PERFORMS AT THE SHEPHERD'S BUSH EMPIRE IN 2006.

The Replacements

Before Wilco, Goo Goo Dolls, Green Day, or Nirvana, there were the Replacements. Catch them on stage one night, and they would hit you with 90 minutes of potent punk rock that would leave you gasping for air. The next night they might be so drunk that they could barely get through a song. When they did manage to finish a song, it was apt to be anything from Petula Clark to Bad Company to Robyn Hitchcock.

As a songwriter, Paul Westerberg was beloved as the patron saint of angst-ridden, white, suburban, middle-class kids who grew up on punk rock but weren't ashamed to cry in their milk because no one understood them.

In these contradictions lay one overriding point: Something noble and beautiful can be salvaged from failure—a sense that anything is possible, that you have something important to say, even if you are a drunk from Minneapolis.

GREATEST HITS	
YEAR	SONG
1993	"We Are the Normal"
1995	"Name"
	"Naked"
1998	"Iris"
	"Slide"
1999	"Black Balloon"
2000	"Broadway"
2002	"Here Is Gone"

GREEN DAY

1989–

irvana's explosion into the mainstream proved the hit potential of punk-influenced music and created the genre "alternative rock." The best and most successful of these bands was Green Day. Green Day combined the elements of the first generation of punk—the Sex Pistols, Buzzcocks, the Clash—with some of the angst of the Replacements and Husker Du. They created a sound that spoke to the alienated and disaffected youth of the '90s, without preaching and with a sense of humor.

Green Day guitarist Billie Joe Armstrong, bassist Mike Dirnt, and drummer Tre Cool emerged from Berkeley's punk rock scene in 1989. The band, whose name was inspired by the members' affection for marijuana, issued two albums on Lookout Records in 1991 and 1992, which did respectably for independent releases. Their music was longer on melody and craft than many of their punk contemporaries, and attracted the attention of Reprise Records in 1994. The band's major label debut, *Dookie*, was a blockbuster, selling more than 12 million copies, and yielding five singles, three of which went Top 10 on the Modern Rock charts.

Sales of subsequent albums dropped off considerably, although they maintained a fairly steady presence on modern rock radio. In 1997, they scored a hit with

FROM LEFT: TRE COOL (DRUMS), BILLIE JOE ARMSTRONG (GUITAR, VOCALS), MIKE DIRNT (BASS). GREEN DAY WAS ONE OF THE MOST SUCCESSFUL BANDS TO EMERGE FROM THE '90S ALTERNATIVE ROCK SCENE.

an uncharacteristic acoustic ballad laden with strings, "Good Riddance (Time of Your Life)."

In 2004, Green Day released a punk rock opera called *American Idiot*, a thinly-veiled criticism of Bush Administration policies. It was a massive success, topping the album charts and spawning five singles, including two Top 10 hits, "Boulevard of Broken Dreams" and "Wake Me up When September Ends." In 2006, they recorded a duet with U2, "The Saints Are Coming."

With the success of *American Idiot*, Green Day has evolved into elder statesman of punk rock. To record their most potent work 16 years into their career is something that eludes many classic rock acts, to say nothing of punk bands.

GREATEST HITS

Year	Song
1994	"Basket Case"
	"When I Come Around"
1995	"J.A.R. (Jason Andrew Relva)"
	"Geek Stink Breath"
1996	"Walking Contradiction"
1997	"Good Riddance (Time Of Your Life)"
2004	"Holiday"
	"Wake Me Up When September Ends"
	"Jesus of Suburbia"

Punker-than-Thou

Green Day's roots date back to a not-for-profit, volunteer, all-ages club in Berkeley called 924 Gilman Street, that reflected a do-it-yourself code of ethics espoused by many first-generation punk bands. It spawned a number of bands including AFI, Rancid, and Operation Ivy.

Gilman Street is also called the Alternative Music Foundation with an orthodox code of ethics (Former Dead Kennedys front man and owner of uber-independent label Alternative Tentacles was beaten up at the club because he was considered a "sellout". Their Web site notes, "We strive to provide a violence, alcohol and drug-free environment. We will not book or support racist, misogynist, or homophobic bands or performances" and bands must submit their lyrics before getting booked.

The club will also not book bands that are signed to major labels, thus barring many of the club's most successful offspring from returning.

AL GREEN

APRIL 13, 1946–

"My songs come from within. At first, I didn't know where I was going. Now, I know what the plan is. I've got it all straightened out with the man on high."—Al Green

The history of soul music has always been fraught with tension between the sacred and the secular. So when Al Green sings in the bridge to "Tired of Being Alone," "Needing you had proven to be my greatest dream," is he singing about a girl or God? Presumably it's a girl, but the yelp that follows is straight out of church.

The tension between the spirit and the flesh fueled Al Green. Almost every song was a plea for salvation. His voice was the most powerful in soul music since Otis Redding. And to slam the message home, he had the bubbling guitar of Teeny Hodges, the syncopated drums of Al Jackson, and the percussive horn charts of the Memphis Horns. To sweeten the message, there was the light touch of strings, helping the music to bridge the gap between gutbucket Southern soul and disco.

GREATEST HITS	
YEAR	SONG
1971	"Tired of Being Alone"
	"Let's Stay Together"
1972	"Look What You Done for Me"
	"I'm Still in Love with You"
	"You Ought to Be with Me"
1973	"Call Me (Come Back Home)"
	"Here I Am (Come and Take Me)"
1974	"Sha-La-La (Make Me Happy)"
1988	"Put a Little Love in Your Heart" (with Annie Lennox)

FEW PERFORMERS WOULD EXPRESS THE TENSION BETWEEN THE SACRED AND THE SECULAR BETTER THAN AL GREEN.

Willie Mitchell

Born in 1928, Mitchell was a trumpeter who played with some of the more popular big bands in Memphis while still in high school. He played on B. B. King's first recordings in 1949, and eventually formed his own big band, which would become a big draw in the West Memphis clubs. At one point, his band included Lewis Steinberg and Al Jackson, who would later go on to form Booker T. & The MGs.

He was hired to produce records at the Home of the Blues label, whose roster at one point included the "5" Royales and Roy Brown. He was then asked to produce at Hi Records, which had been garnering a reputation for cutting hit instrumentals, such as the Bill Black Combo's "Smokey Part 2." He still had designs on a recording career of his own, and cut his own Top 10 R&B hit in 1968, "Soul Serenade." It was around this time that he saw Al Green in Texas, while each was touring with their respective bands.

Willie Mitchell became the guiding force behind Al Green and his label, Hi Records. He emphasized the bass sound of his rhythm section, and had drummer Al Jackson rely on light syncopated beats on the tom-tom drums rather than the snare drum. The result was a mellower sound than the grit of Stax.

This sound would produce hits, not only for Green but for Ann Peebles ("I Can't Stand the Rain," #6, R&B, 1973), Syl Johnson ("Take Me to the River," #7, R&B, 1975, covered by Talking Heads), and Otis Clay ("Trying to Live My Life Without You," #24, R&B, 1972).

After Al Green left Hi Records, Willie Mitchell continued to record minor hits with Peebles, Clay, and George Jackson (who would later cowrite "Old Time Rock N Roll," the classic rock stable sung by Bob Seger). He reunited with Al Green to record I Can't Stop in 2003 and Everything's OK in 2005.

At age 9, Green joined the family gospel quartet called the Green Brothers that his father had formed, but was kicked out after getting caught listening to Jackie Wilson records. Green went on to create Al Green & the Soul Mates in high school and scored a Top 10 R&B hit with "Back Up Train" in 1967.

While on tour in 1968, he impressed R&B bandleader Willie Mitchell, who was touring behind his hit, "Soul Serenade." Mitchell, one of the guiding forces behind Memphis-based Hi Records, invited Green to record for the label, where he would have seven Top 10 pop hits between 1971 and 1974.

Tragedy struck in 1974 when a former girlfriend, distraught that Green would not marry her, doused him with boiling grits (or boiling water to make grits, depending on who's telling the story) while he was bathing. He suffered second-degree burns on his stomach, back, and arm. The woman then killed herself.

In 1976, he joined the ministry, and bought a local church in Memphis and named it the Full Gospel Tabernacle, where he preaches to this day. He would still record secular music until he slipped from a stage in 1979 and narrowly avoided serious injury. He took this as a sign from God that he should sing only for the Lord.

But it didn't stick, and he recorded a cover of the Jackie DeShannon hit "Put a Little Love in Your Heart" with the Eurythmics' Annie Lennox, which made the Top 10 in 1988. He would record a criminally underrated comeback album, Don't Look Back, in 1993 with member of the Fine Young Cannibals, which wouldn't be released in the U.S. until 1995 (with a different title and track lineup). He reunited with Willie Mitchell for a pair of albums in 2003 and 2005 that sounded, well, exactly like Al Green's '70s records.

HALL & OATES

1972–

Devotees of Motown and Philly soul, Hall & Oates merged the slicker strains of R&B with elements of pop and rock, and in the process sold more records in the '80s than all but three artists—Michael Jackson, Prince, and Madonna.

Daryl Hall (née Hohl) met John Oates during a race riot at a Philadelphia dance in 1967. Hall fled to a freight elevator where he found Oates, a fellow student at Temple University. Oates, who played in a number of local R&B acts, recognized Hall as a member of one of the city's best-known white soul acts, the Temptones. The two joined forces in 1972 and soon signed to Atlantic Records. Although their debut album didn't sell well, "Fall in Philadelphia" was a hit in their hometown.

They honed their songwriting skills and came up with a soul ballad, "She's Gone," musically inspired by Philadelphia acts like Harold Melvin & the Blue Notes, and lyrically inspired by Hall's divorce. The Tavares took "She's Gone" to the top of the R&B charts in 1974, giving Hall & Oates some cachet in the music business. Two years later, Hall & Oates would take their own version to the Top 10 of the pop charts.

DARYL HALL (LEFT) AND JOHN OATES PERFORM IN 1976. AT THE TIME, "SARA SMILE" AND "SHE'S GONE" WERE CLIMBING THE CHARTS.

It would be the first of three Top 10 singles in the '70s, the others being 1976's "Sara Smile" and 1977's "Rich Girl," a musical homage to the Spinners' "One of a Kind (Love Affair)." Afterwards, the duo suffered a three-year drought, until they decided to produce themselves for their 1980 album *Voices*. The result was an album that yielded three hit singles, including the #1 "Kiss On My List."

Hall & Oates were virtually omnipresent on Top 40 radio for the next four years, scoring twelve Top 10 hits. They would revisit the Top 10 once more with "Everything Your Heart Desires" in 1988 and "So Close," cowritten with Jon Bon Jovi, peaked at #11.

After a seven-year layoff, they reunited in 1997 to record *Marigold Sky* on their own label, which sold poorly. They worked on solo projects, before regrouping in 2003 to record more frequently. They have toured regularly since 2005.

GREATEST HITS	
YEAR	SONG
1976	"Sara Smile"
	"She's Gone"
1977	"Rich Girl"
1980	"You've Lost that Lovin' Feeling"
1981	"Kiss on My List"
	"You Make My Dreams"
	"Private Eyes"
	"I Can't Go for That (No Can Do)"
1982	"Maneater"
1983	"Say It Isn't So"
1984	"Out of Touch"
1988	"Everything Your Heart Desires"

Careers of the Backup band

T-Bone Wolk: Shortly before joining Hall and Oates, Wolk played bass on Kurtis Blow's 1980 hit "The Breaks," often cited as one of the first hip-hop hits. In 1986, he was asked to join the house band for *Saturday Night Live* by fellow Hall & Oates alumnus G.E. Smith. Wolk is now Hall & Oates' musical director.

G.E. Smith: Guitarist Smith got his start touring with Dan Hartman for following his first hit, "Instant Replay," in 1978. He became the pit guitarist for Gilda Radner's Broadway show *Gilda Live* in 1979. Hall & Oates hired him in 1979, and he stayed with the band until *Saturday Night Live* hired him as a musical director in 1986. Beginning in 1988, he toured for two years as Bob Dylan's lead guitarist.

WHITNEY HOUSTON

August 9, 1963–

Whitney Houston represented the next important step for gospel-influenced R&B singing, following Aretha Franklin. Although Franklin had a more limited vocal range, she became known for the feeling she could inspire within those limitations. Houston had no limitations in her voice. Every note is An Event—so much so that this effect sometimes upstages the words she's singing. But these are mere quibbles in the face of a career that has made her not only one of the best-selling artists of the '80s and '90s, but also the benchmark against which every other female vocalist is judged, regardless of the genre.

Whitney is the daughter of Cissy Houston, who scored several minor R&B hits in the '70s and was the lead singer in the estimable backup group Sweet Inspirations. By age 11, Whitney was singing in the New Hope Baptist Junior Choir in Newark, New Jersey, and by her teenage years she was singing backup for such legendary R&B acts as Lou Rawls and Chaka Khan. She was discovered in a nightclub by Arista Records poobah Clive Davis, who has overseen her career since. Between 1985 and 1988, she scored seven consecutive #1 hits.

Album sales dipped somewhat after her second album *Whitney*, but songs she's contributed to soundtracks have been huge hits. Her cover of Dolly Parton's "I Will Always Love You," from the film *The Bodyguard*, is one of the biggest hits of all time. "Exhale (Shoop Shoop)" from *Waiting to Exhale* was another chart-topper.

In 1998, she released *My Love Is Your Love*, which featured some contemporary hip-hop and R&B artists, including Babyface, Wyclef Jean, and Faith Evans. The album exceeded expectations, yielding three Top 10 singles, even though it didn't reach the stratospheric levels of her first two albums.

"My business is sex, drugs, rock and roll . . . Trust me. I partied my tail off . . . you get to a point where . . . the party's over." —Whitney Houston

WHITNEY HOUSTON PERFORMS AT THE BRIT AWARDS IN 1999. AT THIS POINT "HEARTBREAK HOTEL," "IT'S NOT RIGHT BUT IT'S OKAY," AND "MY LOVE IS YOUR LOVE" WERE CLIMBING THE CHARTS.

GREATEST HITS

Year	Song
1985	"Saving All My Love for You"
	"How Will I Know"
1986	"Greatest Love of All"
1987	"I Wanna Dance with Somebody (Who Loves Me)"
	"Didn't We Almost Have It All "
	"So Emotional"
1988	"Where Do Broken Hearts Go"
1990	"I'm Your Baby Tonight"
	"All the Man That I Need"
1992	"I Will Always Love You"
1995	"Exhale (Shoop Shoop)"
1999	"It's Not Right but It's Okay"

Houston, We Have a Problem . . .

The tumult in Houston's personal life started after she married R&B singer Bobby Brown in 1992. There were allegations that Brown abused her— "I do the hitting," Whitney would quip in a 1999 interview in *Redbook*. In 2002, she admitted to ABC's Diane Sawyer that she had used marijuana, cocaine, alcohol, and prescription drugs. In 2000, she was fired at the last minute from the Oscars broadcast by Burt Bacharach. She was also a no-show at the annual Rock and Roll Hall of Fame Dinner that year, in which her mentor Clive Davis, founder of Arista Records, was being inducted. She was supposed to sing at the dinner as a tribute, but she begged off, claiming "voice problems." Finally in 2006, after a stormy 14-year marriage, she filed for divorce from Brown. The divorce was finalized in April of 2007.

THE IMPRESSIONS

1958–1975

Although Chicago is better known for exports of such bluesmen as Muddy Waters and Howlin' Wolf, from 1961 to 1968 the city would produce a strain of soul music that amalgamated both the Memphis and Detroit styles of rhythm and blues. This sound would be perfected by the Impressions.

The Impressions were formed by Jerry Butler and Curtis Mayfield, two friends who had sung with the Northern Jubilee Gospel Singers at the Traveling Souls Spiritualist Church in Chicago. Initially a forum for Butler's smooth baritone, the group would score

GREATEST HITS

Year	Song
1958	"For Your Precious Love"
1961	"Gypsy Woman"
1962	"Grow Closer Together"
1963	"It's All Right"
1964	"Keep on Pushing"
	"Amen"
1965	"People Get Ready"
	"Meeting Over Yonder"
1967	"We're a Winner"
1968	"We're Rolling On"
	"This Is My Country"
1969	"Choice of Colors"

Superfly

When Curtis Mayfield went solo in 1970, his music became increasingly concerned with the problems of society. Taking cues from the darker tones of Sly & the Family Stone's *There's a Riot Goin' On*, "Freddie's Dead" and "Superfly" would have moral (some might say "preachy") cores compared with songs from other blaxplotation films. Mayfield's long funky vamps and carefully orchestrated arrangements would help usher in disco later in the decade.

"Being a young black man, observing and sensing the need for race equality and women's rights, I wrote about what was important to me." —Curtis Mayfield

a Top 10 R&B hit (#11, Pop) with the classic ballad "For Your Precious Love" in 1958. After Butler left to pursue a solo career, Mayfield took the reins and created a string of hits around his quasi-falsetto gospel tenor.

Although Mayfield initially wove narratives about love and loyalty, starting in 1963 he borrowed more heavily from gospel to address issues of freedom and equality raised by the growing civil rights movement. The best of these songs, "People Get Ready," would reach #14 on the pop charts and #3 on the R&B charts.

Mayfield never abandoned love songs, but the veil of symbolism in his lyrics grew increasingly thin. There would be little doubt what "Keep on Pushing" (#10, Pop, 1964), "We're a Winner," and "We're Rolling On" were about. He dropped the symbolism altogether (not coincidentally after the death of Martin Luther King) in 1968 and 1969, with a pair of singles, "This Is My Country" and "Choice of Colors," two of the most eloquent statements of pride and equality in R&B.

Curtis Mayfield left the Impressions to start a solo career in 1970 and continued to perform into the '80s. In 1990, while performing at an outdoor concert in Brooklyn, a strong wind blew over a lighting scaffold that crushed Mayfield beneath it leaving him paralyzed for life. In 1998, he lost his right leg to diabetes, and a year later he was gone at age 57, leaving behind a legacy of social consciousness in R&B that would form the bedrock of hip-hop in the future.

CURTIS MAYFIELD (THIRD FROM LEFT) EMPHASIZED CIVIL RIGHTS ISSUES IN HIS LYRICS.

JANET JACKSON

May 16, 1966–

Janet Jackson grew up in the shadow of one of the most successful entertainers of all time. By the late '80s she surpassed her brother Michael both artistically and commercially, by more adeptly updating her sound, more convincingly embracing samples and hip-hop, and projecting an image that was sexy, fiercely independent, and thoughtful.

At age 11, Janet won the role of "Penny Gordon," the abused child on the sitcom *Good Times*. She also got parts in *New Kind Of Family* and *Diff'rent Strokes* but in 1982, she was persuaded by her father to pursue music. Her first album, *Janet Jackson*, was a dance-pop album without distinction or identity and was quickly disavowed by the singer. Her second album featured a cameo by brother Michael and help from Jesse Johnson, a former member of the Time, but it too sank without a trace. She became better known for her marriage to James DeBarge, from the R&B act DeBarge. She was divorced after seven months.

For the next album, she was paired with the production team of Terry Lewis and Jimmy Jam, both veterans of the Time, who'd been freelance producers working with R&B groups like Klymaxx and the S.O.S.

Flyte Tyme

Terry Lewis and Jimmy Jam are one of the most successful production teams in the history of music, with 15 chart-topping pop hits and 25 #1 R&B hits. Their clients include Mariah Carey, Boyz II Men, Mary J. Blige, and Sting. They got their start with the Minneapolis R&B group the Time, who, under the tutelage of Prince, had four Top 10 R&B singles. The group began to pursue freelance production work and by 1983, they'd scored their first Top 10 R&B hit with the S.O.S. Band. They were promptly fired by Prince, allegedly for missing a gig, although Jam has suspected that they were becoming too much of a threat to his Royal Purpleness. By 1985, they had established their own production and publishing company, Flyte Tyme. A year later, Janet Jackson sought their services, and they turned one another into hot properties in R&B and pop.

JANET JACKSON DANCES IN LOS ANGELES IN 2001.

JANET JACKSON PERFORMS ON NBC's "TODAY SHOW" IN 2006.

GREATEST HITS	
YEAR	SONG
1986	"What Have You Done for Me Lately"
	"Nasty"
	"When I Think of You"
1989	"Miss You Much"
1990	"Escapade"
	"Black Cat"
1993	"That's the Way Love Goes"
	"If"
1997	"Together Again"
2000	"Doesn't Really Matter"
2001	"All for You"
2006	"Call on Me"

Nasty!

In 2004, Janet Jackson was named to the coveted bill at the Super Bowl halftime show to perform with Justin Timberlake. During the choreography of the performance, Timberlake was to tug at Jackson's outfit, but when he did, parts of her bosom were revealed, violating the morals of the tens of millions of people watching and sparking a debate on vulgarity in the media. Timberlake pleaded ignorance to what went down in history as a "wardrobe malfunction." He apologized and was allowed back into the good graces of the community, and took home two Grammys later that month. Jackson didn't apologize and her career nosedived thereafter.

Band. As they discussed the album and her life, the key theme of her new album took form, exemplified by its title, *Control*. The 1986 album was effectively her declaration of independence. She cowrote the songs, played keyboards on the album and was present for the assembling and mixing of the music. The result was five Top 10 singles.

Her 1989 album *Rhythm Nation 1814* was even more successful, with seven Top 10 hits—more than half the songs on the album—and included her ruminations on race, crime, education, and homelessness. While the lyrics didn't necessarily add to the well of human knowledge on any of these affairs, it indicated that these subjects were not exclusive to the rock and rap boys' club, and indeed demonstrated more ambition than many R&B acts in similar stratas of success.

Janet marked the beginning of her identity as a sex symbol, with her topless image emblazoned on the cover. But the music inside the cover was her most compelling yet, including the scorching ballad "That's the Way Love Goes."

The Velvet Rope topped the charts in 1997 and yielded a #1 single, "Together Again." It took her independent image and expanded it in her most personal and sexually explicit work, with allusions to deviances and bondage.

The Velvet Rope also marked a turn toward more personal matters. Each album that followed began to have the feel of diary entries rather than pop music. But few seemed to mind, as the 2001 album *All for You* included the chart-topping title track and the #3 hit "Someone to Call My Lover." *Damita Jo* in 2004 sold worse than its predecessors and failed to yield a Top 10 pop hit. But by then Janet Jackson had lost much of her credibility, if not her audience, because of the so-called "wardrobe malfunction" that exposed her breast at the 2004 Super Bowl halftime show. This was an ironic dénouement since she'd been much more explicit on her albums for years.

JANET JACKSON SIGNS COPIES OF *20 Y.O.* IN *2006* AT VIRGIN MEGASTORE IN NEW YORK.

MICHAEL JACKSON

AUGUST 29, 1958–

After the court cases, the marriages, the babies (and the dangling thereof), it's hard to remember that at one point (well, several points, really) Michael Jackson was the brightest hope for pop music. With the Jackson 5, he effectively carried Motown in the early '70s. He ushered R&B out of the disco era with *Off the Wall*. And by 1983, his *Thriller* album was selling a million records a week. He consolidated the very best of rhythm and blues from the '70s and, with the help of Quincy Jones, made irresistible pop music that broke down the color line at MTV.

We didn't just love Michael Jackson. We wanted to be Michael Jackson, whether we were black or white. Some of us bought the red "zipper" jacket, learned to moonwalk, or learned every single dance step from the "Thriller" video. He brought soul back to singing with *Off the Wall*. He was the '80s version of Elvis: the one thing that all music fans could agree on. And, like Elvis, when the fall came, it came hard.

Michael was the seventh of nine children born to Joe and Katherine Jackson in Gary, Indiana. Joe worked in a steel mill during the day and played in his own band at night. He wasn't shy about encouraging his kids' musical hobbies. In fact, he was a stern

MICHAEL JACKSON WAS ONE OF THE MOST POPULAR ARTISTS OF THE '70S AND '80'S.

GREATEST HITS

YEAR	SONG
1972	"Ben"
1979	"Don't Stop 'Til You Get Enough"
	"Rock with You"
1983	"Billie Jean"
	"Beat It"
	"Say Say Say" (with Paul McCartney)
1987	"The Way You Make Me Feel"
1988	"Man in the Mirror"
1991	"Black or White"
1995	"You Are Not Alone"
2001	"You Rock My World"

"Looking back, I can view the whole tapestry and see how Off the Wall *prepared me for the work we would do on the album that became* Thriller. Off the Wall *had sold almost six million copies in this country, but I wanted to make an album that would be even bigger."* —Michael Jackson

taskmaster when it came to their musical aspirations, aggressively grooming the children for talent contests, then nightclubs, and eventually Amateur Night at the Apollo Theater in New York City.

They passed their audition for Motown in 1968 with a sound inspired by the rock and soul of Sly & the Family Stone, but slicker and more melodic. The first two singles, "I Want You Back" and "ABC," were built around a chicken-scratch guitar and fluid, James Jamerson–inspired basslines with Michael Jackson's updated Frankie Lymon–styled tenor on top. The two songs were the first of four consecutive #1 hits. In 1971, Michael began forging his own solo career with Top 10 singles, "Got to Be There," "Rockin' Robin," and "Ben," while still fronting the Jackson 5.

Jackson's first fully-realized solo album, *Off the Wall*, was an exquisite collection of R&B and dance-pop with more layers and density than the disco that preceded it. And if it lacked the political and spiritual ambition of Stevie Wonder, who until *Off the Wall* was the standard bearer for R&B, it made up for it in the sheer execution of diverse music, ranging from the soul ballad "Rock with You" to the

MICHAEL JACKSON AND THE JACKSON 5 WERE ONE OF MOTOWN'S BIGGEST HIT-MAKERS IN THE EARLY '70S.

irresistible disco groove of "Don't Stop 'Til You Get Enough."

But no one was prepared for the juggernaut that was *Thriller*, a de facto greatest hits collection in which seven of nine tracks were Top 10 hits. The album invited everyone in. Rock and rollers loved "Beat It," with its Eddie Van Halen guitar solo. Dance-pop kids loved "Wanna Be Starting Something." Heck, parents even liked "The Girl Is Mine," a duet with Paul McCartney. And when Jackson appeared on the Motown 25th Anniversary television special with a magical set of dance moves that borrowed in equal parts from James Brown and break dancers, a whole generation swooned. To teenagers growing up in the '80s, it was the equivalent of '60s teens seeing the Beatles on *The Ed Sullivan Show*. The long-form "Thriller" video exploded the possibilities of what that medium could do for music. *Thriller* remains one of the best-selling albums of all time.

Thriller's follow-up *Bad* may be the only album to sell 15 million copies, yield five #1 hits, and still be considered a disappointment. More disconcerting was the bleached-out look of Michael's skin and other cosmetic changes. Nevertheless, the album featured a similar diversity of styles as *Thriller*, including the rockish "Dirty Diana" and the smooth soul of "The Way You Make Me Feel."

On the 1991 album *Dangerous*, he hooked up with contemporary R&B producers, including New Jack Swing auteur Teddy Riley, who updated his sound and added hip-hop elements. The result was four Top 10 singles, including "Black or White," a great rock number and his most explicit song about race.

Jackson vs. Sony

Michael Jackson's sales had been on a decline, albeit from colossal levels, since 1983's *Thriller*. When *Invincible* was released, it spawned only one Top 10 single and disappointing sales. In July 2002, Jackson blamed his label, Sony Music, for not promoting the album well enough, which made him merely the latest in a rich tradition of artists blaming labels for an album's weak sales. But Jackson took his claims one step farther. He held a rally in front of Sony's headquarters and called Sony Music's president Tommy Mottola "racist" and "very very devilish." "Industry sources" (read: Sony flaks) claimed that they spent $55 million to promote the album (including production costs). In the end, Jackson hasn't gone anywhere. He continued to release compilations through Sony, but no new music.

MICHAEL JACKSON PERFORMS DURING THE *VICTORY* TOUR IN 1984.

In 1993, Jackson was accused of molesting a 13-year-old boy. Before the case went to trial, he settled out of court with the boy's family. He married Elvis Presley's daughter, Lisa Marie, in 1994 for about seven minutes. He issued a two-disc set *HIStory* in 1995, which featured one greatest hits disc and a disc of new material, including "Scream," a duet with his sister Janet Jackson. But evidently deciding he hadn't had enough controversy, he included the lines "Jew me, sue me," and "Kick me, kike me" in the song "They Don't Care about Us," which didn't endear him to the Jewish community. He eventually changed the lyrics.

Invincible came out in 2001 and yielded one Top 10 hit, "You Rock My World." But by then his offstage exploits were upstaging his music. There was talk of a Jackson 5 reunion in 2003, but nothing arrived on the shelves but another Michael Jackson compilation. Later that year, he was charged with another case of child molestation, but he was acquitted in 2005. Chatter has surfaced from time to time of a new album, but when it will arrive is anyone's guess.

Quincy Jones

Bringing together the rock, funk, and R&B elements in the production of *Thriller*, one of the top-selling records of all time, would probably be enough to warrant immortality. But add to that equation: expert trumpeting with Lionel Hampton and Count Basie; master arranging with Frank Sinatra, Miles Davis, and Ray Charles; and almost single-handedly integrating the Hollywood soundtrack talent pool, and you don't have an artist. You have a force of nature.

Jones grew in up in Seattle where he played trumpet from the age of 13. He formed a combo with Ray Charles that played everything from be-bop to boogie-woogie to R&B to pop standards. In 1951, he accepted an offer to play trumpet and arrange songs for Lionel Hampton, which, in turn, led to a flourishing career as a freelance arranger for the likes of Dinah Washington, Tommy Dorsey, Count Basie, and Duke Ellington.

In 1957, Jones moved to Paris to study with one of the world's preeminent composers, Nadia Boulanger, who also trained such luminaries as Aaron Copeland and Philip Glass. There, Jones learned lessons that would give his arrangements with Miles Davis and Frank Sinatra more depth. With that kind of musical vocabulary at his command, there was nothing Jones couldn't accomplish in pop music.

He became the head talent scout and music director for Mercury Records in 1961. One of his most successful signings was Lesley Gore, proving that his touch was not limited to strictly jazz or standards. His soundtrack for Sidney Lumet's *The Pawnbroker* was his first of 33 soundtracks, breaking down the race barrier in that industry.

When Michael Jackson tapped him to produce *Off the Wall* in 1979, executives were concerned about Jones' jazz background. They needn't have worried; he produced one of the greatest R&B albums of decade, which wasn't surprising given his apprenticeship with Ray Charles and blues singer Wynonie Harris. He also helmed several albums under his own name, featuring the vocals of a wide range of talent, including James Ingram, Ray Charles, and Chaka Khan.

THE JAM

1977–1982

"When people say it's important to go to the States, there's only one reason and that's purely for money." —Paul Weller

From left: Paul Weller (guitar, vocals), Rick Buckler (drums), Bruce Foxton (bass, vocals). Although relatively obscure in the U.S., the Jam was one of the biggest hitmakers to come out of the U.K. punk movement.

O f the first generation of Johnny Rotten's spiritual descendents, the Jam, would be his most successful progeny from a sales perspective. From an artistic standpoint, the Jam's front man, Paul Weller, would go way beyond his predecessor, reinventing himself several times throughout his career and creating a body of work that was diverse and powerful.

In the U.S., the Jam was ignored by all but a small cult following. But, in the U.K., nine of ten singles released between 1979 and 1982 went to the Top 10. Four of them topped the charts. Weller scored seven Top 10 hits with the Style Council and would earn five more as a solo artist.

Although the Jam's energy was reminiscent of punk rock, they actually positioned themselves more as heirs to the mod throne. The songs were so rooted in British mores and class struggles that U.S. audiences were almost

GREATEST HITS	
Year	Song
1977	"All around the World"
1978	"Down in the Tube Station at Midnight"
1979	"The Eton Rifles"
1980	"Going Underground"
	"Start"
1981	"Absolute Beginners"
1982	"Town Called Malice"
	"Beat Surrender"

PAUL WELLER (LEFT) AND MICK TALBOT WERE THE GUIDING FORCE OF THE STYLE COUNCIL.

Style Council

The fans who mourned the passing of the Jam and were shocked by Paul Weller's new direction as the front man of the Style Council were simply not paying attention. Songs like "The Bitterest Pill," "Beat Surrender," "Town Called Malice," and "Trans-Global Express" had far more in common with the sound that would be identified with the Style Council.

Eminently danceable and a far cry from the Jam's punk-influenced early years, the Style Council, which included keyboardist Mick Talbot and vocalist D.C. Lee, harkened back to '70s R&B. The music included elements of cocktail jazz and house along with British power-pop sensibility. Weller also eschewed some of the subtleties of the Jam's narratives and more impressionistic writing in favor of outright criticism of the British conservative government.

Stylistically, Paul Weller was becoming something of a British equivalent of Neil Young, hopping from genre to genre and alienating much of his audience. The Style Council's last album, *Modernism: A New Decade*, reflected his infatuation with house music, which was a burgeoning subculture on both sides of the Atlantic featuring pulsating electronic beats and often repetitive lyrics that were designed not only to dance to but to enhance the experience of taking hallucinogenic drugs. The album, recorded in 1989, was rejected by Polydor. Although widely bootlegged, it wouldn't be officially released until 1998 as part of the box set *The Complete Adventures of the Style Council*.

completely excluded. Weller, bassist Bruce Foxton, and drummer Rick Buckler used the Who's *My Generation* as their touchstone, and combined it with pared-down instrumentation, a love for '60s R&B, sharp suits from Carnaby Street, and revved-up tempos borrowed from punk to create the Jam's sound.

The Jam was associated with the punk movement, but Weller was uncomfortable with orthodoxy of any kind. He played this card to the extreme early in their career when he proclaimed that he would vote Tory in an upcoming election. His stance invoked the wrath of many leftward-leaning punks—the Clash's "White Man in Hammersmith Palais" was said to be about Weller. Years later, the Jam's front man would back off those remarks, and, in fact, would form a collective of musicians called Red Wedge that advocated a progressive agenda.

Writer's block prevented Weller from building on the band's initial success with *In the City* and the follow-up single, "All Around the World." But he would return to peak form in 1978 with *All Mod Cons*, which went to #6 in the British album charts and began their dominance in the U.K. The 1979 concept album *Setting Sons* dealt with three childhood friends and the different directions their lives took and gave the band their first Top 10 single with "The Eton Rifles." Their first #1 hit came with "Going Underground," arguably the band's finest moment, in which Weller rages against the both the vagaries of British life and the country's political policies in the Thatcher era. It also began the band's most experimental period.

Breaking out of the power-trio format, the Jam began to add horn sections to some of their hits, further distancing themselves from other punk bands. But Weller's lyrics wouldn't lose any of their bite or their penchant for social comment. The Jam's biggest hit of the period was "Town Called Malice," which topped the U.K. charts in 1982. Their rhythms belied Weller's fascination with contemporary R&B, and by the time they issued their last single, "Beat Surrender," in 1982, the stage had already been set for the Style Council. Weller disbanded the Jam in late 1982.

Paul Weller

The demise of Style Council sent Paul Weller underground to battle again with writer's block. When he reemerged in 1991, his music had more in common with classic rock than anything else he'd done. Gone were most of the dance rhythms and the aggressive punk rock of the Jam. His songs, mostly mid-tempo, and often rooted in acoustic guitar, became more introspective. By golly, the Modfather had become, well, a singer-songwriter. His solo albums included homages to the Beatles' more baroque years and included some intricately arranged touches à la Brian Wilson. He would also purvey some tributes to '60s soul music in his vocal stylings. *Stanley Road* was hugely successful in the U.K. in 1995. Oasis' Noel Gallagher, among others, cites Weller as an important influence. Weller continues to record solo albums in the classic rock vein, with 2005's *As Is Now* being a particularly strong collection.

JAY-Z

DECEMBER 4, 1969–

Jay-Z was not only one of the most popular hip-hop stars of the 2000s, he also became one of its most powerful players—a producer of note, the owner of his own record label, and eventually president of Def Jam Records, the most venerable label in rap music. His lyrics depicted much of his experience as a crack dealer prior to getting a record deal. Unlike early "gangsta rap," there weren't many political overtones. Everything was recited in a matter-of-fact manner and combined with slick, compelling samples and beats.

Jay-Z's (Shawn Carter) 1996 full-length debut *Reasonable Doubt* rose to #3 on the R&B/Hip-Hop charts, and yielded three singles, including "Ain't No Nigga," which introduced the world to Foxy Brown, who became a hip-hop star in her own right.

JAY-Z PROMOTES HIS COMEBACK ALBUM *KINGDOM COME* AT VIRGIN MEGASTORE IN HOLLYWOOD.

GREATEST HITS	
YEAR	SONG
1996	"Aint No Nigga" (with Foxy Brown)
1998	"Can I Get a . . ."
	"Hard Knock Life (Ghetto Anthem)"
1999	"Jigga My Nigga"
	"Heartbreaker" (with Mariah Carey)
2000	"Big Pimpin'"
	"I Just Wanna Love U (Give It 2 Me)"
2001	"Izzo (H.O.V.A.)"
	"Girls, Girls, Girls"
2002	"'03 Bonnie & Clyde" (with Beyonce Knowles)
2003	"Excuse Me Miss"
2004	"Change Clothes"
	"Dirt Off Your Shoulder"
2006	"Show Me What You Got"

The 1997 follow-up *Vol. 1: In My Lifetime* was a commercial disappointment and was criticized by hip-hop magazines as being too soft. But Jay-Z rebounded in 1998 with *Vol. 2: Hard Knock Life*, with a title track that became a huge hit anchored by a sample from the *Annie* musical number of the same name.

The Black Album, his so-called farewell album in 2003, was believed by many to be his finest hour. It included the Top 10 hits, "Change Clothes" and "Dirt off Your Shoulder." He launched his "comeback" in 2006 with *Kingdom Come*, which failed to meet the sales of previous records.

Shades of Grey:

By the late '90s and early 2000s, DJ culture had evolved from scratching and sampling to so-called mashups—grafting vocals of one song over the music of a completely different and often incongruous song. These mashups were often released as bootleg collections, because they were believed by some to run afoul of copyright laws.

Jay-Z, however, approved of the burgeoning art form, going so far as to issue a cappella versions of his raps from his 2003 set, *The Black Album*. In doing so, he was effectively inviting DJs and mixers to apply their own accompaniment. One legendary mashup that resulted was *The Grey Album* by DJ Danger Mouse, who layered Jay-Z's rhymes over musical samples from the Beatles' *White Album*. The album spread like wildfire over the Internet, and even ended up on some year-end, best-of-2004 polls. The Beatles' label, EMI, brought the hammer down with a "cease and cesist" order, claiming that the album violated the Fab Four's copyright.

To this day, use of samples and mashups remain a point of contention among artists and labels, but there's little question about the cleverness and legitimacy of the art form.

BILLY JOEL

MAY 9, 1949–

Unlike other confessional singer-songwriters of the era, Billy Joel's beacon wasn't really Bob Dylan or the folkies. He was taken by the more baroque pop of the Beatles, as well as the simple but powerful rock and roll sound of the Brill Building. Later he reached back even further to include shades of Tin Pan Alley. Others could rock harder (Springsteen, Browne, Costello). But not many were as crafty as Joel.

In 1971, he recorded his first solo album, *Cold Spring Harbor*, which started Joel on the path of the sensitive, piano-playing troubadour. But because of production problems, the songs were recorded at the wrong speed. His follow-up, *Piano Man*, would fare better, with the title track becoming one of his signature songs, a waltz-time, beer-swigging song that humorously recounted his years working as a cocktail pianist in bars.

"It's better to fail at different things and build up the lessons that result than to stop taking risks."—Billy Joel

BILLY JOEL STARTS THE FIRE AT THE WEMBLEY ARENA IN 1990.

GREATEST HITS	
YEAR	SONG
1974	"Piano Man"
1977	"Just the Way You Are"
1978	"My Life"
1980	"You May Be Right"
	"It's Still Rock and Roll to Me"
1982	"Allentown"
1983	"Tell Her about It"
	"Uptown Girl"
1986	"A Matter of Trust"
1989	"We Didn't Start the Fire"
1990	"I Go to Extremes"
1993	"The River of Dreams"

Joel's next two albums wouldn't succeed from a sales perspective but showed impressive growth in his songwriting, from his cynical take on the music business in "The Entertainer" to "New York State of Mind," which became a virtual theme song for the city in the '70s. But legitimate pop success wouldn't come until 1977 when "Just the Way You Are" hit the Top 10. The

My Life

After his parents split, Joel grew up in a working-class part of Long Island, robbing stores and picking fights. Like most teenagers of the '60s, he was inspired by the rock and roll of the Beatles and the Rolling Stones. He joined a white soul band in the late '60s called the Hassles, who recorded two albums before disbanding. Not long after, he formed a progressive rock duo called Atilla, which recorded an album in 1970. Around this time, he tried to commit suicide by drinking furniture polish and checked himself into a mental hospital for three weeks. Convinced that he wasn't as bad off as the other patients, he checked himself out and eventually set off on his career as a solo artist.

album from which the song came, *The Stranger*, would become one of the best-selling albums of the '70s and establish Joel as a top-tier performer.

His subsequent hits would come in a variety of styles, from Beatlesque pop in "Moving Out" or bona fide rock and roll in "You May Be Right." In 1980, he would absorb some new wave and punk influences on his *Glass Houses* record, which included the chart-topping "It's Still Rock and Roll to Me." He allowed himself to become more experimental on *The Nylon Curtain* album, which featured impressive production flourishes as well as an emerging penchant for social commentary on "Allentown" and "Goodnight Saigon." *An Innocent Man* in 1983 was a pastiche of the music that Joel had listened to growing up in the '50s and '60s. It yielded three Top 10 singles, including the #1 hit "Tell Her about It."

His reign on the pop charts continued until 1994, when he retired from recording rock albums and devoted himself instead to recording classical music. Still, he never quit playing rock concerts and would sometimes perform on a double bill with Elton John. He went through a tough patch in 2002 when in the midst of a three-month-long drinking binge following a breakup with a girlfriend, he crashed his Mercedes and checked into a rehab center. He did a second stint in rehab in 2005. He has been touring seemingly nonstop for the past 15 years, including a triumphant 12-night run at Madison Square Garden in 2006, documented on the album *12 Gardens*.

Grammy Awards:
1978 "Just the Way You Are," Song of the Year
1978 "Just the Way You Are," Record of the Year
1979 *52nd Street*, Best Pop Vocal Performance, Male
1979 *52nd Street*, Album of the Year
1980 *Glass Houses*, Best Rock Vocal Performance, Male

ALTHOUGH HE HAD CLAIMED HE WAS RETIRING FROM RECORDING ROCK MUSIC, JOEL CONTINUED TO TOUR TIRELESSLY THROUGHOUT THE 2000s.

"PIANO MAN" WAS BASED ON JOEL'S EXPERIENCES AS A COCKTAIL PIANIST BEFORE HE BECAME A POP STAR.

Origins of a Piano Man

After Billy Joel's progressive rock duo Atilla split, he was offered a deal with entrepreneur Artie Ripp. With Ripp, Joel recorded his debut album *Cold Spring Harbor*, which hinted at the directions he would later take by combining pop ballads with piano-based rock and roll numbers. But the album was pressed onto vinyl at the wrong speed, which led to Joel sounding like Alvin and the Chipmunks. He also discovered that Ripp owned his publishing rights. In protest, he moved to Los Angeles and began performing in bars incognito under the name Billy Martin. During the six months that followed, he played in cocktail bars and accumulated enough stories and images to create the lyrics for his first hit, "Piano Man." When Ripp realized that he wasn't going to get Joel back into the studio, Columbia Records brokered a compromise in which Joel would be signed to the label and for many years to come, Ripp would get a cut from Joel's subsequent recordings, a fact that niggled at Joel for a long while.

ELTON JOHN

MARCH 25, 1947–

What made Elton John a talented songwriter was his ability to draw on blues and rock and roll, as well as the British music hall tradition, and to dress his masterful creations with Gus Dudgeon and Paul Buckmaster's string arrangements. But Elton's dynamic performances, which were equal parts camp, spectacle, and quality rock and roll, were what made him a pop star. No one sold more records in the '70s.

Reginald Dwight began playing piano at age 4 and grew up with eclectic tastes ranging from Tennessee Ernie Ford to Little Richard. He was classically trained at the Royal Academy of Music, but dropped out of school at age 14 to form Bluesology, one of many blues revival bands that cropped up in Britain in the mid-'60s. When he left Bluesology, he took the name of the group's saxophone player Elton Dean and combined it with John from Long John Baldry to give himself a new stage name of Elton John.

Elton was signed on at Dick James Publishing to write songs, and was paired with lyricist Bernie Taupin. His 1970 album, *Elton John*, contained his first major hit "Your Song." But the album didn't sell until Elton performed a showcase at the famed Los Angeles club the Troubadour late that year. In front of a live audience, John turned into an uncaged beast—pounding on the piano like Little Richard, kicking his piano stool à la Jerry Lee Lewis, and doing handstands off the piano keys—stunts that would eventually become mainstays of his performances. The Troubadour shows represented a turning point and the resulting publicity helped "Your Song" rocket into the Top 10.

Fourteen of the 16 singles he released from 1972 to 1976 went Top 10, and none peaked lower than #14. His costumes became more garish and his performances campier, helping to make him one of the most consistent live draws throughout the '70s. The pace of hits slowed into the '80s, although he still

ELTON JOHN PERFORMS IN THE MID '70S AT THE HEIGHT OF HIS POPULARITY.

had seven Top 10s. He had throat surgery in 1987, which robbed him of most of his higher register. He also began to de-emphasize the campier elements of his shows, although he remains an explosive performer.

In the '90s, he branched out into composing for films and theatre. He wrote the music for the blockbuster Disney film *The Lion King*, which earned him his first Oscar and went on to huge success on Broadway. He also composed

> **NUGGET:** Although Elton John has had nine #1 hits in the U.S. between 1972 and 1997, he would not score a chart-topper in the U.K. until 1990's "Sacrifice."

Disco Days

After splitting with Bernie Taupin in 1977, John went into the studio with renowned R&B producer Thom Bell to record songs in a disco vein, including the Top 10 hit "Mama Can't Buy You Love." Three of the songs remained unreleased until 1989. In 2004, a song from the 1977 session, "Are You Ready For Love" was rereleased and became a huge hit in dance clubs.

Bernie Taupin

While John was attracted to raucous rock and roll and the sinewy sounds of Motown as a child, Bernie Taupin grew up listening to folk and blues. And rather than mastering an instrument, Taupin devoted himself to poetry. At the suggestion of a record executive in 1967, he mailed about 20 of his poems and narratives to Elton John, who was then an unknown songwriter. John promptly set them all to music and began to peddle them to other songwriters through a publishing deal with Dick James Music. From then on Taupin became the Brown Dirt Cowboy to John's Captain Fantastic. From 1972 to 1976, the two were rarely absent from the Top 10. Taupin recalled seeing Elton John performing at a stadium in Los Angeles in 1976. While watching him, Taupin thought, "Where do we go from here?" After Elton announced one of his several "retirements," the two parted ways. But they reunited in 1980 and continue to work together to this day. Taupin has also had success writing lyrics for Starship ("We Built This City") and Heart ("These Dreams"). John and Taupin signed a $39 million publishing deal with Warner/Chappell music in 1992, the largest advance ever in the music business at that time. Some of their most personal work was written in 2006's *The Captain And The Kid*.

ELTON JOHN HAS ALWAYS PRIDED HIMSELF ON HIS SHOWMAN-SHIP. THIS GET-UP HAS NOTHING ON THE DONALD DUCK COSTUME HE WORE DURING A 1980 PERFORMANCE IN NEW YORK'S CENTRAL PARK

music for the Broadway production *Aida*. His 1997 rewrite of "Candle in the Wind," a tribute to the late Princess Diana, is the one of the best-selling singles of all time. Although his hits have dried up in recent years, his shows are still consistent sellouts.

ELTON JOHN'S CALLING CARD WAS HIS USE OF CAMP, GARISH COSTUMES, AND STUNTS SUCH AS HANDSTANDS OFF THE PIANO.

GREATEST HITS	
YEAR	SONG
1970	"Your Song"
1972	"Rocket Man"
	"Honky Cat"
	"Crocodile Rock"
1973	"Daniel"
	"Goodbye Yellow Brick Road"
1974	"Bennie and the Jets"
	"The Bitch Is Back"
1975	"Philadelphia Freedom"
1976	"Don't Go Breaking My Heart" (with Kiki Dee)
1988	"I Don't Wanna go on with You Like That"
1997	"Candle in the Wind 1997"

CAROLE KING

February 9, 1942–

The apotheosis of the singer-songwriter movement was Carole King's *Tapestry*, not because it was more honest or confessional than any other work in the same genre—although it was certainly both honest and confessional. It wasn't because it sold more than 25 million copies and counting—although that would make it one of the best-selling albums of all time. It was the craft that separated King from other songwriters.

Majestic chords on a grand piano swept us into her world on "So Far Away." The steady R&B beat propelling "I Feel the Earth Move" compelled us. The fragility with which she handled one of her signature Brill Building hits, "Will You Love Me Tomorrow," revealed not only a plea for loyalty after a one-night stand, but a deeper transcendent commitment.

King, along with her first husband, Gerry Goffin, honed her craft in the cubicles of the Brill Building in New York City, where publishing houses worked feverishly to supply pop acts with slices of teen life boiled down to three minutes each. "Will You Love Me Tomorrow," recorded by the Shirelles in 1960, was Goffin and King's first #1 hit and allowed them to quit their day jobs. They would both join the staff at Don Kirshner's Aldon Music. King and Goffin

"Say it simply, say it truthfully, and make it rhyme."—Gerry Goffin's advice to Carole King

CAROLE KING PERFORMS IN 1974. AT THE TIME, HER #2 HIT "JAZZMAN" WAS CLIMBING THE CHARTS.

The Locomotion

It was 1962, two years after Gerry Goffin and Carole King scored their first #1 hit with "Will You Love Me Tomorrow." The husband-and-wife songwriting team was trying to capitalize on dance songs like Chubby Checker's "The Twist." As usual, King was tinkering with a melody on the piano, while Goffin toyed with lyrics. Their 19-year-old babysitter, Eva Boyd, started dancing to the piano's beat. Goffin tried to set words to her dance steps: "Everybody's doin' a brand new dance now . . ." And when Goffin and King had finished, they asked Boyd to record a rehearsal tape of their new song, "The Locomotion," which they had been planning to submit to Dee Dee Sharp ("Mashed Potato Time," #2 Pop, 1962). But they liked Boyd's rendition so much, they recorded her version. Boyd, who soon became Little Eva, took the song to the top of the charts.

CAROLE KING AND GERRY GOFFIN WERE ONE OF THE MOST IMPORTANT SONGWRITING TEAMS TO EMERGE FROM THE BRILL BUILDING IN THE '60S. THEIR HITS WOULD INCLUDE "WILL YOU LOVE ME TOMORROW," "UP ON THE ROOF," AND "ONE FINE DAY." BRILL BUILDING

divorced in 1968, and King headed to Laurel Canyon in Los Angeles, where a bohemian artist community was blossoming. Here she formed a group called the City with a young unknown guitarist named Danny Kortchmar, who would later go on to greater fame and fortune playing with the likes of James Taylor, Jackson Browne, and Don Henley. The City's debut album made no impression on the public or the critics.

After a mediocre attempt at a solo album, *Writer*, King constructed 1971's *Tapestry*, which juxtaposed stripped-down versions of her older hits such as "Will You Love Me Tomorrow" and "Natural Woman," with newer solo ballads such as "So Far Away" and "You've Got a Friend," which became a #1 hit for James Taylor. And for good measure, she paid tribute to her R&B roots with such up-tempo songs as "I Feel the Earth Move" and "Smackwater Jack." Her voice was too nasal and thin to match the singers who originally scored hits with those songs, but she invoked a vulnerability and intimacy that resonates to this day.

If you fell in love with a rock and roll song from the late '50s or early '60s, there's good chance that song was conceived in the Brill Building.

Here, songwriting teams like Carole King and her husband, Gerry Goffin, Jerry Lieber and Mike Stoller, Doc Pomus and Mort Shuman, Burt Bacharach and Hal David, Ellie Greenwich and her husband, Jeff Barry, and Barry Mann and Cynthia Weil, would cram into tiny offices and cubicles and compose songs to audition for record executives.

All of these songwriters had different styles, but what they shared was a love for early '50s rhythm and blues records. Pomus and Shuman favored Latin colorings to their music, as is evident in their big hits for the Drifters. Two Jewish kids, Lieber and Stoller, espoused black patois so accurately that their stories and songs sounded natural coming out of the lips of the Coasters. Greenwich and Barry created narratives that felt like mini dramas, such as "Leader of the Pack." Burt Bacharach and Hal David used Dionne Warwick as their canvas, and were one of the few teams that eschewed rhythm and blues forms in favor of pop and less obvious song structures. And few could encapsulate the histrionic swings of adolescence like Goffin and King.

It would take producers like Phil Spector, Jerry Wexler, and others to turn these songs into timeless classics, to say nothing of heavenly voices like Ben E. King, Aretha Franklin, and Dionne Warwick. But the inspiration came from the Brill Building.

GREATEST HITS	
YEAR	SONG
1962	"It Might as Well Rain Until September"
1971	"It's Too Late"
	"I Feel the Earth Move"
	"So Far Away"
	"Smackwater Jack"
1972	"Sweet Seasons"
1974	"Jazzman"
	"Nightingale"
1980	"One Fine Day"

She would never again match the success of *Tapestry*, but she would revisit the Top 10 three more times with "Sweet Season," "Jazzman," and "Nightingale" before the end of the decade. In 1983, she retreated to Idaho where she became an environmental activist. She also supported John Kerry's presidential campaign in 2004, and continues to be active in the Democratic Party.

MADONNA

AUGUST 16, 1958–

People have always said, "Madonna's greatest talent is her ability to manipulate the media." If this were true, which it isn't, Madonna would still be one of the many—including David Bowie, R.E.M., the Beatles, the Rolling Stones, and Elvis Presley—who use image to their advantage. One wonders if Madonna would receive the same criticism if she were a man. In any case, Madonna was indeed the best of all pop artists at playing cat and mouse with the public's expectations of a pop star.

All this would be meaningless without a cache of songs that ranks with the very best that the '80s and '90s have to offer. Madonna started by updating the disco and club sounds of New York for a mass audience and ultimately became the best practitioner of '80s dance pop. She was also one of the more underrated ballad singers of the decade. Helped by powerful videos and a constantly changing image, she was easily the best-selling female artist of the '80s.

Madonna Louise Ciccone grew up in Pontiac, Michigan, and went to the University of Michigan on a dance scholarship. She quit school after two years to come to New York to study with dance instructor Alvin Ailey. She eventually won a spot in the disco troupe Patrick Hernandez Revue, which had a minor hit with "Born to Be Alive." In the early '80s she played drums and sang in several groups, before splitting off with boyfriend Stephen Bray and compiling audition tapes with dance tracks. Those tapes led to a record deal with Sire Records and the stratospheric sales of her debut album *Madonna*, although it took over a year for sales to explode. When she appeared on *American Bandstand* in 1983, she was asked by Dick Clark what her ambition was. Her reply without a shred of irony was: "I want to rule the world."

Dance pop king Nile Rodgers, formerly of Chic, was called in to produce the next album, *Like a Virgin*, which filled out her sound and gave her vocals even more punch. Meanwhile, her songs became pithier. "Like a Virgin" was an ingenious juxtaposition of promiscuity and commitment. Teenage girls dressed

MADONNA, PICTURED HERE AT THE TIME OF "LIKE A VIRGIN," WAS ONE OF THE BEST PRACTITIONERS OF '80S DANCE POP.

like her, and teenage boys alternated between fear of, and lust for, this powerful woman who wore her lingerie on the outside and dressed in bangles and belts that said, "Boy Toy." If "Holiday" represented the hope of what America could be in the '80s, "Material Girl" was the reflection of what it became.

Her 1986 single "Papa Don't Preach" was a compelling dance groove, which featured a lyric in which the teenage narrator becomes pregnant. The song left suburban parents across middle-class America to blanch while their teenage daughters sang triumphantly, "I'm keepin' my baby." Madonna's lyrics made a significant impression not only on pop fans, but music critics, and social commentators. And it didn't hurt that "Papa Don't Preach" was a great song.

By 1989, Madonna had hit her stride both musically and as a media figure. Pepsi Cola filled her pockets with millions of dollars of sponsorship money, only to take her commercial off the air when she had the bad manners to suggest in the video for "Like a Prayer" that Jesus was black. The video was also seen as blasphemous for its interweaving of sexual and sacred images. She followed it up with one of her greatest R&B workouts, "Express Yourself," a thinly veiled allegory of empowerment and independence for women.

Like Prince before her, Madonna used sex not only to titillate, but also to grab attention. Her limited edition *Sex* book, laden with explicit photos of bondage scenes and other deviant sexual archetypes, was savaged by critics, but under the "no such thing as bad publicity" edict, Madonna was never more popular.

M for Madonna

Madonna is no stranger to shocking people with what she wears, from bustiers to lingerie to, well, nothing. Still, few expected the Versace and Gaultier-wearing pop star to show up as the pitch woman for Swedish cut-price fashion line H&M. Sure enough, in June 2006, the company announced she would design a line of track suits. The following December she launched a complete line called "M for Madonna." The line helped H&M boost its sales, and was yet another avenue of exposure for the versatile and enterprising performer.

MADONNA CONCERTS WERE ELABORATE AFFAIRS, FEATURING EXQUISITE CHOREOGRAPHY AND OFTEN SUGGESTIVE CONTENT.

GREATEST HITS	
Year	**Song**
1983	"Holiday"
1984	"Like a Virgin"
1985	"Crazy for You"
1986	"Live to Tell"
	"Papa Don't Preach"
	"Open Your Heart"
1987	"Who's That Girl"
1989	"Like a Prayer"
1990	"Vogue"
	"Justify My Love"
1992	"This Used to Be My Playground"
1994	"Take a Bow"
1998	"Ray of Light"
2000	"Music"
2005	"Hung Up"

MADONNA, PICTURED HERE AROUND THE TIME OF *DICK TRACY*, CHANGED HER IMAGE FREQUENTLY, WHICH KEPT HER ON THE COVER OF BOTH FASHION AND MUSIC MAGAZINES.

MADONNA'S 2005 ALBUM *CONFESSIONS ON THE DANCE FLOOR* HEARKENED BACK TO THE DANCE POP OF THE '80s.

The video for "Justify My Love," which included explicit homoerotic scenes, was banned from MTV and encouraged a new round of "Has Madonna Gone Too Far?" debates. Meanwhile, the song topped the charts.

By the early '90s, Madonna was alternating between seductive dance grooves (and bawdy videos) and placid soul ballads like "Take a Bow." This set her up for her role in *Evita*, which yielded a Top 10 version of "Don't Cry for Me Argentina." By the late '90s, her position as a serious artist was assured. She explored techno-inspired dance grooves on the *Ray of Light* album, earning her more rave reviews. *Music* in 2000 showed no signs of letting up, with two Top 10 singles and a sold-out tour that was easily one of the hottest tickets of 2001. Her 2003 album *American Life* was the first unqualified disappointment of her career. But her latest album, *Confessions on the Dance Floor,* was viewed as a back-to-basics move (or if you're a cynic, a nostalgia ploy) that hearkened to the dance pop days of her debut. It yielded a Top 10 single, a feat her previous album failed to achieve.

"What kids see in me is another rebel kid who says what she wants and does what she wants and has a joy in life. The girls that dressed like me all got the joke—it was their parents who didn't. You didn't see those girls going off and doing awful things because they bought my records. What I've learned from all the controversy is that you can't expect everyone to get your sense of humor."—Madonna

The Movies

While Madonna's music career has been more or less a linear upward trajectory, her film career has had peaks and valleys. Her role as a the sexy bohemian in *Desperately Seeking Susan* won her positive notices and helped reinforce her star power (the song "Into the Groove" didn't hurt either). The follow-up *Shanghai Surprise* with her then-husband, Sean Penn, bombed at the box office and helped usher producer and former Beatle George Harrison out of the film business (he'd previously had success with such films as *Mona Lisa* and *Monty Python's Life Of Brian*). The highly stylized *Dick Tracy* in 1990 got mixed reviews, but Madonna's role as Breathless Mahoney was generally well received. She worked regularly in both independent and big budget Hollywood films throughout the '90s. Her acting triumph came in 1996 in the title role of *Evita*, for which she won a Golden Globe.

BARRY MANILOW

Jun 17, 1946–

Frank Sinatra's optimistic assessment of Barry Manilow was: "He's next." Manilow was a skilled performer, singer, arranger, and composer. Favoring dramatic vocal turns and lush arrangements, Manilow showed no shortage of emotion. He helped create and define the so-called adult contemporary subsection of pop music, along with Karen and Richard Carpenter.

And even if no one in the rock community wants to admit it, he had a way with a ballad. "Weekend in New England," "Looks Like We Made It," and "Trying to Get the Feeling Again" demonstrate an ability to take somewhat mediocre material and turn it into inspired pieces of drama. Those were just three of eleven Top 10 hits spanning 1974 to 1980.

When his string of hits ended, Manilow genre-hopped from jazz to swing to Broadway tunes. He toured regularly until 2005, when he finally landed the gig it seemed he was groomed to do from the outset. He became the house show for the Las Vegas Hilton.

In 2006, he recorded two albums of cover songs from the '50s and '60s. They peaked at #1 and #2, respectively. Although he said he has retired from touring, he did a three-night sold-out stand at Madison Square Garden in January 2007.

BARRY MANILOW'S MUSIC HAS ALWAYS BEEN POWERED BY HIS EMOTIONAL INTENSITY.

GREATEST HITS

Year	Song
1974	"Mandy"
1975	"I Write the Songs"
1976	"Tryin' to Get the Feeling Again"
	"Weekend in New England"
1977	"Looks Like We Made It"
1978	"Can't Smile without You"
	"Copacabana"
	"Somewhere in the Night"
	"Ships"
1980	"I Made It Through the Rain"

The Early Years

Even Manilow's beginnings have the making of show business myth. He started in the mailroom at CBS, while he was studying music at Julliard. At 18 years old, he was discovered by a director who asked him to arrange a series of public-domain songs for a musical called *The Drunkard*. Instead he wrote an entire score for the musical, which would run for eight years.

After that, he was the musical director for a New York television show called *The Callback*. He penned several commercial jingles for several companies including State Farm Insurance ("Like a good neighbor . . .") and Band-Aid ("I am stuck on Band-Aids . . ."). In 1972, he became Bette Midler's musical director and co-produced her first two blockbuster albums *The Divine Miss M* and *Bette Midler*, both of which went Top 10 and the former of which yielded the Top 10 cover of the 1941 Andrews Sisters hit "Boogie Woogie Bugle Boy."

PAUL McCARTNEY

JUNE 18, 1942–

There are few performers saddled with as large a legacy as Paul McCartney who have managed not only to survive but thrive in their follow-up careers. He scored 22 Top 10 hits from 1971 to 1985. Even more amazing is that he managed that run by playing in a style that was distinct from the musical vocabulary he invented while a member of the Beatles.

As the Beatles were fracturing, McCartney sequestered himself in a home studio in 1969 and made work tapes playing all of the instruments himself. A far cry from the ornate arrangements of the Beatles' last recorded work, *Abbey Road*, these modest recordings revolved around his acoustic guitar. The songs, which became his debut album, *McCartney*, had the feel of a man who has nothing to lose. As a result, they would be the most easygoing and natural recordings of McCartney's solo career.

It would be nearly 20 years before he reached such off-handed charm again. After *McCartney*, his albums began to sound like he was wrestling with his past. His hits alternated between straight-up rock and roll and lighter fare.

McCartney formed another band, Wings, that would grow into one of the most successful arena rock bands of the '70s. Wings' *Band on the Run* would yield three Top 10 hits in 1973 and 1974 including the title track, "Helen Wheels," and "Jet."

By 1985, he seemed to be losing touch with the zeitgeist. A year after McCartney's wife Linda died in 1998, Paul released *Run Devil Run*, an album predominantly consisting of rock and roll covers that was quickly recorded with a pickup band including Pink Floyd guitarist David Gilmour. Some consider to be the best album of his career, even though it would be his worst-selling studio album in the rock vein since 1986's *Press to Play*.

PAUL McCARTNEY HAD THE MOST COMMERCIALLY SUCCESSFUL SOLO CAREER OF ANY OF THE BEATLES. HIS SUCCESS WAS WON LARGELY BY ESCHEWING THE MUSICAL MODES HE PIONEERED WITH THE FAB FOUR.

Post-Beatle Highlights

John Lennon: The stark and harrowing 1970 album *Plastic Ono Band* and early singles "Instant Karma" and "Cold Turkey" stake Lennon's claim to being the arty, passionate Beatle. Aiming to explode the myth of the Beatles and fame, Lennon effectively recorded his own nervous breakdown, and ushered in a new era of the singer-songwriter in the process.

George Harrison: Armed with a large backlog of songs that never made it onto Beatles records, George Harrison's first post-breakup album was 1970's *All Things Must Pass*, a sprawling set that ranged from spiritual concerns to the dissolution of the Beatles to gorgeous straightforward pop songs.

Ringo Starr: A pair of fine singles, "It Don't Come Easy" and "Back Off Boogaloo," both hit the Top 10 in 1971 and 1972, and began a string of seven consecutive Top 10 hits. Three of those hits would come from his next album, *Ringo*, a star-studded affair that included songs penned by John Lennon, the Band's Robbie Robertson, and George Harrison.

GREATEST HITS	
YEAR	SONG
1971	"Uncle Albert/Admiral Halsey"
1973	"My Love"
1974	"Band on the Run"
	"Junior's Farm"
1975	"Listen to What the Man Said"
1976	"Silly Love Songs"
1978	"With a Little Luck"
1980	"Coming Up"
1982	"Ebony and Ivory"
1983	"Say, Say, Say"

GEORGE MICHAEL

June 25, 1963–

George Michael was considered a teen idol in the mode of Ricky Nelson in the '50s or the Monkees in '60s. And like both of those acts, George Michael is perfect for the time capsule for his respective decade—in his case, the booming drum sounds, the synth pop hooks, the feel-good lyrics, and the distinctive fashions of the '80s. And like both Nelson and the Monkees, Michael was underrated in his time. In reality, he was a skillful white soul singer who took the best sounds of Motown and fused them with '80s dance pop.

Georgios Kyriacos Panayiotou, the son of Greek immigrants, met classmate Andrew Ridgeley when they were 11 years old and discovered that they had compatible tastes in music. By 1982, the duo had become Wham! and with the support of MTV, worldwide success was theirs by 1984, with "Wake Me up Before You Go-Go." By the follow-up single, the writing was on the wall, or rather the record label, which credited "Careless Whisper" to "Wham! Featuring George Michael." By 1986, Wham! was finished.

The following year, Michael reconstructed his career as a serious artist, with *Faith*, which went from style to style like a moth bouncing off a lightbulb. Each one of those styles made it to the top of the charts, whether it was the Buddy Holly cop "Faith" or the Prince homage "I Want Your Sex" or the soul ballad "Father Figure." In all, the album yielded six Top 10 hits, four of which went to #1.

GEORGE MICHAEL PERFORMS AT LIVE AID IN 1985.

GREATEST HITS

Year	Song
	WHAM
1984	"Wake Me Up Before You Go-Go"
	"Careless Whisper"
1985	"Everything She Wants"
	"Freedom"
	"I'm Your Man"
1986	"The Edge of Heaven"
	GEORGE MICHAEL
1987	"I Want Your Sex"
	"Faith"
1988	"Father Figure"
	"One More Try"
	"Monkey"
1990	"Praying for Time"

In the last 10 years, Michael has been better known for his April 1998 arrest for engaging in a lewd act in a public bathroom in Los Angeles.

Michael vs. Sony

With his sophomore solo effort, *Listen Without Prejudice, Vol. 1*, Michael wanted to play down his image as a sex symbol and make music that wasn't as accessible as his previous work. Furthermore, the photogenic star refused to appear on the album cover or in any of the videos for the album, which sold a fraction of what *Faith* had, even though that fraction still added up to more than five million copies. Michael ended up suing Sony Music to get out of his contract, accusing the company of not promoting the record and claiming that the label was hindering his artistic progress. After the suit lingered for years, a London court ruled against Michael. He eventually bought his way out of the contract in 1995 and signed with DreamWorks, for whom he delivered two Top 10 singles, "Jesus to a Child" and "Fastlove."

MOBY

September 11, 1965–

Moby represented some of the best that the DJ and techno subculture had to offer in the '90s and became one of the first stars of the genre. Beats and samples had been a staple of hip-hop and dance culture since the '80s. In fact, hip-hop producers like Dr. Dre, Hank Shocklee from Public Enemy, and the Beastie Boys had been advancing the form for years. The aural colleges that Moby created established a benchmark. He deconstructed a variety of musical forms from blues to jazz to pop to gospel and layered guitars and punk rock influences into brilliant creations with propulsive rhythms. While some would criticize him for watering down the form, he could also claim credit for bringing the music to the widest audience ever.

Moby started studying classical music and jazz at age 10, learning bass, drums, guitar, keyboards, and programming. He briefly sang in the seminal punk band Flipper as a teenager, but by the mid-'80s he discovered house music. His 1991 single, "Go," has since become one of the staples of the genre. Shortly thereafter, he became one of the most sought-after remix artists. He also earned a reputation as one of

MOBY HELPED BRING TECHNO AND DJ CULTURE TO THE MAINSTREAM IN THE 2000S.

the most dynamic performers of the genre, sometimes smashing his equipment at the end of a performance like a postmodern Pete Townshend.

His 1995 major label debut, *Everything Is Wrong*, got wildly positive reviews in the U.S. His follow-up, *Animal Rights*, a hard-rock, guitar-driven album, had little in common with the music he'd been making for the better part of the previous 10 years. But in 1999, he released *Play*, the beacon for the genre, mixing blues, gospel, rock, and pop into hypnotic and compelling dance music. The album was among the best to be released in the '90s.

None of his follow-ups sold as well as *Play*. He has spent an increasing amount of time as an advocate for animal rights, environmental groups, and liberal causes.

GREATEST HITS

Year	Song
1992	"Go"
1993	"Move"
1995	"Into the Blue"
1997	"James Bond Theme"
1999	"Bodyrock"
	"Why Does My Heart Feel So Bad"
2000	"Natural Blues"
	"Porcelain"
	"South Side" (with Gwen Stefani)

NUGGET: Moby, or Richard Melville Hall, is a distant relative to Herman Melville, author of the epic *Moby-Dick*. Moby has never finished reading the novel.

Remix Man

Moby has remixed songs for many artists including Erasure, the B-52's, Brian Eno, Orbital, Aerosmith, Metallica, and Smashing Pumpkins. "Was It Worth It" for the Pet Shop Boys, "Dead Man Walking" for David Bowie, and "They Don't Care about Us" for Michael Jackson are among the best known.

THE MONKEES

1966–1996

By the mid-'60s, most pop stars had learned to use television as a medium to sell records, and began fashioning memorable images to match their music. But the Monkees were one of the first groups to be assembled explicitly for a television show. The group initially didn't play their own instruments or write their own songs. But they were charismatic and attractive and could sing and harmonize well. It didn't hurt that the finest songwriters in Los Angeles and New York constructed some of the best pop songs of the era for them to sing.

The Monkees were the invention of publishing impresario Don Kirshner, who held auditions in 1965 for a television comedy he was creating about a pop band modeled after the Beatles and inspired by their film *A Hard Day's Night*. Davy Jones was a horse jockey and actor from London. Micky Dolenz was a child actor. Michael Nesmith was a country music fan from Texas. And Peter Tork was a folk musician in New York.

Kirshner planned to release records to promote the television show. But when the first single, "Last Train to Clarksville," shot to the top of the charts, it turned out the show itself promoted the singles. "Clarksville" was the first of six Top 10 hits, three of which went to #1. At their peak, the Monkees were selling more records than the Beatles or the Stones.

GREATEST HITS	
YEAR	SONG
1966	"Last Train to Clarksville"
	"I'm a Believer"
	"I Wanna Be Free"
	"(I'm Not Your) Steppin' Stone"
1967	"A Little Bit Me, a Little Bit You"
	"Pleasant Valley Sunday"
	"Words"
	"Daydream Believer"
1968	"Valleri"

The Comeback

In 1986, MTV began running reruns of the television series, sparking a resurgence of interest in the Pre-Fab Four. It seemed appropriate because the Monkees' television show foreshadowed the power of music video by about 15 years. Capitalizing on this resurgence, Jones, Dolenz, and Tork reunited for a highly successful tour. Dolenz and Tork even scored a Top 20 single that year with "That Was Then, This Is Now." Over the course of their 1986 revival, all of their original albums managed to claw their way back on to the sales charts, some 20 or so years after they were first released, a virtually unprecedented feat.

The show was a hit for two seasons, but the Monkees endured a backlash because they didn't actually play their instruments on their recordings—the height of hypocrisy, since such critical darlings as the Byrds and the Beach Boys also relied on session musicians for their early records.

Nevertheless, Nesmith made a grand statement in 1967 that the Monkees would forge a career as a "real band" and play their own instruments. The album, *Headquarters*, didn't sell as well as their first two. Nevertheless *Headquarters* became a favorite of many Monkees devotees. They played their instruments on their subsequent albums augmented by session musicians.

They continued to have a steady flow of hits until the television show was cancelled. The Monkees starred in the 1968 film *Head*, which was panned at the time. Nevertheless, the film has since acquired cult status for being an enjoyable if surreal product of the hazy '60s.

After the band broke up 1969, Nesmith had the biggest musical success, going on to record with his own country-rock band. He would later be instrumental in the creation of the modern-day music video. The other three Monkees tour the revival circuit periodically. All four Monkees got together for an album of self-composed material in 1996, but without the tie-in of the television show the album sold poorly.

FROM LEFT: MICHAEL NESMITH, MICKY DOLENZ, PETER TORK, DAVY JONES. ALTHOUGH THEY DID NOT WRITE THEIR OWN SONGS OR PLAY THEIR OWN INSTRUMENTS, THEY CHARMED AMERICA WITH UNDENIABLY GREAT POP CONFECTIONS.

RICKY NELSON

May 8, 1940–December 31, 1985

Ricky Nelson unwittingly created the template for child actors to make the transition to teen pop stars. And he did so with a derivative but convincing brand of rock and roll, made all the more credible by the tasty guitar licks of James Burton.

Nelson got his start at age 8 on the popular radio program *The Adventures of Ozzie and Harriet*, which starred his parents, Ozzie Nelson, a popular bandleader, and vocalist Harriet Hillard. Ricky and his older brother, David, joined the show in 1948, and four years later the show moved to television, where it became one of the most successful sitcoms from the early days of television.

A fan of Elvis Presley, Nelson made his musical debut with a cover of Fats Domino's "I'm Walkin'," which peaked at #4 in 1957. It would be his first of 19 Top 10 hits. He used television as a mode to promote his music, and thus became the first rock and roll star whom audiences saw and heard on a regular basis. He was equally comfortable crooning pop ballads and mid-tempo songs as he was yelping his way through rockabilly numbers.

Nelson's career was short-circuited for a couple of years by the arrival of the Beatles, which cleared the decks of many teen pop idols. In 1966, *Ozzie And Harriet* was cancelled. Teen idols weren't supposed to buck trends or surprise their audiences, which made Nelson's next move a bold one: an album of

RICK NELSON ABANDONED HIS TEEN POP IMAGE BY THE '70s AND STRUCK OUT AS A COUNTRY ROCK TROUBADOUR.

> *"When you sing rock and roll, or country. It comes from your soul . . ."*—Rick Nelson

country songs. The new style earned him a whole new audience and, in 1972, gave him his first Top 10 hit in eight years with "Garden Party."

He continued to tour 250 nights a year through the '70s and '80s, but on New Year's Eve in 1985, his plane crashed, killing him, his fiancée, and his band. Cocaine was found in his bloodstream, leading many media reports at the time to question whether freebasing was a factor in the crash. In fact, the plane's demise was probably due to a faulty heating system that caused mechanical problems.

GREATEST HITS

Year	Song
1957	"I'm Walkin'"
	"A Teenagers's Romance"
	"Be-Bop Baby"
1958	"Poor Little Fool"
	"Lonesome Town"
1961	"Travelin' Man"
	"Hello Mary Lou"
1972	"Garden Party"

Can't Please Everyone

Against his better judgment, Rick Nelson was persuaded to play a rock-and-roll nostalgia show at Madison Square Garden in New York that also featured Chuck Berry, Bo Diddley, and Bobby Rydell. When Nelson appeared, his performance was a far cry from the rockabilly days of yore. Although he played some of his best-known songs, he also played a series of light country-rock fare with his Stone Canyon Band. He was allegedly booed vociferously halfway through the set (some stories suggest there was police activity at the back of the hall that caused the booing). The incident inspired the song "Garden Party," and its lines "if memories were all I sang, I'd rather drive a truck" and "you can't please everyone, so you got to please yourself." The song would be one of the more eloquent expressions of self-determination among pop stars, even if the music he was playing wasn't as popular.

OLIVIA NEWTON-JOHN

OLIVIA NEWTON-JOHN WAS THE BEST-SELLING FEMALE ARTIST OF THE '70S.

GREATEST HITS	
YEAR	SONG
1973	"Let Me Be There"
1974	"If You Love Me (Let Me Know)"
	"I Honestly Love You"
1975	"Have You Never Been Mellow"
1978	"You're the One that I Want" (with John Travolta)
	"Hopelessly Devoted to You"
	"Summer Nights" (with John Travolta)
	"A Little More Love"
1980	"Magic"
	"Xanadu" (with ELO)
1981	"Physical"
1983	"Twist of Fate"

Olivia Newton-John conjures up a number of images from the '70s and '80s: the pop chanteuse that cooed "I Honestly Love You," the sexpot from *Grease*, the leather-clad rocker of *Totally Hot*, and the bandana and legwarmers-wearing sylph from the video for her biggest hit, "Physical." These seemingly disparate images are a testament to her ability to succeed in many styles. With a smoother and more airy voice than many other female singers, she became the best-selling female artist of the '70s.

Born in the U.K., she grew up in Australia listening to country star Tennessee Ernie Ford, as well as the R&B of Ray Charles and the pop stylings of Dionne Warwick. After winning a talent contest in 1965 she won a trip back to the U.K., where she formed a pop duo with Pat Carroll. Billed as Pat & Olivia, they recorded a single for Decca that went nowhere on the charts.

Don Kirshner, the creator of the Monkees,

Grease Is The Word

"None of us dreamt it would be the phenomenon it turned out to be," Allen Carr, the producer of the film *Grease*, reminisced. The musical, written by Jim Jacobs and Warren Casey, started in a small experimental theater in Chicago in 1971. On tour, a 17-year-old John Travolta played the minor role of Doody. The musical caught the attention of Allen Carr, who bought the film rights at a bargain. The movie was one of the biggest hits of the era, trafficking an idyllic image of the '50s that included no tension, no parents, and nothing but an innocent love of fast cars, true love, and rock and roll.

assembled a British made-for-movies band called Toomorrow and named Newton-John as the group's female singer. The movie sank without a trace, but Newton-John caught on as a regular on U.K. pop legend Cliff Richard's variety show, *It's Cliff*. Based on the success of the show, she scored major international hits with "Let Me Be There," "If You Love Me (Let Me Know)," and "I Honestly Love You." In the United States, she was marketed as a country artist and even won a Grammy in 1973 for best country vocal performance with "Let Me Be There."

In 1978, she won a starring role in the film version of *Grease*, which yielded three Top 10 songs and was a blockbuster movie. After that, she remade her image as a rock and roll chick (think Joan Jett lite) and scored her fourth-consecutive Top 10 tune with "A Little More Love." Her second major film, *Xanadu*, a roller disco movie, was released in 1980, after the craze had ended, and proved less successful at the box office, although she would score two Top 10 songs from the film. In 1981, she came out with "Physical," one of the biggest hits of the '80s.

98 • LEGENDS OF POP

OASIS

To any student of pop music, Oasis will sound instantly familiar. Few songwriters have a better gift for stitching hooks together than Noel Gallagher. Every song is like a beautiful streamlined machine. The lyrics and melodies take you exactly where you want to go. Oasis synthesized the best of British pop music from the Beatles to the present.

Liam Gallagher, bassist Paul "Guigsy" McGuigan, guitarist Paul "Bonehead" Arthurs, and drummer Tony McCarroll were schoolmates in Manchester when they formed a band called the Rain. Liam invited Noel to join the band. The older brother agreed, with the condition that he be given complete creative control over the band.

When Oasis came together in 1994, headed by Noel Gallagher, the band might have been classified as anti-grunge. In the wake of the suicide of Nirvana's Kurt Cobain, they polished an image of good-time blokes who liked to tipple and didn't shy away from a fight. The Top 10 U.K. single "Live Forever" vaulted them to stardom in the U.K. and garnered heavy MTV play in the U.S.

This set the stage for Oasis' *What's the Story (Morning Glory)*, which quickly became one of the

OASIS COMBINED THE BEST ELEMENTS OF POST-BEATLES ROCK INTO A SINGLE STREAMLINED MACHINE.

best-selling albums in British history, yielding four Top 10 singles in the U.K. and a Top 10 hit on the other side of the Atlantic with "Wonderwall." Despite numerous personnel changes over the years, the band continues to sell well in the U.K.

GREATEST HITS

Year	Songs
1994	"Live Forever"
	"Cigarettes and Alcohol"
	"Whatever"
1995	"Some Might Say"
	"Roll with It"
	"Wonderwall"
1996	"Don't Look Back in Anger"
1997	"D'You Know What I Mean"
1998	"All Around the World"
2000	"Go Let It Out"
2005	"Lyla"

Brit Pop at a Glance

Suede: Predating Oasis by a good two years and the brainchild of vocalist Brett Anderson and guitarist Bernard Butler, Suede was credited with ushering British pop music away from the Manchester sound of the Stone Roses and Happy Mondays and toward a style rooted in '70s British rock. Their touchstones were David Bowie, Public Image Limited, and the Smiths.

Blur: Blur front man Damon Albarn prided himself on a British-centric view in his lyrics, thus the group remained relatively obscure in the U.S., with the exception of "Song 2." Musically, Blur drew on a wider scope of influences than its rivals, including elements of techno, dance music, electronica, and eventually indie-rock.

Elastica: Justine Frischmann's group was the most punk-influenced and arguably the best of the '90s crop of Brit pop bands. Brazenly lifting riffs from Wire and the Stranglers, Frischmann's style was similar to the Pretenders' Chrissie Hynde, with whom she shared the ability to both detach emotionally from her lyrics and yet sound sultry and sexy at the same time.

LEGENDS OF POP • 99

THE O'JAYS

1963–

Throughout much of the '60s, the pulse of rhythm and blues could be felt in one of three places: Memphis, New Orleans, and Detroit. But by the early '70s, R&B, like most popular music, began to fragment. Some fine R&B was made in Miami or Muscle Shoals, Alabama. Certainly Al Green and Willie Mitchell would tell you that soul music never left Memphis. But in terms of a cohesive sound that would portend the next major move for popular music in the '70s, you would have to look to Philadelphia. It was there that the key bridge between funk and disco would be built, and the greatest practitioners of this new sound were the O'Jays.

Eddie Levert and Walter Williams got their start in the late '50s singing gospel music on a radio station in Canton, Ohio. In 1959, they were joined by three schoolmates, William Powell, Bobby Massey, and Bill Isles, and became a secular harmony group.

Their career was guided in their early years by a Cleveland disc jockey, Eddie O'Jay, who renamed the group the O'Jays. They recorded a string of singles for the Imperial and Bell labels including the Top 10 R&B hit "I'll Be Sweeter Tomorrow (Than I Was Today)." But nothing they did made much of a dent in the pop charts until they met producers Kenny Gamble and Leon Huff backstage at the Apollo Theatre in 1968. By this time Isles had left the group. Gamble & Huff would issue the O'Jays' "One Night Affair," which went Top 20 on the R&B charts in 1969.

Shortly thereafter, Columbia Records gave Gamble & Huff seed money to start the Philadelphia International imprint in 1971. The song that put them on the pop charts was the O'Jays' "Backstabbers," which went to #3 on the pop charts. Here the Philadelphia International formula began to take shape. On top of a sinuous, funky groove, Gamble & Huff layered string and horn arrangements modeled on their jazz background.

It was smoother in places than anything Motown had conceived of at that point. Inspired by Sly & the Family Stone's *There's a Riot Goin' On* and the growing Black Power movement, Gamble & Huff spun yarns of treachery and hypocrisy. In songs like "For The Love of Money," the seeds of hip-hop were sown—seeds that would be reaped later in songs like "The Message" and "White Lines" by Grandmaster Flash & the Furious Five.

The O'Jays topped the charts in 1973 with "Love Train," a song as hopeful and optimistic as anything the hippie movement would create, but with a beat that

THE O'JAYS, THE GREATEST PRACTITIONERS OF THE SOUND OF PHILADELPHIA, BUILT THE BRIDGE BETWEEN FUNK AND DISCO.

GREATEST HITS

Year	Songs
1967	"I'll Be Sweeter Tomorrow (Than I Was Today)"
1969	"One Night Affair"
1972	"Backstabbers"
1973	"Love Train"
	"Put Your Hands Together"
1974	"For the Love of Money"
1975	"I Love Music"
1978	"Use Ta Be My Girl"

was unrelenting. That train would ride on into the '70s and influence a new generation of music in Donna Summer and other disco performers.

They continued to have success on the R&B charts through the '90s, including a fabulous cover of Bob Dylan's "Emotionally Yours."

THE O'JAYS SOWED THE SEEDS OF HIP-HOP IN SONGS LIKE "FOR THE LOVE OF MONEY."

TSOP

The architects of the Sound of Philadelphia were the songwriting team of Kenny Gamble and Leon Huff. Gamble was a record store owner in the '60s and ran errands for local disc jockeys. He also fronted a harmony group, Kenny Gamble & the Romeos, which included future conspirators Thom Bell, a songwriter and arranger, and session pianist, and fellow songwriter Leon Huff (his piano graces the Ronnettes' "Baby I Love You").

Gamble and Huff began writing together at first for local groups, eventually penning "I'm Gonna Make You Love Me" for Dee Dee Warwick, sister of Dionne. The song was covered in a near-identical version by the Supremes and the Temptations in 1968 and went to #2 on the pop charts.

Like many songwriting and producer teams, Gamble & Huff starting writing and producing songs for other labels, scoring hits with "Expressway to Your Heart," by the Soul Survivors. When Wilson Pickett's string of hits ran out in Muscle Shoals and Miami, Atlantic Records sent him to Philly to record Gamble & Huff's "Don't Let the Green Grass Fool You." And Jerry Butler, an alumnus of the Impressions, had a five-year drought before Gamble & Huff would deliver him back to the Top 10 with "Only the Strong Survive."

In 1971, Gamble & Huff set up Philadelphia International. Anchored by the O'Jays, the label would define the sound of soul music in the '70s. Harold Melvin & the Blue Notes, headed by the sonorous baritone of Teddy Pendergrass, would have two Top 10 pop hits with "If You Don't Know Me by Now" and "The Love I Lost". "TSOP (The Sound of Philadelphia)" recorded by the Philly International house band MFSB became the theme song for the national dance show *Soul Train*.

As disco flourished in the '70s many strains of R&B would fall by the wayside. CBS Records was having success with their own acts such as Earth, Wind & Fire, The Isley Brothers, and Michael Jackson, and no longer considered Philly International a priority. But from 1971 through 1975, there was no more dominant sound in pop music than The Sound of Philadelphia.

P. DIDDY

November 4, 1969–

Diddy (or Puff Daddy, P. Diddy, or Sean "Puffy" Combs), is one of the best selling hip-hop artists of all time. His skills and influence can be heard everywhere in the current hip-hop scene. He established Bad Boy Records in 1996 and eventually became one of the genre's most important and successful businessmen since Russell Simmons. As a producer, he's worked with with Mary J. Blige, Notorious B.I.G., Li'l Kim, Usher, Janet Jackson, and Mariah Carey.

P. DIDDY IS ONE OF THE MOST IMPORTANT HIP-HOP PRODUCERS OF THE '90S AND 2000S.

> **NUGGET:** Diddy has branched out into fashion with his Sean John clothing line. He also has a film production company. He has taken up acting with roles in *Monster's Ball* and *A Raisin in the Sun* on Broadway.

Diddy was studying for a business degree at Howard University when he first started to promote concerts. He quit school and took a job as an intern at Uptown Records. He rose through the ranks and ultimately became one of the label's most successful producers.

GREATEST HITS

Year	Singles
1997	"Can't Nobody Hold Me Down" (with Ma$e)
	"I'll Be Missing You" (with Faith Evans)
	"Mo Money Mo Problems" (with Notorious B.I.G. and Ma$e)
	"It's All about the Benjamins" (with the Family)
1998	"Been around the World" (with The Family)
	"Come to Me" (with Jimmy Page)
	"Lookin' at Me" (with Ma$e)
1999	"All Night Long" (with Faith Evans)
	"Satisfy You" (with R. Kelly)
2002	"I Need a Girl (Part One)" (with Usher and Loon)

He eventually started his own label, Bad Boy, whose roster included Notorious B.I.G., Li'l Kim, and Ma$e. Diddy would make appearances on virtually all of his artists' songs.

He has had some run-ins with authorities along the way. An event he promoted at City College in 1991 featuring Heavy D and the Boyz ended in tragedy when nine people were crushed to death in a stampede. Eight years later, Diddy was accused of opening fire in a crowded club, although acquitted in this case, he has periodically found himself entangled in troubling situations with the law.

Diddy scored his biggest musical successes by taking complete choruses or verses of older songs and building raps and productions on top of them. The most popular example is "I'll Be Missing You," which lifted the music from the Police's "Every Breath You Take" and rewrote the words as a tribute to his murdered friend, Notorious B.I.G. He even found ways to make Carly Simon's "You're So Vain," Led Zeppelin's "Kashmir," and Christopher Cross' "Sailing" sound funky.

Bad Boy vs. Death Row

From the early '90s, Diddy's Bad Boy Records, whose most promising star was Notorious B.I.G., had a rivalry with Marion "Suge" Knight's Death Row Records, home to legendary hip-hop act 2Pac. Diddy and B.I.G. traded barbs with Knight and 2Pac through the media. But the rivalry turned ugly when 2Pac survived being shot five times in the lobby of a Times Square recording studio. He blamed the shooting on Diddy and B.I.G. According to press reports, the labels became proxies for a 30-year bloody rivalry between the two gangs, the Crips and the Bloods. The Crips were affiliated with Bad Boy and the Bloods were linked with Death Row. The rivalry often broke out in public, as it did at the 1996 Soul Train Music Awards where members of B.I.G. and 2Pac's respective entourages scuffled. That summer, a gang of Crips beat and robbed one of 2Pac's bodyguards. A month later, 2Pac and his posse retaliated by beating up one of the Crips in Las Vegas. Later that night, 2Pac was killed in a drive-by shooting. In March 1997, Notorious B.I.G. was murdered after a party. Neither assailant has been found.

PET SHOP BOYS

1984–

In the early '80s, several musical styles—American disco, the German electronic music of Kraftwerk, David Bowie's gender-bending, identity-shifting personas, and Joy Division's angst—began to converge. When the concoction was complete, a whole era of synth pop was born, led by the likes of Depeche Mode and New Order, who combined the misanthropy and angst of modern English society and set it to danceable but dehumanized beats. It was this world that gave rise to Pet Shop Boys. They emerged as one of the only bands of the era (along with Erasure) that had a sense of humor intact as well as skills at mixing and layering sounds. This socially relevant music gave synth dance pop more depth than it ever had.

Keyboardist Chris Lowe was an architecture student when he met Neil Tennant, a writer for the British magazine *Smash Hits*. Lowe turned Tennant on to dance music and persuaded the writer to try his hand at writing lyrics to Lowe's songs. The duo attracted the attention of an American disco producer, Bobby "O" Orlando, who produced their first single "West End Girls," which was a minor hit in the U.S. dance clubs in 1984, but Pet Shop Boys parted ways with Orlando over a legal dispute. After they landed a deal with EMI-Manhattan, they

Losing My Musicians

When assembling her 1989 comeback album *Results*, Liza Minnelli called on Pet Shop Boys to produce. Although it may seem like an incongruous collaboration, Minnelli said that she was a fan of their work and claimed to know all of the words to "West End Girls." "I went into the studio, but there were only Neil, Chris, Julian (Mendelsohn, coproducer) and me," she told the *New York Times* in 1989. "I asked when the musicians would arrive. And Neil said: 'Are you mad? There are no musicians: it's all machines, darling.'" The pairing scored a surprise dance hit with a cover of Stephen Sondheim's "Losing My Mind" from the musical *Follies*.

recorded another version of "West End Girls" that topped the charts on both sides of the Atlantic.

The follow-up "Opportunities (Let's Make Lots of Money)" injected a cunning and ironic send-up of capitalism into the Top 10 at a time when the Reagan and Thatcher regimes were doing their best to root out the equitable distribution of wealth wherever it could be found. Although Pet Shop Boys were capable of political insight, they also knew the value of a great pop song, such as "What Have I Done to Deserve This," which featured soul chanteuse Dusty Springfield. And they also knew the value of a good joke, like their cover of Elvis Presley's "Always on My Mind," a Top 10 hit both in the U.S. and the U.K.

Techno and house music would take computerized dance music one step further, but few could match the wit of Pet Shop Boys.

GREATEST HITS

Year	Song
1986	"West End Girls"
	"Opportunities (Let's Make Lots of Money)"
1987	"It's a Sin"
	"What Have I Done to Deserve This" (with Dusty Springfield)
1988	"Always on My Mind"
	"Heart"
	"Domino Dancing"
1991	"Where the Streets Have No Name"

PET SHOP BOYS' NEIL TENNANT BROUGHT WIT AND SOCIAL COMMENTARY TO DANCE MUSIC IN THE '80S.

WILSON PICKETT

MARCH 18, 1941–JANUARY 19, 2006

WILSON PICKETT DOES THE SHING-A-LING IN THE '70S. BY THIS TIME, HE'D FOUND SUCCESS WITH THE PHILADELPHIA INTERNATIONAL PRODUCTION TEAM.

GREATEST HITS	
YEAR	SONG
1965	"In The Midnight Hour"
	"Don't Fight It"
1966	"634-5789 (Soulsville, USA)"
	"Ninety-Nine and a Half (Won't Do)"
	"Land Of 1,000 Dances"
	"Mustang Sally"
1967	"Funky Broadway"
	"I'm in Love"
1971	"Don't Let the Green Grass Fool You"
	"Don't Knock My Love–Pt. 1"

Wilson Pickett had two styles of singing: hard and harder. The man could scream on key. And with amazing bands like the MGs and the Muscle Shoals rhythm section, he fused James Brown's untamed vocal style with the precision of Southern soul.

The Wicked Pickett was born in Prattville, Alabama, but moved to Detroit as a teenager. He sang with the Violinaires, a gospel group that recorded with Chess Records. In 1960, he made the jump to secular music with the Falcons, one of the most underrated R&B combos of the '60s, that also included Eddie Floyd ("Knock On Wood") and Mack Rice (the original "Mustang Sally"). With Pickett singing lead, the Falcons scored a Top 10 R&B hit with "I Found A Love."

Pickett went solo shortly thereafter and signed with Atlantic Records, who sent him down to Memphis to record with the Stax Records rhythm section. There he collaborated with Stax guitarist Steve Cropper to write "In the Midnight Hour," his first #1 R&B hit. He recorded three more hits with Stax before Atlantic took him farther south to Muscle Shoals, which is where he scored his first Top 10 pop hit, "Land Of 1,000 Dances." He recorded eight Top 10 R&B hits in Muscle Shoals, including his only other Top 10 pop hit "Funky Broadway."

He continued to have hits through the early '70s, including two under the auspices of Kenny Gamble and Leon Huff at Philadelphia International. But the string ended in 1973. He would be immortalized as the inspiration for Roddy Doyle's novel *The Commitments* (and the Alan Parker film of the same name).

"(My family) would say, 'You should come back to God' . . . . When I started buying my mother all these homes, like a second home in Kentucky, where I moved most of my family, they began to rely on my wallet. They didn't say much after that!" —Wilson Pickett

Don't Fight It

In an incident described in Atlantic Records executive Jerry Wexler's autobiography, Pickett was having trouble recording a vocal track when Percy Sledge ("When a Man Loves a Woman") came into the studio and said, "You sound good, Pickett. Man, you sounding like Otis (Redding)."

"I don't sound like nobody, except me," Pickett seethed.

Sledge was shown the door, but an hour later Sledge returned and quipped, "It's sure enough Otis in there, but now I'm hearing some James." Pickett, who hated James Brown, went after Sledge with both fists. According to Wexler, Sledge, once a professional boxer, held his own.

THE PLATTERS

1953–

Following in the mode of their heroes the Ink Spots, the Platters adopted a hybrid of gospel music and pop that made them one of the most popular acts of the '50s. Their R&B and gospel voicings gave songs like "Twilight Time" and "Smoke Gets In Your Eyes" a contemporary feel that put them in a league with other popular harmony groups, such as the Coasters and the Dominoes. But the smooth orchestrations also gave them an appeal to the generation before rock and rollers. Led by former parking attendant Tony Williams' beautiful tenor, they were easily the most successful ensemble of the '50s.

The Platters' manager, Buck Ram, who had worked with the Ink Spots in the '40s, got them a deal at Mercury Records in 1955. Ram penned the Platters' first hit "Only You (and You Alone)," which rose to #5. Their follow-up, "The Great Pretender," was one of the greatest songs of the doo-wop era. Musically, it was little more than the basic 6/8 time triplets that formed the foundation of most R&B ballads of the era. But when Tony Williams' soaring tenor took control employing dramatic flourishes juxtaposed with tense restraint, the song became otherworldly.

After their initial hits, they turned their attention to covers, such as a note-perfect copy of the Ink Spots' 1939 hit "My Prayer," the Three Suns' "Twilight Time," which dates back to 1944, and "Smoke Gets in Your Eyes," a hit for Paul

THE PLATTERS COMBINED GOSPEL MUSIC WITH THE SOUNDS OF TIN PAN ALLEY.

Whiteman's Orchestra in 1934. In 1959, four of the group's members were arrested and accused of using drugs and soliciting prostitutes. This dampened their popularity. Tony Williams left the group in 1960 for a solo jaunt, which spelled the end of both Williams' and the Platters' careers, although the Platters would hit the Top 20 once more with Sonny Turner as the lead tenor on "With This Ring." Bass singer Herb Reed is the only living member of the original group, and he continues to tour with revolving personnel.

GREATEST HITS

YEAR	SONG
1955	"Only You (And You Alone)"
	"The Great Pretender"
1956	"(You've Got) The Magic Touch"
	"My Prayer"
1958	"Twilight Time"
	"Smoke Gets in Your Eyes"
1960	"Harbor Lights"
1967	"With this Ring"

The Ink Spots

The foundation of most rhythm and blues harmony singing in the '50s can be traced to the Ink Spots, one of the first black harmony groups to attract a white audience. They started performing in 1932, first as a swing group called the Four Riff Brothers. Tenor Bill Kenny was brought into the group in 1936. With his quavering tenor in the forefront, they had their first hit in 1939 with the ballad "If I Didn't Care." They became one of the most popular bands of the '40s with such hits as "My Prayer," "When the Swallows Come Back to Capistrano," and "Address Unknown."

ELVIS PRESLEY

January 8, 1935–August 16, 1977

"Who do you sound like?" asked Marion Keisker, a recording engineer at Memphis' Sun Studios, of the young man who wandered in one day in 1953.

"I don't sound like nobody," replied Elvis Presley.

And he was right.

A year later, Elvis Presley exploded the boundaries between blues and country. In so doing, he delivered rock and roll to a national audience and created a culture that turned rebellion, individuality, and sexual energy into a worldwide industry (although he still called elders "sir" or "ma'am," and loved his mother more than anyone else). This white musician also crossed the race lines in the South and helped to integrate popular music. And when he took on pop ballads, standards, gospel, and country, he managed to dominate those styles as well.

Elvis Presley was born in Tupelo, Mississippi, in 1935 to a poor Pentacostal family. He grew up singing gospel hymns in church, listening to the Grand Ole Opry out of Nashville, devouring blues and hillbilly music on local Memphis radio stations, driving a truck, and dreaming of a life better than the one he was living.

Sun Studios and the accompanying Sun Records aimed to record so-called race records by local musicians. It also offered professional recording services to anyone who wanted to record a vanity single for him—or herself. In the summer of 1953, Presley recorded "My Happiness" and "That's When Your Heartaches Begin," both originally recorded by the Ink Spots, a popular gospel proto–rhythm and blues combo. A year later, the label's proprietor, Sam Phillips, asked Presley to return for a professional recording session. After a long day of recording backed by guitarist Scotty Moore, and bass player Bill Black, Elvis started playing a chugging rhythm, goofing on an old Arthur "Big Boy" Crudup song he

LEFT: ELVIS PRESLEY WAS PREDOMINANTLY A FILM STAR IN THE '60s.

RIGHT: ELVIS PRESLEY'S SOUND LAID THE GROUNDWORK FOR ROCKABILLY MUSIC.

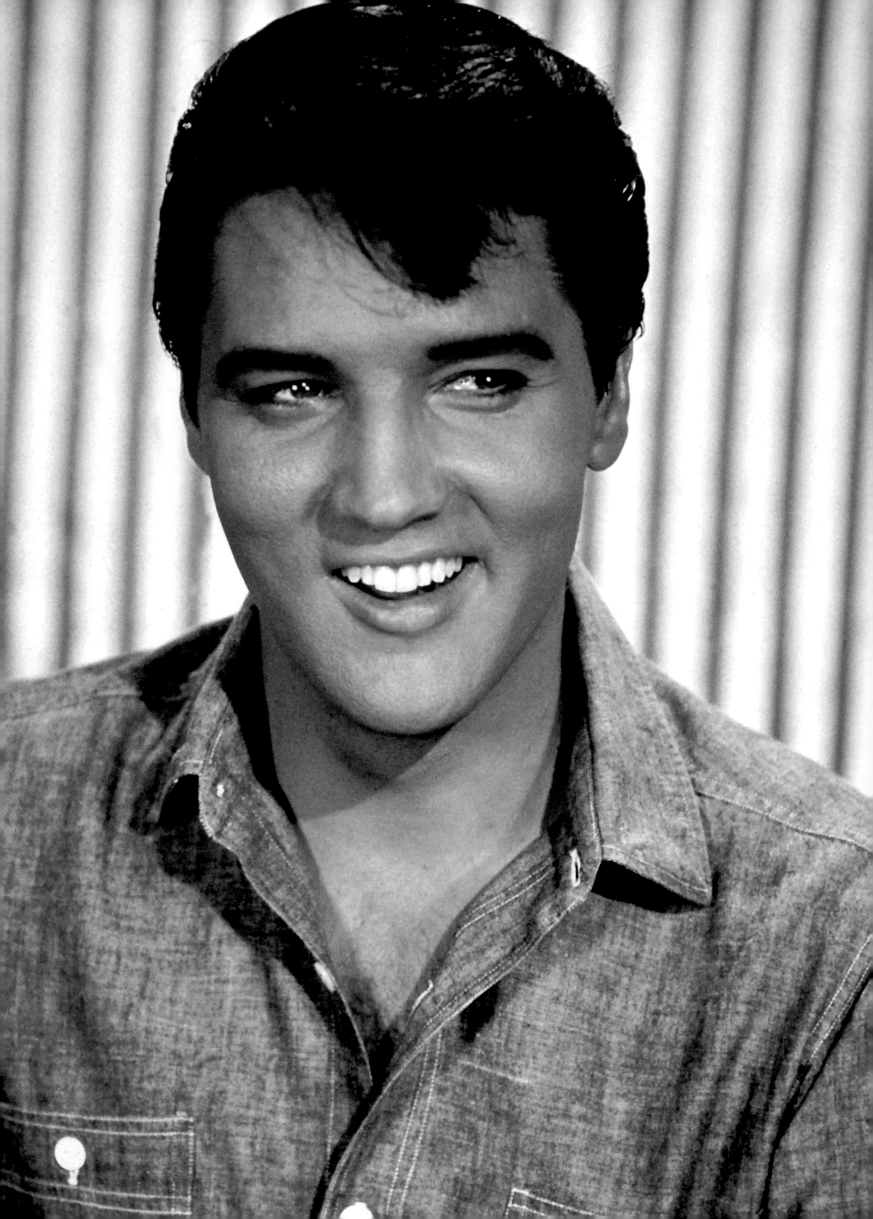

A 7-YEAR-OLD ELVIS PRESLEY STANDS WITH HIS FATHER, VERNON, AND HIS MOTHER, GLADYS. THE LATTER WAS THE STRONGEST NON-MUSICAL INFLUENCE IN HIS LIFE.

knew called "That's All Right, Mama." The song became Presley's first local hit.

Phillips recorded a series of singles between 1954 and 1955. These are considered by some to be among Presley's best—songs that formed the very foundation of rockabilly music, which was later taken up by Carl Perkins, Eddie Cochran, Gene Vincent, and a host of other early rock and rollers.

Presley left Sun for RCA Records, where he recorded the hits that would define the era. Sometimes the music would hearken back to the breathless energy he exuded at Sun, such as on "Hound Dog" or "Jailhouse Rock." On

GREATEST HITS	
YEAR	SONG
1956	"Heartbreak Hotel"
	"Don't Be Cruel"
	"Hound Dog"
	"Love Me Tender"
1957	"All Shook Up"
	"Let Me Be Your Teddy Bear"
	"Jailhouse Rock"
1960	"Stuck on You"
	"Are You Lonesome Tonight"
1961	"Surrender"
1962	"Good Luck Charm"
1969	"Suspicious Minds"
1972	"Burnin' Love"

other songs, he began to croon in the manner of pop singers like Dean Martin. These songs—"Don't Be Cruel," "Love Me Tender," and "All Shook Up" among others, would be his biggest hits. His manager, Colonel Tom Parker, began to soften Presley's image so that he would be palatable to more than just kids.

"I'm afraid I'll go out like a light, just like I came on." —Elvis Presley

Colonel Tom Parker

Thomas A. Parker liked to tell people that he was born in West Virginia and ran away to join the Great Parker Pony Circus as a small boy. In reality, he was born Andreas Cornelis van Kuijk in Breda, the Netherlands, in 1909. He worked on the docks of Rotterdam in the mid '20s before working his way to America in 1929 and settling in the South. It's been said that he discouraged Presley from touring outside the U.S. because Parker was afraid that if he left the country, he might never be allowed to return.

A crude and pugnacious man, Parker was also fiercely loyal to, and ambitious for, his clients, and he expected complete control and fealty in return. In 1948, he used his carny connections to get the governor of Louisiana, Jimmy Davis, to make him an honorary colonel. From then on, he insisted on being called "the Colonel" by everyone, even in casual conversation. After agreeing to manage Elvis, he eventually dropped his other pursuits to commit himself solely to Elvis. Parker was a skillful negotiator and compensated himself handsomely for his efforts, sometimes taking as much as a 50-percent commission from Presley. Parker's first move was to extricate Presley from Sun Records. He was blamed for steering the musician away from rock and roll and toward adult pop and movies, although there's no evidence to suggest that Presley himself didn't want these things. After Elvis died, Parker became an advisor to Hilton Hotels in Las Vegas. He died at age 87 from a stroke.

Presley appeared on Steve Allen's television show in tails to sing "Hound Dog" to, well, a hound dog. On *The Ed Sullivan Show*, he was only shown from the waist up, for fear that his swiveling hips would incite a riot. He would pay his first of many visits to Las Vegas in 1956. He starred in several films, including *Jailhouse Rock*, one of his few movies that was an unqualified critical success. In December 1957, he was drafted into the army, leading many to believe that it was the end of the line for the pop star. They underestimated him.

Throughout the two years he served in the army, Presley left enough tracks in the pipeline to ensure a steady stream of Top 10 hits, including "Hard Headed Woman," "A Big Hunk o' Love," and "I Got Stung." When he returned, he resumed his career both in music, with hits like "Stuck On You" and "Are You Lonesome Tonight," and in Hollywood, churned out films largely without distinction, although most did well at the box office. With the arrival of the Beatles, Presley's popularity took a hit.

His 1968 *NBC Comeback Special*, was supposed to signify his return from Hollywood to assume his rightful place atop the rock pantheon. Some of the show consisted of campy pre-recorded production numbers that added little to Presley's legacy. But parts of the show were recorded live in front of an invited studio audience. Presley's live music would be his most potent in more than 10 years, and it opened up a resurgence for him on the charts, including the #1 hit "Suspicious Minds."

He returned to Vegas in 1969 for a well-received run of shows at the International Hotel. Over the next eight years, the halls got bigger, the concerts became more rote, and Elvis appeared to grow more distant. He scored one more Top 10 hit in 1972 with "Burnin' Love" but his shows were erratic, and often featured him practicing karate moves. Still he inspired devotion in his fans, whether they were coming out to participate in a ritual long since codified and calcified, or whether they still believed in Elvis' power to inspire. The question was rendered moot in August 1977 when he died of a heart attack, brought on by an overdose of prescription pills.

BY THE '70S, ELVIS PRESLEY HAD EMBRACED MOST OF THE TRAPPINGS OF THE VEGAS-STYLE PERFORMANCE.

Sam Phillips

Sam Phillips lived his life bucking every trend and beating all the odds, not dissimilar to Elvis Presley. Phillips was a fan of black spirituals, big band jazz, and blues records. He eventually became a disc jockey in Muscle Shoals, Alabama, and moved up to Memphis in 1945. He opened Sun Studios in 1950 as a place to record black artists who had nowhere else to record. He would lease those records—by such artists as Howlin' Wolf, Ike Turner, and Jackie Breston—to other labels. Since Phillips, an iconoclast himself, encouraged individuality and independence in the artists he produced, the studio earned a reputation for recording some of the best local talent in so-called race records.

In 1953, he established his own independent label and scored local hits with Rufus Thomas, the Prisonaires, and Little Junior Parker. But he would also record amateurs who wanted copies of their own singles. Elvis Presley was one such amateur. His success would also attract other budding artists to Sun. Soon, the label's roster expanded to include Johnny Cash, Carl Perkins, and Jerry Lee Lewis. He sold Presley's contract for $40,000, gambling that Carl Perkins would be able to compensate for the loss of Presley's talent. A car accident unfortunately derailed Perkins' career temporarily. By 1960, most of his big-name acts had moved on to major labels. He sold the label and its catalog in 1969.

PRINCE

JUNE 7, 1958–

No pop star of the '80s covered as much ground, drew on as broad a scope of influences, or brought them to bear on their music as ingeniously as Prince did. Prince melded rock and soul, like no one since Sly & the Family Stone. For a while, the pop world would struggle to keep up with him. Then as the '80s gave way to the '90s he went his own way, caring not one whit who followed (and many didn't). He remains to this day one of the most innovative artists in pop.

Prince Rogers Nelson, born in Minneapolis in 1958, was the son of two jazz musicians who played in the Prince Rogers Trio. By junior high school, he was proficient at the piano, guitar, and drums. And by the time he was 18, he was fronting his own band, Grand Central, which later changed its name to Champagne. He landed a deal with Warner Brothers, which offered him tremendous artistic control. From the git-go, he insisted that he not be marketed solely as a black artist.

PRINCE BROKE THROUGH ON THE POP CHARTS IN 1983 WITH "1999" AND "LITTLE RED CORVETTE."

GREATEST HITS	
YEAR	SONG
1983	"Little Red Corvette"
	"Delirious"
1984	"When Doves Cry"
	"Let's Go Crazy"
1985	"Raspberry Beret"
1986	"Kiss"
1987	"U Got the Look"
1988	"Alphabet St"
1989	"Batdance"
1990	"Thieves in the Temple"
1991	"Cream"
1992	"7"
1994	"The Most Beautiful Girl in the World"

The Artist Formerly Known as Prince

On his 35th birthday in 1993, Prince began writing his name as an unpronounceable symbol. He initially described it to writers as a way of coming to grips with his identity. But later it emerged that he was having trouble with his record company. For one thing, he was recording 10 songs for every song that was released, which meant his vault was filling up with unused material that he wanted the public to hear. But Warner Brothers refused to issue more than one album a year, claiming the market would be "oversaturated" if albums were released more frequently. He also became perturbed that his master recordings of released works were owned by the label, not by him. At the time, this was fairly standard procedure in the record business. But it galled Prince, who took to appearing in public with the word "Slave" written on his face. He quipped in interviews: "If you don't own your masters, your masters own you." He also explored alternate ways of distributing his music, including direct sales through a 1-800 number. He eventually negotiated his way out of his contract with Warner in 1996 and produced a series of records with a variety of labels.

PRINCE PERFORMS AT WEMBLEY ARENA IN LONDON IN 1990.

Dirty Mind in 1980 was Prince's artistic breakthrough, an amalgam of Elvis Costello, the Rolling Stones, and George Clinton, but with lyrics right out of *Penthouse Forum*. Subject matters included oral sex, promiscuity, and incest.

His commercial breakthrough came in 1983 with the album *1999*, whose title track was one of the best expressions of Cold War fears. The next album, *Purple Rain*, topped the charts for 24 weeks, yielded four Top 10 singles and was the soundtrack to one of the few artistically and commercially successful rock films ever made. The album made him a sort of Rorschach inkblot. To rockers, he was the new Jimi Hendrix. To R&B fans, he was James Brown, Otis Redding, and Stevie Wonder all rolled into one. Girls and boys, blacks and whites, all flocked to his shows.

"I never grew up in one particular culture. I'm not a punk, but I'm not an R&B artist either— because I'm a middle-class kid from Minnesota, which is very much white America." —Prince

He short-circuited his skyward trajectory with *Around the World in a Day*, which eliminated some of the obvious hooks that dominated his last four albums. In their place were mysterious psychedelic textures. His next move was the vanity film project *Under the Cherry Moon*, which stiffed at the box office. The accompanying album *Parade* fared much better, featuring a more stripped-down and straight-ahead funk sound.

Although this effectively marked the end of his most commercially successful period, his artistic renaissance was just beginning. *Sign 'O' the Times* was one of the greatest albums of the decade, a double album that moved with ease from funk to soul to jazz and rock and roll. With new personnel in his backup band, including percussionist Sheila E, his music began to loosen up and fulfill all of its initial promise. *The Black Album* and *Lovesexy* had some of the most exciting funk he'd ever make. The hits tr ailed off after 1994, as he battled with his record company and began to release less accessible music. In 2004, Prince began to claw his way back into the mainstream with *Musicology*. And *3121*, released in 2006, became his first #1 album since *Batman* in 1989.

What Time Is It?

At the peak of his popularity, not only was Prince a prolific recording artist, but he also became an important magnet for talent in the R&B world, inking deals throughout the '80s with acts such as Mavis Staples, George Clinton, Chaka Khan, and Vanity 6. He also penned a number of hit songs for other performers including the Bangles, Sheena Easton, Sheila E., and Sinead O'Connor. But the most successful of these projects was the Time. While Prince was mixing rock and soul and other styles, the Time was unadulterated R&B, hard and fast, headed by the charismatic Morris Day. The group had four Top 10 singles on the R&B charts in the '80s, but was better known for their explosive live shows. In fact, they were so successful opening for Prince in the mid-'80s, he took them off the bill. After they broke up, guitarist Jesse Johnson scored five Top 10 R&B hits, while bassist Terry Lewis and keyboardist Jimmy Jam went on to become one of the most important production teams in pop music.

PRINCE'S *PURPLE RAIN* IN 1984 SET THE HIGH-WATER MARK FOR HIS POPULARITY.

BONNIE RAITT

November 8, 1949–

BONNIE RAITT'S 1989 ALBUM *NICK OF TIME* WAS A TRIUMPHANT RETURN AFTER A ROUGH PATCH IN HER CAREER.

Bonnie Raitt had the broadest skill set of anyone to emerge out of the '70s singer-songwriter movement. She's an expressive soulful singer. She can cut with any of the great slide guitarists. She's an adept songwriter. And she was one of the best interpretive singers to come out of the era. What made her story even more amazing is that after losing the plot in the '80s as a result of alcoholism, she staged a comeback that gained her more popularity than she'd ever had before—the prototype of the VH1 *Behind the Music* story.

Raitt's first love was folk and blues. By the late '60s she had met and earned the respect of such blues legends as Mississippi Fred McDowell, Sippie Wallace, John Lee Hooker, and Skip James and absorbed lessons, both good and bad, from all of them—whether it was how to phrase her singing, how to play slide guitar, or how to polish off several fifths of whiskey.

Bonnie sang Motown singles, Robert Johnson covers and her own blues originals with unshakable authority. She made several attempts to fashion her blues roots into a mainstream sound with quality results, but sales still lagged.

After a long battle with alcoholism, she dried out and in 1989 released *Nick of Time*, an album of some of her most personal songs. The album became her first #1 and picked up three Grammys, including Album of the Year. The 1991 follow-up *Luck of the Draw* was an even stronger record, and 20 years into her career she scored her first Top 10 hit with "Something to Talk About." She continues to tour and record regularly with moderate success in the adult contemporary market.

GREATEST HITS

Year	Song
1977	"Runaway"
1979	"You're Gonna Get What's Coming"
1989	"Thing Called Love"
1990	"Have a Heart"
	"Nick of Time"
1991	"Something to Talk About"
	"I Can't Make You Love Me"
1992	"Not the Only One"
1994	"Love Sneakin' Up on You"
	"You"
1995	"You Got It"
1998	"One Belief Away"

Giving It Back

Bonnie Raitt has never been shy about her political views, vociferously supporting Democratic candidates, and anti-nuclear causes among others. But in music, perhaps her most lasting contribution was her early support of the Rhythm and Blues Foundation. The not-for-profit group emerged out of royalty negotiations between R&B legend Ruth Brown and her former label Atlantic Records. Part of that resolution was Atlantic Records founder Ahmet Ertegun's donation of $1.5 million to establish a foundation to recognize, financially support, and preserve rhythm and blues. Bonnie Raitt has sat on its board of directors since its inception in 1988 and been one of its most vocal supporters. Programs include grants to provide medical care, musical instruments, and, if necessary, funeral arrangements for artists in need.

CLIFF RICHARD

October 14, 1940–

If you were a kid in Britain in the late '50s, Cliff Richard may well have been the first bit of rock and roll you ever heard. The Peter Pan of Pop was certainly the first British-born rock and roll star. He was often called the U.K.'s answer to Elvis Presley; indeed only the King sold more records in the U.K. He's had more Top 10 U.K. hits than the Beatles and the Rolling Stones put together. Until the Beatles arrived in 1962, he set the standard against which all British popular music was based.

Richard was born Harry Webb in Lucknow, India, and moved to the U.K. shortly after India declared independence in 1947. He started in a five-piece harmony group called the Quintones. At age 16, he worked in a lamp factory, and sang nights with the Dick Teague Skiffle Group. Inspired by Presley, he formed a rock group called the Drifters in 1958 and changed his name to Cliff Richard. The band eventually changed its name to the Shadows to avoid confusion with the U.S. R&B group. His debut single "Move It!" topped out at #2 on the British charts, the first of 66 Top 10 hits.

He continued to dominate the British charts, moving away from rock and roll and into more traditional

CLIFF RICHARD SCORED 66 TOP 10 HITS IN THE U.K.

pop forms. Although the hits tailed off after the onset of Beatlemania in 1963, he still managed #1 hits in 1965 with "The Minute You're Gone" and 1968 with "Congratulations." He had a resurgence in 1976 with "Devil Woman," his first Top 10 hit on both sides of the Atlantic. In the late '80s and '90s, he returned to the #1 slot in the U.K. with a series of Christmas singles. While he's relatively obscure in the U.S., he remains one of the most-loved pop artists in British history.

GREATEST HITS

Year	Song
1958	"Move It!"
1959	"Living Doll"
	"Travelin' Light"
1960	"Please Don't Tease"
	"I Love You"
1962	"The Young Ones"
	"The Next Time"
	"Bachelor Boy"
1963	"Summer Holiday"
1976	"Devil Woman"
1979	"We Don't Talk Anymore"
1999	"Millennium Prayer"

The Black Knight

Richard was frustrated by a lack of respect from radio stations in the '90s. A DJ who interviewed him called Richard boring and rude had his records banned from being aired on Virgin Radio. So, Cliff Richard hatched a plan. His 1998 single "Can't Keep This Feeling In," a light R&B number, was released under the pseudonym Black Knight. Not knowing who the shadowy figure was, the cut began to get airplay on some R&B stations and eventually made it to #10 on the British charts. Upon the revelation of the identity of the Black Knight, the song was subsequently dropped from radio station playlists. In fact, two DJs who played the song in the face of the ban were taken off the air.

LIONEL RICHIE

JUNE 20, 1949–

If Motown took R&B and made it palatable for pop audiences, Lionel Richie helped give R&B a smooth easy sound to make it palatable for the adult contemporary audience. An expert singer who absorbed influences ranging from country to gospel to soul to rock, Richie got his start as the leadman of the funky '70s group the Commodores. When they needed a ballad, Richie wrote to order. When it became clear that his songs were all turning out to be the group's biggest hits, he went solo and became one of the most successful performers of the '80s.

After nine Top 10 hits as a member of the Commodores, Richie claimed that he was unsure of himself when he went solo. He would have been the only one. Starting with the chart-topping "Endless Love" with Diana Ross, Richie scored 13 consecutive Top 10 singles at a time when popular music was at its most competitive with the likes of Michael Jackson, Prince, and Bruce Springsteen all at the peak of the their powers. He also penned "We Are the World" with Michael Jackson to aid Ethiopian famine relief.

Then in 1987, Richie disappeared for nearly 10 years. In that time he dealt with a number of personal

LIONEL RICHIE OPENED UP R&B MUSIC TO THE ADULT CONTEMPORARY AUDIENCE.

issues including a divorce, the death of his father, and the death of a close friend to AIDS. He returned to the scene in 1996 with *Louder Than Words*, which incorporated some rap and contemporary R&B songs with his ballads, but the album sold poorly. His 2006 album, *Coming Home*, received some ecstatic reviews as did the concert tour. His appearance at the New Orleans Jazz & Heritage Festival was considered by many to be the highlight of the weekend.

"Tunes are here today and gone tomorrow, and you can't always remember who sang them. Songs are careers. They are timeless."—Lionel Richie

GREATEST HITS

YEAR	SONG
1981	"Endless Love" (with Diana Ross)
1982	"Truly"
1983	"You Are"
	"My Love"
	"All Night Long"
	"Running with the Night"
1984	"Hello"
	"Stuck on You"
	"Penny Lover"
1985	"Say You Say Me"
1986	"Dancing on the Ceiling"
	"Love Will Conquer All"

Commodores

As a teenager at Tuskegee Institute in Alabama, Richie met five other freshmen—William King, Thomas McClary, Ronald LaPread, Walter "Clyde" Orange, and Milan Williams—and together they became the Commodores. The group had designs on becoming the black Beatles. They started their career opening for the Jackson 5, and by 1976, notched two Top 10 singles, "Sweet Love" and "Just to Be Close to You." Richie wrote the three ballads "Easy," "Three Times a Lady," and "Sail On," that became the Commodores' best-known hits.

LINDA RONSTADT

July 15, 1946–

Linda Ronstadt was one the most successful interpretive singers of the '70s, moving easily from country to rock to folk to standards to Chicano music. Her versatile voice can be light and airy for pop standards or gruff and sultry for rock and roll numbers. All of her work shares a slick pristine production, where not a note sounds out of place and nothing is left to chance.

Ronstadt started singing folk music in clubs and cafes around Arizona State University when she formed the Stone Poneys with local musicians Bob Kimmel and Kenny Edwards. Together they would take "Different Drum" to the Top 20 in 1967. In the early '70s, she would become a den mother of sorts for a scene coalescing around the premier folk club in Los Angeles called the Troubadour. There she met aspiring musicians Glenn Frey and Don Henley and hired them to back her up in concert and on her third album, *Linda Ronstadt*. Frey and Henley later formed their own band, the Eagles.

The turning point for Ronstadt came in 1974's *Heart Like a Wheel*. The album had a clean rock sound with more R&B influence than she had ever shown before. She also exposed the mainstream to fresh songwriting talent in J. D. Souther, Kate and Anna McGarrigle, and Little Feat's Lowell George.

In 1983, she'd turned her back on soft rock and recorded three albums of pre-rock pop standards with Frank Sinatra's famed arranger Nelson Riddle, the first of which, *What's New*, went Top 10. Spreading her wings stylistically, she recorded *Trio* with Dolly Parton and Emmylou Harris in 1987, which reached

GREATEST HITS	
YEAR	SONG
1967	"Different Drum" (with the Stone Poneys)
1974	"You're No Good"
1975	"When Will I Be Loved"
	"Heat Wave"
1977	"Blue Bayou"
	"It's So Easy"
1978	"Ooh Baby Baby"
1980	"How Do I Make You"
	"Hurts So Bad"
1986	"Somewhere Out There" (with James Ingram)
1989	"Don't Know Much"

Top 10 on the pop charts, and yielded four Top 10 country singles. Later that year she released a Grammy-winning album of traditional Mexican folk songs, *Canciones de Mi Padre*. A duet album *Cry Like A Rainstorm—Howl Like The Wind* in 1989 with the masterful New Orleans singer Aaron Neville put her back on the pop charts in 1989.

LINDA RONSTADT, PICTURED HERE IN '70S, MOVED EASILY FROM ROCK TO STANDARDS TO COUNTRY.

Is There Any Way You Could Unrecord My Song?

While most writers are appreciative of cover versions, Elvis Costello once called Ronstadt's version of his song "Alison" a "waste of vinyl." Some 18 years later, he admitted that her version, which was on an album that sold some 4 million copies, made more money for him than any of his own recordings at the time. It also was the first exposure that most people in the U.S. had to Costello. Evidently there were no hard feelings; she went on to record three more Costello songs for her next album.

RUN-DMC

1983–2002

Prior to Run-DMC, rap groups took turns at the mic with extended narratives or rhymes. Run-DMC brought almost a gospel style to rap. The exhortations, sometimes a single line or word by Run (Joey Simmons), would be punctuated, echoed, or doubled by DMC (Darryl McDaniels). And underneath would be strong beats and expert scratching by Jam Master Jay (Jason Mizell). When they fused this sound with white rock and roll, they became hip-hop's first act to break through to the Top 10. Run-DMC's sound would pave the way for Public Enemy, N.W.A., Boogie Down Productions—let's face it, just about any hip-hop act you can name owes something to Run-DMC.

Run's career started in 1977 as a DJ and occasional rapper with Kurtis Blow, one of the first stars of the genre. He took tapes of some of these performances back to DMC, and the two took turns MCing and DJing. Soon Jam Master Jay was added as a full-time DJ. Run's brother, hip-hop impresario Russell Simmons, who managed Blow, got Run-DMC a record deal after they finished high school, which they did in 1982. A year later, "It's Like That" was a Top 20 hit on the black charts, although its B-side "Sucker MC's" proved to be one of the most enduring songs in the genre. Follow-up singles "Rock Box" and "King of Rock" helped to establish the formula of commingling heavy electric guitars and

RUN-DMC WAS THE FIRST HIP-HOP GROUP TO REACH THE POP TOP 10.

bass lines into their music, and blurring the lines between rock and rap.

They perfected the style on the album *Raising Hell*, a veritable greatest hits collection unto itself with "My Adidas," "It's Tricky," "You Be Illin'," and "Walk this Way," a collaboration with Aerosmith that almost single-handedly resurrected the hard-rock band's career. *Raising Hell* became the first hip-hop album to crack the Top 10 pop album charts. The members of Run-DMC became elder statesmen of the genre and were still scoring hits through the '90s, until Jam Master Jay was gunned down in 2002 at age 37 in his studio in an unsolved murder.

It's Tricky

In 1986, Run-DMC drew the attention of Tipper Gore, the wife of then-Senator Al Gore. Tipper helped run the Parents Music Resource Center, an organization of wives of legislators seeking to censor popular music. PMRC blamed Run-DMC's lyrics and music for the outbreaks of violence at the group's concerts, although it turned out that no one at the PMRC actually ever listened to their music when they made those claims. Ironically Run-DMC's lyrics regularly decried violence, drug use, and gang life. Little has been heard from the PMRC in recent years, although Run-DMC remain one of the most important groups in popular music.

FRANK SINATRA

December 12, 1915–May 14, 1998

FRANK SINATRA IS BELIEVED BY MANY TO BE ONE OF THE GREATEST SINGERS OF THE 20TH CENTURY.

Before there was Elvis, before there was rock and roll, before there were Grammy Awards or even much of a record industry to speak of, there was Frank Sinatra. He was a teen idol before Ricky Nelson was a gleam in his mother's eye. He held live audiences rapt long before light shows, pyrotechnics, or bustiers became de rigeur. At the peak of his popularity, he caused riots when he walked down the street. He was a "method singer" in the way we think of method actors; he got inside the song, internalized its meaning, and whittled it down to its emotional core. So when he sang, his phrasing became naturalistic, even conversational. On a ballad, he could sound like your closest friend telling you a story. On a swinging number, it was as if hands were reaching out, imploring you to dance. He was arguably the greatest singer of the 20th century.

"Being an 18-karat manic-depressive, and having lived a life of violent emotional contradictions, I have an overacute capacity for sadness as well as elation. Whatever else has been said about me personally is unimportant. When I sing, I believe, I'm honest." —Frank Sinatra

When Sinatra was a teenager growing up in Hoboken, New Jersey, in the early '30s, he was so inspired by a Bing Crosby performance that he dropped out of high school to pursue a career in singing. He was discovered by Harry James, a soon-to-be legendary trumpet player who had left Benny Goodman to form his own band. By the summer of 1939, Sinatra was singing and recording with James. He jumped to Tommy Dorsey's more popular band six months later, where he would score his first #1 hit, "I'll Never Smile Again." In December 1942, he

Riddle Me This, Frank . . .

Frank Sinatra worked with a number of great arrangers over the years, from Quincy Jones to Gordon Jenkins. But his best-known and most emotionally resonant songs—"I've Got You Under My Skin," "Night and Day," "I Get Along without You Very Well"—were arranged by Nelson Riddle.

Riddle's first musical instrument was the piano, although he took up the trombone at 14 and played with a number of big bands, including Tommy Dorsey's. Later, Riddle was a staff arranger for NBC radio and became musical director at Capitol Records, where Sinatra signed in 1953. "I've Got the World on a String," Riddle's first arrangement for Sinatra, was wildly popular and began a very successful partnership. He also worked with Judy Garland, Ella Fitzgerald, Rosemary Clooney, and Nat King Cole, for whom he arranged "Mona Lisa." Riddle spent most of the '60s and '70s scoring film and television. Two years before his death, he was called on to arrange material for Linda Ronstadt, which yielded three successful albums.

appeared as a solo act at the Paramount Theater in New York, opening for Benny Goodman. The reaction was something akin to the Beatles arrival in America: mass hysteria and ensuing fame as a pop idol.

In the mid-'50s, Sinatra recorded his best material. While his voice wasn't the powerful youthful instrument it was in earlier days, he used the limitations to his advantage and began to sing in a more stylish conversational way. With Nelson Riddle's rich arrangements floating behind him, the formula vaulted him to a new level of stardom.

In the '60s, Sinatra's voice began to lose some of its range and his singing became even more mannered. Nevertheless, helped by fellow Rat Packers Dean Martin and Sammy Davis Jr., he remained one of the most beloved entertainers, even as rock and roll was becoming more entrenched in popular music. In the latter half of the '60s, he scored three Top 10 hits with "Strangers in the Night," "That's Life," and "Somethin' Stupid," a duet with his daughter Nancy Sinatra.

Although albums became less frequent in the '70s and '80s, he continued to tour regularly and established residencies in Las Vegas and Atlantic City. In 1993, he scored a surprise hit with the album *Duets*, which featured singing collaborations both with such contemporary artists as Bono and Aretha Franklin and older pop stars like Barbara Streisand and Tony Bennett.

DEAN MARTIN (LEFT) JOKES WITH FRANK SINATRA. THE RAT PACK WOULD EPITOMIZE MASCULINE COOL IN THE '50S.

GREATEST HITS

YEAR	SONG
1955	"Learning the Blues"
	"Love and Marriage"
	"(Love Is) The Tender Trap"
1956	"Hey! Jealous Lover"
1957	"All the Way"
1958	"Witchcraft"
1966	"Strangers in the Night"
	"That's Life"
1967	"Somethin' Stupid" (with Nancy Sinatra)

Sammy Cahn

Sammy Cahn was one of the greatest lyricists to come out of Tin Pan Alley. His gift for a great rhyme and a passionate point of view made him an integral part of Sinatra's greatest material, including "All the Way," "Come Dance with Me," and, in particular, "September of My Years," one of the most touching songs ever to be written about aging and maturity.

Cahn studied violin as a child, playing for a variety of bar mitzvah and wedding bands. When he met his first major collaborator, Saul Chaplin, they began writing songs for vaudeville acts. Their first hit came in 1935 with "Rhythm Is Our Business" for Jimmie Lunceford. Chaplin became a successful arranger in Hollywood, while Cahn took up a partnership with Jule Styne, with whom he scored 19 films between 1942 and 1951, including *Anchors Aweigh* and *Romance on the High Seas*. The pair would also win an Oscar for the song "Three Coins in the Fountain," which became a Top 10 hit for Sinatra in 1954.

Styne split with Cahn to pursue a career writing exclusively for Broadway. Cahn then partnered with Jimmy Van Heusen. Together they would deliver some of Sinatra's best-known songs, including "Love and Marriage," "The Tender Trap," and "All the Way."

SLY & THE FAMILY STONE

1967–1983

SLY & THE FAMILY STONE'S *THERE'S A RIOT GOIN' ON* IS ONE OF THE MOST INFLUENTIAL ALBUMS IN THE HISTORY OF POP MUSIC.

S ly & the Family Stone emerged from the San Francisco scene in 1967 playing a hybrid of James Brown and psychedelic rock. Rallying hippie credos like "You can make it if you try" or "You don't have to die before you live" were more than sloganeering for one of the best and most important interracial bands in pop music. When they sang, "We got to live together," in the 1968 chart-topping single "Everyday People," they were putting those ideals into practice, not just racially but from a gender perspective.

Their prowess is on display in the five-minute-or-so excerpt in the *Woodstock* film taken from the legendary festival in 1969. Sly Stone holds the crowd of 400,000 in his hands. "Higher" resembles a combination of a church revival meeting and a political rally. And it wasn't even the band's peak. That would come in early 1970 with the single "Thank You (Falettinme Be Mice Elf Agin)," a song of pride and purpose set to a beat that even James Brown would envy.

Soon after, there were the death threats from the Black Panthers, who were displeased that Sly wasn't

addressing their political agenda in his lyrics, and who objected to his white Jewish manager. Sly began to show up late for gigs, if he didn't miss them completely. There were financial problems, prompting drummer Greg Errico to quit. There was Sly's obsessive nature in the studio, which held up their next album for two years and led Columbia to stop royalty payments until the album

Sly Returns

Sly Stone made his first public appearance in nearly 20 years on the Grammy Awards telecast in 2006. The event was a tribute to Sly & the Family Stone that included, incongruously, Steven Tyler and Joe Perry of Aerosmith, American Idol contestant Fantasia, and soul revivalist phenom Joss Stone. In the middle of the tribute, members of the original Family Stone came on stage and started playing "I Want to Take You Higher." At Tyler's beckoning, Stone strutted on stage with a 12-inch-high mohawk hairstyle. He took his place behind a keyboard at center stage, sang for about 90 seconds, waved, and disappeared. He has also shown up in the audience at gigs performed by his younger sister, Vet.

SLY STONE'S MUSIC ECHOES IN THE SOUNDS OF GEORGE CLINTON, STEVIE WONDER, AND EVEN MILES DAVIS.

was completed. And then there was cocaine—mountains of it.

On 1971's *There's a Riot Goin' On*, Sly Stone created a new vocabulary for pop music. Its music was a slow languid funk that was disturbing to listeners at first, but went on to influence a generation of performers. The Temptations, in particular, created several hits around this sound, including "Papa Was a Rolling Stone" and "Cloud Nine," albeit in sanitized versions. It resurfaced in the O'Jays' "For The Love of Money" and "Backstabbers." Curtis Mayfield adapted his version of it in "Freddie's Dead" and "Superfly." Miles Davis reinvented jazz (again) using Sly's sound as a template. Even Stevie Wonder's landmark albums of the '70s owe a debt to Stone. But none would ever catch up with Sly.

Between the band's new sound and Sly's unreliable performance record (including some no-shows that resulted in riots), both fans and band members, most notably, bassist Larry Graham, got off the bus. He regained some goodwill with 1973's *Fresh*. But after *Fresh*, most of his albums disappeared without a trace. In addition to other legal woes, he faced a $3.4-million tax lien. Between 1973 and 1989, there was a litany of drug and gun charges. He was in and out of rehab. He poked his head up once in a while, as on Funkadelic's *The Electric Spanking of War Babies* in 1981, but then disappeared again.

There's a Riot Goin' On

When *There's a Riot Goin' On* finally came out after a two year wait in 1971, Sly & the Family Stone had undergone a complete transformation. Rather than the optimistic, idealistic aura of their first four albums, this album was like staring down the barrel of a gun. The music was shrouded in a veil of fog. The grooves were deeper, more rhythmic, almost liquid sounding, but this music didn't invite the audience in. Sly sounded stoned or worse throughout. The words were filled with dread and defeat. Sly would languish over every syllable as if he were uncertain he would make it to the end of the song. The lyrics festered with images of a barren wasteland.

The album would yield a Top 10 single, "Family Affair," but even this song was misleading, for the song was not about the unity and community created by a family but rather about how families rip themselves apart. To put a fine point on it, he closed the album with a remake of "Thank You (Falettinme Be Mice Elf Agin)," only he titled this version "Thank You For Talkin' To Me, Africa." This version was a photo-negative version of the earlier hit. In 1970, the song was a triumphant retelling of Genesis 32:22–32 in which Jacob wrestles with God. Only in Sly's first version, the narrator wrestles with the devil and wins. The 1971 song chugs along languidly like a heroin trip. Sly and the devil are one and no one wins. By the time it ends, Sly seems to have killed off all the hope and optimism that the band helped create at Woodstock.

GREATEST HITS	
YEAR	SONG
1968	"Dance to the Music"
	"Everyday People"
1969	"Stand"
	"I Want to Take You Higher"
	"Hot Fun in the Summertime"
1970	"Thank You (Falettinme Be Mice Elf Agin)"
1971	"Family Affair"
1972	"Runnin' Away"
1973	"If You Want Me to Stay"

BRITNEY SPEARS

DECEMBER 2, 1981–

Judging from the gallons of ink that have been poured into covering her marriages, her children, her behavior, and her clothes, Britney Spears is one of the most important stars in the last 10 years. It almost seems like an afterthought that she was once a talented pop singer and dancer, who at one point won the endorsement of Madonna, a woman who knows a thing or two about being a pop star. Or that ". . . Baby One More Time," was unavoidable in the fall of 1998, along with the video of the innocent Catholic schoolgirl dancing suggestively. Or that "Oops! . . . I Did It Again" was one of the most undeniably great songs of 2000. Few people executed the '90s brand of dance pop better than Britney Spears.

New Orleans–born Spears auditioned for the Mickey Mouse Club when she was 8 years old, but was turned away because she was too young. After spending three summers at the Off-Broadway Dance Center and the Professional Performing Arts School in New York, she successfully auditioned for a part on the Mickey Mouse Club in 1992. Her fellow cast members included Christina Aguilera, *NSYNC's Justin Timberlake, and J. C. Chasez. When the show was canceled two seasons later, she began to assemble demos in hopes of pursuing a singing career.

Her debut album, *Baby One More Time,* was one of the top sellers of 1998 and world domination seemed a foregone conclusion. Her follow-up, *Oops . . . I Did It Again* logged 1.3 million in sales in its first week, a record at the time for a female artist.

In her 2001 album, *Britney,* she tried to shed the innocent teen pop idol image in favor of a more mature and even sexier look. The album debuted at #1, but none of its singles cracked the Top 10. *In the Zone* followed in 2003, but by then her romantic exploits had upstaged her music.

Me Against the Music

It's difficult to pinpoint when Spears made the transition from pop star to phenom whose every move became the subject of gossip pages. It could have been the speculation about her breast enlargements in 1999. It could have been the 2000 MTV Music Awards when she gyrated in a flesh-toned body suit. Maybe it was the 2003 MTV Video Music Awards when she locked lips with Madonna. By the time she wed her childhood friend Jason Alexander in 2004, a union that lasted 55 hours, her behavior was clearly starting to upstage her singing career. Later that year, she married one of her backup dancers, Kevin Federline. Two months after the birth of her second child, she filed for divorce. In early 2007, she was spotted in a tattoo parlor in Los Angeles with a shaved head, an event that was treated like an international crisis by the media. Spears then played now-you-see-me now-you-don't with several drug rehab centers. Integrating her early success with her present difficulties in the face of the media's constant scrutiny will prove a formidable challenge to the once indomitable star.

GREATEST HITS	
YEAR	SONG
1998	". . . Baby One More Time"
1999	"Sometimes"
	"(You Drive Me) Crazy"
2000	"From the Bottom of My Broken Heart"
	"Oops . . . I Did It Again"
	"Lucky"
	"Stronger"
2001	"I'm a Slave 4 U"
2002	"Overprotected"
2003	"Me Against the Music"
2004	"Everytime"
	"Toxic"

BRITNEY SPEARS PERFORMS IN MANCHESTER, U.K., IN 2004.

PHIL SPECTOR

December 26, 1940–

"I get a little angry when people say it's bad music," Phil Spector told Tom Wolfe in 1965. "(Rock and roll) has a spontaneity that doesn't exist in any other kind of music. . . . It has limited chord changes, and people are always saying the words are banal and why doesn't anyone write lyrics like Cole Porter anymore. . . . Actually, it's more like the blues. . . . It's what people respond to today."

Phil Spector understood pop music, so none of the elaborate recordings he created sound contrived or condescending. Because he believed the music was already profound, he was able to enhance it with layers of Latin percussion, elaborate string sections, three drum kits, umpteen guitars, four keyboards, and layer upon layer of vocalists, and still keep the swing and feel of a rhythm and blues song. He took gorgeous churches constructed by Doc Pomus and Mort Shuman, Carole King and Gerry Goffin, Cynthia Weil and Barry Mann, Ellie Greenwich and Jeff Barry, and he turned them into cathedrals.

By the time he was 17, he'd written and produced his first #1 hit, "To Know Him Is to Love Him" recorded by the Teddy Bears. When he was 20 years old, he co-wrote "Spanish Harlem" with Jerry Lieber of the famed Lieber and Stoller songwriting team. The Ben E. King hit was Spector's apprenticeship on how to build a dramatic sound without losing the essence of rock and roll or rhythm and blues.

GREATEST HITS	
YEAR	**SONG**
1958	"To Know Him Is to Love Him" (The Teddy Bears)
1960	"Spanish Harlem" (Ben E. King)
1962	"Uptown" (The Crystals)
1963	"Da Doo Ron Ron" (The Crystals)
	"Be My Baby" (The Ronettes)
	"Then He Kissed Me" (The Crystals)
1964	"You've Lost That Lovin' Feelin'" (The Righteous Brothers)
1966	"River Deep–Mountain High" (Ike & Tina Turner)
1970	"The Long and Winding Road" (The Beatles)
1970	"My Sweet Lord"(George Harrison)
1971	"Imagine" (John Lennon)
1980	"Do You Remember Rock 'N' Roll Radio" (Ramones)

SPECTOR WROTE AND PRODUCED HIS FIRST #1 HIT AT AGE 17.

By the time he was 21, Spector had created his own record company around the powerhouse voice of Darlene Love, the sultry come-hither sound of the Ronettes (whose lead singer Veronica Bennett would become Ronnie Spector after marrying the producer), and a host of other groups. You can hear the beginnings of his legendary Wall of Sound in the opening bars of the Crystals' "Uptown."

By 1962, Phillies Records was a hit factory to rival Motown and Stax. The Crystals, with a revolving host of lead vocalists like Love, Barbara Alston, and La La Brooks, would score with "Da Do Ron Ron" and "Then He Kissed Me." Spector turned the Ronettes into stars with "Be My Baby."

The public had moved on to different styles by 1966, leaving Phil Spector productions sounding outdated.

Spector linked up with the Beatles and rescued their *Let It Be* project, which was collapsing along with the Beatles' partnership in 1970. Both George Harrison and John Lennon would use Spector as a producer for their early solo albums.

Spector gradually retreated into the seclusion of his Los Angeles home. He would rarely emerge over the next 30 years, except for occasional projects with John Lennon, the Ramones, and others.

Spector was known for his violent behavior. He fired a gun over the head of John Lennon during the recording of his *Rock 'n' Roll* album in 1974. Joey Ramone said he brandished a gun during the production of the Ramones' *End of the Century*. These antics took a tragic turn in 2003 when he was arrested for murdering an actress in his home. The case went to trial in 2007.

PHIL SPECTOR'S RONNETTES TOOK "BE MY BABY" TO #2 ON THE POP CHARTS. SPECTOR WOULD EVENTUALLY MARRY LEAD SINGER VERONICA BENNETT (TOP).

Chapel of Love

In moments of braggadocio, Phil Spector would claim that none of the performers would be anything without his production skills. Nowhere was that more patently untrue than with Darlene Love, by far the most skilled of any vocalist Spector worked with other than perhaps Tina Turner.

A church-trained singer, Darlene Wright started singing professionally at age 16 with a female vocal group called the Blossoms, who sang backup for Elvis Presley, Bobby Darin, the Beach Boys, the Mamas & the Papas, and Dionne Warwick throughout the '60s. They were Phil Spector's favorite backup singers. While the Crystals were on tour, Spector fell in love with a song given to him by Gene Pitney called "He's a Rebel." So he had the Blossoms record the song with Wright, whom Spector then dubbed Darlene Love, singing lead and issued the single under the Crystals' name. The song went to #1. Love and her group sang "He's Sure the Boy I Love" under a similar arrangement and peaked at #11. Love would also sing under the name Bob B. Soxx and the Blue Jeans, the act that took "Zip-A-Dee Doo-Dah" to the Top 10. And it isn't Christmas time until you hear Darlene Love singing "Christmas (Baby Please Come Home)" on the radio, easily one of the best rock-and-roll Christmas songs ever

She split with Spector over money (she successfully sued him for back royalties, getting close to $250,000 from him, but still a fraction of what she earned). But the Blossoms were still a hot property as session musicians and eventually toured with Dionne Warwick. After a failed bid at a solo career, Love came on financial troubles in the early '80s, and was reduced to working as a maid. She eventually got a job as a singer on a cruise ship. Around this time, producers started mounting a musical production of Ellie Greenwich songs called *Leader of the Pack*, and Love was invited to participate. The musical flopped when it reached Broadway in 1985, but it brought Love back into the entertainment business full time. She got bit parts in the *Lethal Weapon* film franchise, and by the '90s she was performing weekly at the Bottom Line in New York City, where she was earning rave reviews.

She still appears at Christmas time on the *Late Show with David Letterman* to sing "Christmas (Baby Please Come Home)." In 2005, she won a role in the hit musical *Hairspray*. But for better or worse, she will be remembered as the finest singer to grace a Phil Spector production.

SPICE GIRLS

1996–2000

After several years of earnest, maudlin, shoe-gazing grunge music, the Spice Girls arrived in 1996 like a breath of fresh air. They offered hooky dance beats, a variety of pretty faces each supposed to connote a different style—Sporty Spice, Posh Spice, Ginger Spice, Baby Spice, and Scary Spice—and a vague simulation of gender empowerment that was suitable for teen girls, but still had enough cleavage to appeal to boys who watched MTV. The band would be savaged by holier-than-thou critics for being a cheap marketing ploy, as if Nirvana, R.E.M., or the Beatles never used image to get over. Most of these critics missed what an infectious song "Wannabe" was. Music buyers did not; it topped the charts on both sides of the Atlantic.

GREATEST HITS	
YEAR	SONGS
1997	"Wannabe"
	"Say You'll Be There"
	"2 Become 1"
	"Spice up Your Life"
	"Mama"
1998	"Too Much"
	"Stop"
	"Goodbye"

THE SPICE GIRLS RESCUED POP MUSIC FROM NAVEL-GAZING GRUNGE ROCKERS IN THE LATE '90S.

"Of course I'm a feminist. But I could never burn my Wonderbra. I'm nothing without it."—Emma "Baby Spice" Bunton

better in the U.K. The Spice Girls split in 2000 but the damage was done. Their success ushered in a new era of teen pop that paved the way for Britney Spears, the Backstreet Boys, and *NSYNC.

Victoria "Posh" Adams, Melanie "Scary" Brown, Emma "Baby" Bunton, Melanie "Sporty" Chisholm, and Geri "Ginger" Halliwell were chosen in 1994 by British managers to become a new singing group. But two months after their auditions, they fired their managers for trying to turn the band into a bland pop group. This stoked the media machine and by the time their debut single "Wannabe" reached #1 in the U.K., everyone in Europe knew their names, their personas, and who they were dating. They hit the U.S. six months later and scored three Top 10 hits in a row.

The Spice Girls made the obligatory life-of-a-pop-band feature movie *Spice World*, which was panned by critics and ignored by almost everyone else. The accompanying album was a disappointment in the U.S., although it fared

Life After Spice

Victoria Beckham (née Adams) became best known as the wife of soccer star David Beckham. She also established her own line of clothing.

Geri Halliwell, the first Spice Girl to split from the group in 1998, recorded three solo albums, the first of which did well in the U.K. in 1999. The albums that followed were less successful.

Emma Bunton had a handful of hits in the U.K. including "What Took You So Long" in 2001.

Melanie Chisholm was the only Spice Girl to chart a pop hit in the U.S. (#43) with "I Turn to You." In the U.K. she had two #1 hits.

Melanie Brown scored a #1 U.K. single with "I Want You Back," a duet with Missy Elliott in 1998.

THE SPINNERS

1961–

Neither gritty Southern soul nor fluffy Motown pop, the Spinners were Motown's forgotten men until Atlantic Records picked them up and paired them with Philadelphia songwriter and arranger Thom Bell. The Spinners reorganized the group's doo-wop roots around Bell's lush arrangements and new lead singer Phillipe Wynne. The result was seven Top 10 singles from 1972 to 1980 and a string of 12 straight Top 10 R&B hits.

George Dixon, Henry Fambrough, Billy Henderson, Pervis Jackson, and Bobbie Smith were discovered by doo-wop impresario Harvey Fuqua, who became a key figure at Motown in 1963. But the growing Detroit label had little use for the harmony group other than as chauffeurs and runners of odd jobs for other members of Motown's inner circle. With new lead singer, G.C. Cameron, they would score a hit with the Stevie Wonder-penned and produced "It's A Shame" in 1970. But the group was dropped two years later. Cameron left the group but recommended a replacement lead singer, Philippe Wynne.

On the recommendation of Aretha Franklin, Atlantic Records signed the Spinners. With producer Thom Bell at the helm, the group scored its first Top 10 pop hit with "I'll Be Around" in 1972. They garnered a second hit three months later with "Could It Be I'm Falling in Love." Two years later, the Spinners backed up Dionne Warwick's funkiest single ever with "Then Came You," which topped the pop charts.

Wynne would leave the group in 1977, citing "creative differences" with Bell (read: they fought tirelessly). Bell would follow him out the door two years later, believing he could take them no further. The Spinners, lead by John Edwards, scored two more Top 10 hits with medleys of oldies and new songs "Working My Way Back to You/Forgive Me Girl" and "Cupid/I've Loved You for a Long Time." The Spinners continue to tour the oldies circuit with three original members. Wynne died of a heart attack onstage in 1984 at age 43. Billy Henderson died in 2007 at age 67 of complications related to diabetes.

THE SPINNERS, PICTURED HERE IN THE '60s, FAILED TO FIND SUCCESS UNTIL THEY LEFT MOTOWN FOR ATLANTIC RECORDS IN THE EARLY '70s.

GREATEST HITS

YEAR	SONGS
1970	"It's a Shame"
1972	"I'll Be Around"
	"Could It Be I'm Falling in Love"
1974	"Then Came You" (with Dionne Warwick)
1975	"They Just Can't Stop It (Games People Play)"
1976	"Rubberband Man"
1979	"Working My Way Back to You/ Forgive Me Girl"
1980	"Cupid/I've Loved You for a Long Time"

Thom Bell

Thom Bell was a producer at Cameo-Parkway Records, where one of his first projects was the Delfonics, whose biggest hit was "La-La Means I Love You." He preferred carefully arranged sections of strings to the gutbucket horn sections of Memphis. For the vocals, he drew on the early harmony groups such as the Flamingos and the Orioles, rather than grit of Otis Redding. The song wound up hitting #4 on the pop charts in 1968.

In 1970, he met Linda Creed, a secretary at a Brill Building music publisher struggling to start a career as a lyricist. It would be the beginning of one of Bell's most fruitful collaborations, for in 1971, Bell and Creed would begin a string of hits with the Stylistics.

The Stylistics were so smooth that they made the Delfonics sound like Wilson Pickett. The gorgeous falsetto of Russell Thompkins Jr. was doo-wop headed uptown. Plus the Stylistics had the best use of a sitar since the Beatles, and no one has done it better since.

NUGGET: Linda Creed, lyricist for several Spinners hits, penned the lyrics to "The Greatest Love of All," which became one of Whitney Houston's biggest hits

DUSTY SPRINGFIELD

April 16, 1939–March 2, 1999

Dusty Springfield performs on the BBC at the time of "You Don't Have To Say You Love Me," a Top 10 hit on both sides of the Atlantic.

GREATEST HITS	
Year	**Song**
1964	"I Only Want to Be with You"
	"Wishin' and Hopin'"
1966	"You Don't Have to Say You Love Me"
1967	"The Look of Love"
1968	"Son of a Preacher Man"
1969	"Don't Forget about Me"
	"The Windmills of Your Mind"
	"A Brand New Me"
1987	"What Have I Done to Deserve This" (with Pet Shop Boys)

"Of all the literally hundreds of singers who recorded my songs, Dusty was by far the best."—Carole King

Dusty Springfield cut across a wide swath of styles in pop music. She was equally at home singing Southern soul music, Beatles-style rock and roll, and intricately arranged pop music. Her beehive hairstyle and thick eyeliner made her one of the most enduring images of the '60s. But she is best known for her voice, husky and tender at the same time, capable of both girlish charm and world-weariness. Springfield was one of the most expressive and underappreciated singers of the rock era.

Born Mary Isabel Catherine Bernadette O'Brien, Dusty Springfield's first success came in a folk group called the Springfields. When the Springfields left England to tour the U.S., Dusty was immediately struck by Motown's singers and turned from folk to pop. Her first solo hit was "I Only Want to Be with You," which peaked at #12 in 1964. Her transformation would inspire a host of British female performers, such as Lulu, Cilla Black, and Petula Clark. She also proved her ability to tackle a ballad with her biggest hit, "You Don't Have to Say You Love Me."

Her master stroke was to incorporate the soul singing of Aretha Franklin into pop contexts. Nowhere would she do this better than on *Dusty in Memphis*, which would have the Top 10 hit "Son of a Preacher Man." But this song only scratched the surface of the album's depth. Bringing out the best in songs by Randy Newman; Gerry Goffin and Carole King; and Burt Bacharach and Hal David, she effectively assembled a virtual history of pop music from the rock era on one album.

She returned to the Top 10 in 1987, singing on the Pet Shop Boys hit "What Have I Done to Deserve This?" Springfield was inducted into the Rock and Roll Hall of Fame in 1999. Unfortunately the honor came two weeks after she died of breast cancer at age 59.

Memphis Train

Coming off the pop hits "You Don't Have to Say You Love Me" and "The Look of Love," the strategy of recording the follow-up in Memphis, the home of rhythm and blues, must have seemed incongruous. But that's where she was in 1968, with producer Jerry Wexler unwittingly needling Springfield by incessantly singing the praises of Aretha. Springfield would respond by playing the diva to the hilt. She rejected more than a hundred songs. She refused to sing practice tracks with the backup band to work through arrangements. At the peak of her pique, she hurled an ashtray at Wexler. But when the record was released, *Dusty in Memphis* was hailed a pop masterpiece.

GWEN STEFANI

October 3, 1969–

GWEN STEFANI, WITH HER BAND NO DOUBT, DRAWS ON A BROADER SCOPE OF INFLUENCES THAN MANY OF HER CONTEMPORARIES.

Gwen Stefani may well be the most qualified heir to the throne, when and if Madonna relinquishes her position as reigning queen of pop music. Stefani and her band No Doubt actually draw from a wider scope of influences, from punk to ska to rock to funk to hip-hop to dance pop. Her voice is distinctive, hovering between a shrill punk rock scream, a rap, and a quiver. Her stage show is equal parts calisthenics, punk rock revival, and polished pop production. She's shown an aptitude for transforming her image to keep the interest of both the music and fashion industry. And not a single move seems calculated or dishonest.

Stefani's story starts in a Dairy Queen in Anaheim, California, where Gwen, her brother Eric, and their friend John Spence worked. The three formed a band in 1987 with bassist Tony Kanal, who went to a nearby high school and eventually became Gwen's boyfriend. No Doubt, fronted by Spence and Gwen, rode the wave of a ska revival in California in the late '80s, covering songs by Madness and the Specials and earning a local following. But nine months into their existence, Spence committed suicide. After initially searching for a replacement, Stefani assumed lead singing duties on her own.

Beyond Music

In 2002 Gwen Stefani married Gavin Rossdale, the former lead singer of the Nirvana sound-alike band Bush (and didn't even dump him when his career tanked). She established her own fashion line, L.A.M.B., in 2004 (she has always designed her own clothes). And also in 2004, she made her feature film debut in Martin Scorsese's *The Aviator*, getting positive reviews for her portrayal of Jean Harlow. She had a baby in 2006, fulfilling a wish she'd discussed in many interviews over the years.

"I think I've been able to fool a lot of people because I know I'm a dork. I'm a geek." —Gwen Stefani

After their first album flopped, the band was left to twist in the wind by their label, Interscope Records, which rejected all of the songs for their follow-up. The frustration led keyboardist Eric Stefani to leave the band and take up a career as a layout artist for *The Simpsons*. No Doubt subsequently issued a second album through an independent local label. When relations between Interscope and the band thawed, they issued *Tragic Kingdom*, which took advantage of both the broad palette of styles they brought to the canvas and a loyal local following. No Doubt increasingly became a vehicle for Stefani's vision and persona. As the band's main lyricist, Stefani would parlay her breakup with Kanal into "Don't Speak," which became one of the top hits of the '90s. And her anthem "Just a Girl" was a rallying cry for teen girls (and more than a few adults) in the winter of 1996.

Despite the lack of success of the follow-up, *Return to Saturn*, Stefani managed to stay in the spotlight thanks to appearances on songs by Moby and Eve. The momentum behind those singles helped No Doubt's next album, *Rock Steady*, get them back to the Top 10, with "Hey Baby" and "Underneath It All." The album embraced their ska roots but added elements of dance-pop and hip-hop that would point to Stefani's solo career.

Her solo debut *Love.Angel.Music.Baby* included a virtual who's who of pop music, including hip-hop production team the Neptunes, Andre 3000 from Outkast, hip hop pioneer Dr. Dre, and song doctor extraordinaire Linda Perry, who penned hits for Pink and Christina Aguilera. She intended her solo album to be a dance record,

GWEN STEFANI PROMOTES HER FASHION LINE L.A.M.B.

and she succeeded by every measure with songs like "Rich Girl" and "Hollaback Girl." The album managed the rare feat of hitting the Top 10 on three separate occasions between 2004 and 2006. On *The Sweet Escape* in 2007, she showed no signs of letting up. Despite her solo success, she continued to insist that No Doubt will regroup, possibly in 2008.

Ska Revival

No Doubt rode the crest of a wave that brought the Jamaican antecedent of reggae to the white mainstream in the mid-to-late 1990's. While some would draw more on the syncopated offbeat style than others, all of these bands fused the sound of ska with punk to give a voice to rebellious, angst-ridden, disaffected youth.

Rancid was the best of these bands, mixing both the sound and worldview of the Clash with ska (the Clash borrowed liberally from reggae and dub, themselves). They emerged out of the same Northern California scene that bred NoFX and Green Day. Led by Tim Armstrong and Lars Frederiksen, Rancid would become a staple on modern rock radio and MTV's *120 Minutes*.

Sublime, unfortunately, reached its commercial peak after (or because of) the fatal heroin overdose of its lead singer Brad Nowell, but its biggest hit "What I Got" was absolutely ubiquitous for years afterwards. The band had a devoted following in Long Beach and other parts of southern California among skate and surf punks. The two surviving members went on to form the Long Beach Dub All Stars.

Goldfinger, from Santa Monica, toured frequently with No Doubt in the mid '90s and scored a radio hit with "Here in Your Bedroom" in 1996. Although they never again achieved pop success, they became beloved in the hardcore community.

GREATEST HITS	
YEAR	SONG
	NO DOUBT
1995	"Just a Girl"
1996	"Don't Speak"
2000	"Simple Kind of Life"
2001	"Hey Baby"
2002	"Hella Good"
	"Underneath It All"
	GWEN STEFANI
2004	"What Are You Waiting For"
	"Rich Girl" (with Eve)
2005	"Hollaback Girl"
2006	"Wind It Up"
2007	"The Sweet Escape" (with Akon)
	"4 in the Morning"

ROD STEWART

January 10, 1945–

When Rod Stewart emerged in the late '60s and the early '70s, he looked like he was going to give Mick Jagger a run for his money as Britain's best white blues singer. By the mid-'70s, he virtually abandoned those styles and instead became a pop singer. Although his voice never had the range or subtlety of many blues singers, he acquired a distinctive raspiness that served him as well on pillow-talk ballads as it did on disco and dance-pop hits.

Stewart got his first taste of stardom in 1967 when he joined the Jeff Beck Group. The band, formed by the former Yardbirds' guitarist, was one of the prototypes for heavy metal. He joined the Faces in 1969, which became one of the best rock and roll bands to come out of the U.K.

Stewart, at first, maintained successful careers both as a solo artist and a member of the Faces. But the success of his first solo hit "Maggie May" in 1971 changed the group's dynamics and eventually split up the band. Shortly thereafter, Stewart steered his career away from straight-forward rock and roll and toward pop music, a move that made him one of the most successful performers of the '70s.

Joel Whitburn's *Record Research* ranks him #13 in all-time sales in the rock era. Stewart had 15 Top 10 hits between 1976 and 1993, traipsing through seductive ballads ("Tonight's The Night"), disco ("Do Ya Think I'm Sexy"), ersatz rhythm and blues ("The Motown Song"), and eventually standards.

Stewart recorded an album of pop standards, *It Had To Be You: The Great American Songbook* in 2002, which became his first Top 10 album in nine years and would yield three Top 10 sequels. His latest juggernaut is an album of classic rock covers, which topped the charts in 2006.

GREATEST HITS

Year	Song
1971	"Maggie May"
1976	"Tonight's the Night (Gonna Be Alright)"
	"You're in My Heart (The Final Acclaim)"
1978	"Do Ya Think I'm Sexy"
1980	"Passion"
1981	"Young Turks"
1989	"Downtown Train"
1993	"Have I Told You Lately"
	"All for Love" (with Bryan Adams & Sting)

ROD STEWART HAD A HUGE RESURGENCE IN THE 2000S WITH *THE GREAT AMERICAN SONGBOOK* FRANCHISE.

Ronnie Lane

Frustrated with the Faces' lack of hits and Stewart's burgeoning solo career, bassist Ronnie Lane quit the Faces in 1973 and formed a ragtag group of folk musicians that would record on his farm near the border of Wales. He would have a British hit, "How Come," which went to the #11 in the U.K. charts.

In the late '70s, he was diagnosed with multiple sclerosis, an incurable disease that attacks the nervous system. Eric Clapton helped organize an all-star tour in 1983 to benefit Lane and other victims of MS. Rod Stewart and Ron Wood would help Lane financially through his last years. He died in Colorado in 1997.

His music remained unreleased in the U.S. until 2006, when a compilation, *Just for a Moment*, was finally issued.

BARBRA STREISAND

April 24, 1942–

Barbra Streisand is one of the only artists of her time who was able to break through to a mass audience without incorporating rock and roll, rhythm and blues, or country into her music. Instead, she did it the old-fashioned way, parlaying a career on Broadway into a career in popular music. With her classically trained voice and her skills as an actor, few people could "sell" a song the way Streisand could. And she could sell disco as well as she could sell pop music from the '20s. Then, having made the leap from Broadway to pop music, she leapt again into film, first as an actor, then as a director.

Streisand made her Broadway debut in *I Can Get It for You Wholesale* in 1962. In 1964, she starred in the hit musical *Funny Girl* and became a sensation on Broadway, and "People," from the show, became her first Top 10 hit.

BARBRA STREISAND PARLAYED HER BROADWAY CAREER INTO A SUCCESSFUL CAREER IN POP MUSIC.

GREATEST HITS

Year	Song
1964	"People"
1970	"Stoney End"
1973	"The Way We Were"
1976	"Love Theme from a Star Is Born (Evergreen)"
1977	"My Heart Belongs to Me"
1978	"You Don't Bring Me Flowers" (with Neil Diamond)
1979	"No More Tears (Enough Is Enough)" (with Donna Summer)
1980	"Woman in Love"
	"Guilty" (with Barry Gibb)
1981	"What Kind of Fool" (with Barry Gibb)
1996	"I Finally Found Someone" (with Bryan Adams)

When *Funny Girl* moved to the silver screen, Streisand moved with it and began a highly acclaimed film career. In 1973, she starred in *The Way Were Were* with Robert Redford, and the movie's title song produced her first #1 hit. Then came *A Star Is Born* in 1976, which Streisand starred in and executive-produced. The theme song "Evergreen" shot to the top of the pop charts and won an Oscar for Best Music, Original Song.

By 1978, she was scoring big hits in pop music without film and theater tie-in's, the first of which was "You Don't Bring Me Flowers," a duet with Neil Diamond. A duet with Donna Summer, "No More Tears (Enough Is Enough)," brought her music to the disco audience. Next a collaboration with Barry Gibb of the Bee Gees yielded three Top 10 hits.

Since the '80s, she's earned most of her accolades in film, including acclaim for her directing of *The Prince Of Tides* and *The Mirror Has Two Faces*, although *The Broadway Album* in 1985 was a massive success on the album charts.

DONNA SUMMER

December 31, 1948–

Donna Summer was the undisputed queen of disco. She had the most disco hits of anyone who wasn't a member of the Gibb family and took advantage of everything that the genre had to offer: mechanical beats and riffs that borrowed from both soul and funk music and a slick, detached, almost decadent outlook on sex and love. Nowhere would this be better executed than on "Love to Love You Baby," a 17-minute groove, replete with wordless coos and moans. Summer never got enough credit for her singing; "Hot Stuff" is by far one of the most soulful readings of the genre.

In the mid-'70s, she was recording commercial jingles in Munich, when producer Giorgio Moroder took a liking to her voice and asked her to sing on some of his demos. In 1975, she had an idea for a melody of a song. Moroder constructed music around it. They had no lyrics so Summer began to improvise and eventually lay on the floor moaning as a joke. Moroder left the vocalizing in and the song became Summer's first hit "Love to Love You Baby."

In 1978, she got a role in *Thank God It's Friday*, the next in a line of films that sought to cash in on the success of *Saturday Night Fever*. The soundtrack was one of the highlights of the era, thanks to Summer's "Last Dance," which nearly 30 years later is a mainstay of weddings, proms, bar mitzvahs, and probably even a few funerals. Her *Bad Girls* album established her as not just a product of the disco era, but as a formidable R&B singer as well.

Although the pace of her hits dropped off after she parted ways with Moroder, "She Works Hard for the Money" was ubiquitous on the radio in the spring and summer of 1983. She also had a big hit in 1989 with "This Time I Know It's for Real."

DONNA SUMMER, THE QUEEN OF DISCO, BREAKS IT DOWN AT THE PEAK OF HER CAREER.

GREATEST HITS

YEAR	SONG
1975	"Love to Love You Baby"
1977	"I Feel Love"
1978	"Last Dance"
	"MacArthur Park"
1979	"Heaven Knows"
	"Hot Stuff"
	"Bad Girls"
	"Dim All the Lights"
	"No More Tears (Enough Is Enough)"
1980	"On the Radio"
	"The Wanderer"
1983	"She Works Hard for the Money"
1989	"This Time I Know It's for Real"

Enough Is Enough

Donna Summer had just finished performing eight nights in Los Angeles, when she arrived in the studio to sing "No More Tears (Enough Is Enough)" with Barbra Streisand. Toward the end of the song a high note was to be held by both singers, but during the recording, Summer failed to catch her breath and passed out. "I hit the floor . . . and she didn't stop holding her note," she told *Billboard* in 1994. "It was the height of professionalism." Only when she was done singing did Streisand notice that Summer had passed out. "She thought I was playing around," Summer said. The song went to #1 in 1979.

THE SUPREMES

1962–1976

FROM LEFT: CINDY BIRDSONG, MARY WILSON, DIANA ROSS—THE SUPREMES IN 1968. DIANA ROSS WOULD SOON LEAVE TO PURSUE A SOLO CAREER.

Diana Ross had one of the most expressive voices at Motown. Whether it was the come-hither seduction of "Come See about Me," the vulnerability of "Where Did Our Love Go," or the girlish charm of "Baby Love," she and the

GREATEST HITS

YEAR	SONG
1964	"Where Did Our Love Go"
	"Baby Love"
	"Come See about Me"
1965	"Stop! In the Name of Love"
	"Back in My Arms Again"
	"I Hear a Symphony"
1966	"You Can't Hurry Love"
	"You Keep Me Hangin' On"
1967	"The Happening"
1968	"Love Child"
1969	"Someday We'll Be Together"

Supremes charmed their way to the top of the pop charts 12 times, five times in a row between 1964 and 1965.

When the Supremes started, Mary Wilson, Florence Ballard, and Ross all shared lead vocal duties, with many believing Ballard to have the best voice. But prior to Motown founder Berry Gordy's active involvement with the Supremes, the highest they would climb on the charts was to #23 with "When the Lovelight Starts Shining in His Eyes." This was the first of their songs to be written by Lamont Dozier and brothers Brian and Eddie Holland. (Their previous songs were written by Gordy and Smokey Robinson.)

Their next single, "Where Did Our Love Go," made full use of the Holland-Dozier-Holland signature of a simple backbeat, in this case composed of foot stomps, and a melodic but rhythmic bass line courtesy of James Jamerson. Ross the full-time lead singer by this point, would coo over the top, while Wilson and Ballard exhorted behind her.

Gordy lavished what other Motown acts perceived to be an inordinate amount of attention on Ross (the two had a baby in 1971). By 1967, the group was dubbed Diana Ross & the Supremes. At the same time, Ballard was battling depression and alcoholism and was replaced by Cindy Birdsong. Ballard died in 1976 at age 32 of cardiac arrest.

Holland-Dozier-Holland left the Motown stable in 1967, which not coincidently ended the Supremes' reign at the top of the charts. The Supremes would earn two more #1's after the team's departure: "Love Child" and "Someday We'll Be Together," which was, ironically, the final Supremes single to feature Ross.

As a solo artist, Ross would score a number of hits in the '70s with a more lush pop and less R&B derived sound, including "Ain't No Mountain High Enough," "Touch Me In the Morning," and "Theme From Mahogany (Do You Know Where You're Going To)." In 1980, with the help of Chic's Nile Rodgers and Bernard Edwards, Ross would embrace disco and score big hits with "I'm Coming Out" and "Upside Down." Her duet with Lionel Richie, "Endless Love," is one of the top-selling hits of all time.

Ross continued to record and perform in the '80s and early '90s with modest success on the R&B charts, but little success on the pop charts. She announced a reunion tour with Wilson and Birdsong in 2000, but they never performed because of money disputes. Two Supremes alumni from the post-Ross years were hired, but the tour was cancelled due to weak sales.

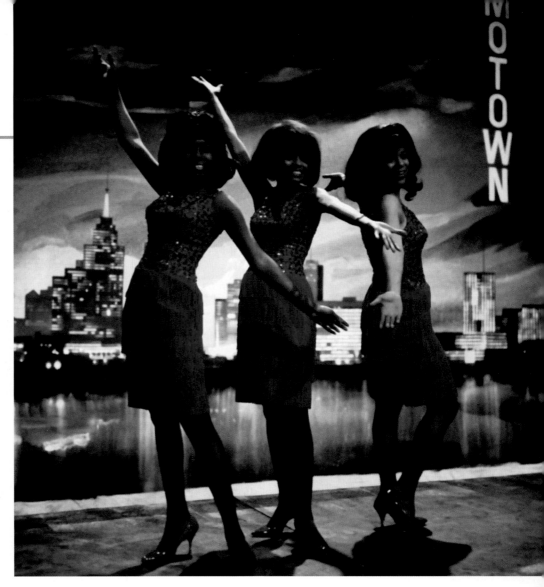

THE SUPREMES SCORED 12 TOP-10 HITS BETWEEN 1964 AND 1967, TEN OF WHICH TOPPED THE CHARTS.

The Sound of Young America

Motown was a sound: the fluid bassline of James Jamerson, the gunshot crack of Bennie Benjamin and "Pistol" Allen's snare drum, matched by the tambourine of Jack Ashford, the subtle piano touches of Joe Hunter and Earl Van Dyke's piano, the incessant staccato, percussive guitars that rarely soloed but existed to accentuate the rhythms, the horn and string sections that became voices themselves, and the oddball rhyming dictionary lyrics of Smokey Robinson that roll off the tongue as naturally as if they were poetry. (Bob Dylan once called Robinson his favorite poet.)

And then there were the voices: Marvin Gaye, Stevie Wonder, Smokey Robinson, Martha Reeves, Diana Ross, Levi Stubbs, David Ruffin, and Mary Wells. Their names can only be breathlessly listed here, but their stories fill volumes. They dominated the charts with nearly 80 Top 10 hits over a 10-year run.

But before all that, there was Berry Gordy Jr.

Gordy penned Jackie Wilson's first six hits, including the Top 10 "Lonely Teardrops." But he envisioned controlling all aspects of the product: finding talent, recording the talent, writing the songs, and managing the acts. So he borrowed $800 from his parents and launched Motown. His friend Smokey Robinson would score the label's first #1 R&B hit with "Shop Around" in late 1960. The song also reached #2 on the pop charts. Shortly after that, the floodgates opened: "Please Mr. Postman" by the Marvellettes, "My Guy" by Mary Wells, "My Girl" by the Temptations, "I Can't Help Myself" by the Four Tops, "I Want You Back" by the Jackson 5.

As the '60s turned into the '70s, the balance of power would shift from the production and songwriting teams to the artists, led by visionaries Marvin Gaye and Stevie Wonder. Motown would certainly benefit from their assertion of creative control, with hits like Gaye's "What's Goin' On" and Wonder's run of hits, including "Superstition" and "You Haven't Done Nothin.'" Norman Whitfield and Barrett Strong continued to write massive hits for the Temptations into the '70s, such as "Papa Was a Rolling Stone." The Jackson 5 would carry the torch into the '70s with "I'll Be There" and "Never Can Say Goodbye." Lionel Richie provided most of Motown's success in the '80s. Richie would hit the Top 10 an amazing 13 times in a row. Even into the '90s, groups like Boyz II Men kept the Motown flame alight with nine Top 10 hits, including "End of the Road."

JAMES TAYLOR

March 12, 1948–

James Taylor is one of the most successful performers in the singer-songwriter genre, which usually consists of hyper-literate lyricists setting their innermost feelings to a melodic acoustic guitar accompaniment. Picking up the mantle from Joni Mitchell, who briefly dated Taylor, and Paul Simon, James Taylor approached his calling with sincerity and humor.

One of the first outside artists signed to the Beatles' Apple label in 1968, James Taylor broke through to pop audiences in 1970 with "Fire and Rain." The song, which went to #3, ruminates on the death of a friend, Taylor's attempts to kick heroin, and his experiences in a mental institution.

One of Taylor's trademarks was the lilting acoustic guitar that would form the centerpiece to most of his biggest hits. But the other, which tends to get less attention, is his love for rhythm and blues. To further this aspect of his music, he used some of the best session musicians in Los Angeles as his accomplices,

NUGGET: The song "Suite for 20 G" from *Sweet Baby James* is so named, because Taylor would not be paid until he delivered the album. He stitched portions of three songs together to complete the final song.

James Taylor had success with his own ballads as well as a host of R&B covers.

GREATEST HITS

Year	Singles
1970	"Fire and Rain"
1971	"You've Got a Friend"
1972	"Don't Let Me Be Lonely Tonight"
1974	"Mockingbird" (with Carly Simon)
1975	"How Sweet It Is (To Be Loved by You)"
1976	"Shower the People"
1977	"Handy Man"
1981	"Her Town Too" (with J. D. Souther)

such as guitarist Danny Kortchmar (who would later hit paydirt collaborating with Don Henley), bassist Lee Sklar, and drummer Russ Kunkel. This rhythm section would back many West Coast songwriters throughout the '70s.

While not every R&B excursion would be successful, Taylor reached #5 with a cover of Marvin Gaye's "How Sweet It Is (To Be Loved by You)," and he made more than his share of hay with adult contemporary covers of Jimmy Jones' "Handy Man," and the Drifters' "Up on the Roof."

James Undercover

Although he is loved for his personal, intimate songwriting, some of James Taylor's best-known songs were authored by others. "You've Got a Friend" was written by Carole King, and "(What a) Wonderful World" by Sam Cooke.

JUSTIN TIMBERLAKE

JANUARY 31, 1981–

After the Spice Girls put the kibosh on the alternative rock, they opened up the gates to a resurgence of teen pop. One of the most enduring figures from that movement was Justin Timberlake. His group, *NSYNC, was initially compared to the late '80s phenomenon New Kids on the Block, but the *NSYNC boys were more skillful singers, influenced by the silky harmonies of Boyz II Men from the mid-'90s, as well as hip-hop, and dance pop. When it appeared that *NSYNC was approaching its sell-by date, Timberlake embarked on a promising solo career.

Justin Timberlake appeared on the television show *Star Search* at age 11, singing country music. Although he didn't win, he later successfully auditioned for the Disney Channel's *The Mickey Mouse Club*, where he appeared alongside Britney Spears, Christina Aguilera, and future *NSYNC member J. C. Chasez. After moving to Orlando, Timberlake and Chasez recruited Chris Kirkpatrick, Joey Fatone, and Lance Bass to complete *NSYNC. They broke in Europe first, and got their first Top 10 in the U.S. with "(God Must Have Spent) A Little More Time on You." But *No Strings Attached* in 2000 vaulted them to stardom with three Top 10 hits, including the chart-topper "It's Gonna Be Me." They recorded one more album, *Celebrity,* in 2001, which yielded the Top 10 single "Girlfriend."

Timberlake went solo in 2002 and revamped his image from a well-scrubbed teen idol to a sex symbol. Helped by popular production teams like the Neptunes, he scored two hits with "Like I Love You" and "Cry Me a River," the latter of which was allegedly about the end of his romance with Britney Spears. In 2006, he attached himself to top-notch producer Timbaland and released the blockbuster *Future Sex/Love Sounds.*

Backstreet Boys

The teen pop craze of the late '90s was presaged by the Backstreet Boys, whose 1996 debut album *Backstreet Boys* was a massive hit outside the U.S. In America, success would come two years later—about nine months before *NSYNC broke through and a year before Britney Spears' first hit. Their antecedent was Boyz II Men, who dominated the charts earlier in the decade with a blend of doo-wop, contemporary R&B, and hip-hop. The Backstreet Boys scored eight Top 10 hits between 1997 and 2000 (although they would never have a #1 hit).

GREATEST HITS

YEAR	SONG
	*NSYNC
1998	"(God Must Have Spent) A Little More Time on You"
1999	"Music of My Heart"
	"Bring It All to Me"
2000	"Bye Bye Bye"
	"It's Gonna Be Me"
2002	"Girlfriend"
	JUSTIN TIMBERLAKE
2002	"Like I Love You" (featuring Clipse)
	"Cry Me a River"
2003	"Rock Your Body" (featuring Lene)
2006	"SexyBack" (featuring Timbaland)
	"My Love" (featuring T.I.)
2007	"What Goes Around . . . Comes Around"

JUSTIN TIMBERLAKE CROONS AT THE **2003** BRIT AWARDS.

TLC

1992–2002

From left: Lisa "Left Eye" Lopes, Rozonda "Chilli" Thomas, Tionne "T-Boz" Watkins. From 1992 to 1999, TLC had nine Top 10 hits, including four #1's.

Of the groups that combined contemporary R&B with hip-hop in the '90s, few were more successful than TLC. By their second album, they'd gone from a teen pop act to a skilled trio. They could emote with the best of soul singers, as on "Waterfalls," or they could swagger through upbeat songs like "Creep." They tallied nine Top 10 hits from 1992 through 1999.

Lisa "Left Eye" Lopes met Tionne "T-Boz" Watkins at a 1991 audition for an R&B group. After an audition for LaFace Records owner Antonio "L.A." Reid, Rozanda "Chilli" Thomas was added to the mix and the group took the name TLC. They went on to score three Top 10 singles out of the chute that emphasized their more irreverent side. Their second album, *CrazySexyCool*, outperformed their debut, spawning four Top 10 hits. A year later, the group filed for bankruptcy as part of a tactic to renegotiate the terms of their record contract.

Before recording their third album, *Fanmail*, Lopes quit the group, frustrated that her songs were being rejected. After LaFace records froze their finances, she came back to the fold, although she would frequently grouse in the press about her groupmates. She eventually made a challenge which was the equivalent of pistols at sunset. Each singer would record a solo album, and the one that sold the most would get a $1.5 million contract from LaFace. Nothing came of the challenge, although Lopes did record a solo album, which wasn't released in the U.S. TLC's *Fanmail* yielded two #1 hits, "No Scrubs" and "Unpretty."

The group was in the middle of recording their fourth album when Lopes died in a car accident. They completed the album without her and then disbanded.

> *"I hope we go down in history for being something more than just another famous act that got ripped off....This is a cutthroat business full of greedy individuals who take advantage of naive young artists."* —Lisa Lopes

GREATEST HITS

Year	Song
1992	"Ain't 2 Proud 2 Beg"
	"Baby-Baby-Baby"
	"What About Your Friends"
1994	"Creep"
1995	"Red Light Special"
	"Waterfalls"
	"Diggin' on You"
1999	"No Scrubs"
	"Unpretty"

NUGGET: Lisa "Left Eye" Lopes would often appear in concert with a condom over her left eye.

Burning Down The House

In the early morning hours on June 9, 1994, firefighters were summoned to a $2 million home in a tony suburb of Atlanta. The house was owned by Andre Rison, Lisa "Left Eye" Lopes' boyfriend. Less than 24 hours later, Lopes surrendered and was charged with arson. She pleaded guilty and was sentenced to five years on probation. The couple reconciled a week after the fire and were engaged to be married at the time she was sentenced. The prosecutor at the time believed that Rison had beaten Lopes prior to the fire.

SHANIA TWAIN

August 28, 1965–

Strutting through the door that Garth Brooks opened, Shania Twain became one of the most successful country artists to cross over to the pop charts. Using a combination of hooky classic guitar riffs, heavy beats, Def Leppard's producer, just a touch of country stereotyping, and a lot of revealing clothing, the Timmins, Ontario, native became the face (and body) of country music in the late '90s.

From the time Twain (née Eileen Regina Edwards) was 8 years old, her parents roused her from bed at 1 a.m. to sing in the local bars after liquor sales had stopped. Her parents died in a car accident when Shania was 21, leaving her in charge of her three younger siblings. She supported her family by singing at a nearby resort, performing everything from pop hits to Broadway tunes. As her siblings got older and moved out, she pursued a career in country music. Her 1993 debut album *Shania Twain* attracted the attention of rock producer Robert "Mutt" Lange, who had been looking to expand into country music. Twain and Lange had phone conversations about music and then began cowriting songs long distance. When they met two months later, they fell in love and eventually married.

The Woman in Me, was a blockbuster album, the first in a series of successes spawned by Twain and Lange. Women were attracted to her fiercely independent lyrics, while the men ogled her videos and stage act. *Come On Over* sold even better, yielding three Top 10 pop hits. While she would be criticized by many inside and outside Nashville for using her looks to advance her career (iconoclast Steve Earle once called her "the highest paid lap dancer in Nashville"), she would hardly be the first country star to do so. She eventually won the endorsements of June Carter Cash and Reba McEntire.

> *"I was the kid that always went to school without a lunch. I could relate to country music a lot."* —Shania Twain

Nothin' But a Hound Dog

Prior to working with (and marrying) Shania Twain, Robert John "Mutt" Lange was one of the most successful producers in pop music. Twain represented his debut into country music, although he applied the same techniques that would lead many acts that he worked with to the top of the charts: booming drums, anthemic guitars, and an overall bright, slick sound. His most popular efforts include, AC/DC's *Back In Black*, Foreigner's *4*, Def Leppard's *Pyromania*, and individual tracks on The Corrs' *In Blue*, Backstreet Boys' *Millennium,* and Britney Spears' *Oops...I Did It Again*.

SHANIA TWAIN IS ONE OF THE MOST SUCCESSFUL COUNTRY CROSSOVER ARTISTS.

GREATEST HITS	
YEAR	SONG
1995	"Any Man of Mine"
	"Whose Bed Have Your Boots Been Under?"
	"(If You're Not in It for Love) I'm Outta Here!"
1997	"Love Gets Me Every Time"
	"Don't Be Stupid (You Know I Love You)"
1998	"You're Still the One"
	"From This Moment On"
1999	"That Don't Impress Me Much"
	"Man! I Feel Like a Woman"
2002	"I'm Gonna Getcha Good!"

DIONNE WARWICK

DECEMBER 12, 1940–

Dionne Warwick achieved the perfect balance between pop and pulpit. And if that wasn't enough, she managed to make awkward lines like, "What do you get when you kiss a guy/You get enough germs to catch pneumonia/After you do they never phone ya," sound elegant.

In fact, Brill Building stalwarts Burt Bacharach and Hal David would never find a better (or more successful) canvas on which to paint their angular melodies and off-beat lyrics. Warwick's elegant phrasing and light timbre would raise the level of their songwriting from the often ridiculous to the sublime, a feat even the best rock singers would fail to match. (As great a singer as Elvis Costello is, even he stumbles over the lyrics in "I'll Never Fall in Love Again.") The formula would yield twelve Top 10 hits over 20 years.

Warwick began singing with the nationally known gospel group the Drinkard Singers as a child. As a teenager, she formed the Gospelaires with her sister Dee Dee, who would later have some success of her own on the R&B charts, and her aunt Cissy Houston, who later gave birth to Whitney Houston.

When she wasn't studying at Hartt School

DIONNE WARWICK POSSESSES ELEGANT PHRASING AND IS INSPIRED AS MUCH BY POP MUSIC AS GOSPEL.

GREATEST HITS	
YEAR	SONGS
1963	"Anyone Who Had a Heart"
1964	"Walk on By"
1966	"Message To Michael"
1967	"Say a Little Prayer"
1968	(Theme from) "Valley of the Dolls"
	"Do You Know the Way to San Jose"
1969	"This Girl's in Love with You"
	"I'll Never Fall in Love Again"
1974	"Then Came You" (with the Spinners)
1979	"I'll Never Love this Way Again" (produced by Barry Manilow)
1982	"Heartbreaker"
1985	"That's What Friends Are For"

of Music, she would sing backup on sessions in New York with Bobby Darin, Chuck Jackson, and the Drifters. It was during one of these sessions with the latter in 1960 that arranger Burt Bacharach noticed her powerful instrument and asked her to sing on demos he was producing with David. This led to a deal with Scepter Records in 1962, which began her string of successes.

After parting ways with Bacharach and David, she would revisit the Top 10 three more times between 1974 and 1982. One of those hits was the chart-topper "Then Came You" with the Spinners, on which Warwick would never sound more funky.

She reunited with Bacharach in 1985 for "That's What Friends Are For," which included Elton John, Stevie Wonder, and Gladys Knight.

Bacharach-David

By the early '60s, most pop music of the rock era are had a fairly simple musical structure of verse-chorus-verse-chorus, sometimes with a bridge thrown in and usually consisting of three or four chords. These were the rules under which Burt Bacharach operated when he scored one of his earliest hits with the Shirelles' "Baby It's You."

With his partner, Hal David, the songwriting team would go on to obliterate those rules, adding dissonant chord structures borrowed from jazz, changes in time signature that were influenced by Brazilian music, and melodies that had more to do with Tin Pan Alley and Broadway than rock and roll.

Aside from their work with Warwick, they penned two Top 10 hits for Gene Pitney, "The Man Who Shot Liberty Valance" and "Only Love Can Break a Heart" in 1962. They worked on film soundtracks, including the #1 hit "Raindrops Keep Falling on My Head" for the film *Butch Cassidy and the Sundance Kid* in 1969.

NUGGET: Warwick's 1982 hit "Heartbreaker" was written by Barry, Robin, and Maurice Gibb, otherwise known as the Bee Gees.

JACKIE WILSON

June 9, 1934–January 21, 1984

Jackie Wilson was one of the most dynamic performers of the '50s, shimmying, flirting, leaping into the crowd, and doing what he could to connect with his audience rather than just perform for them, a sort of Marvin Gaye or Bruce Springsteen of his day. Despite his showmanship it was always Wilson's voice, which combined the wildness of Little Richard with the smoothness of Sam Cooke, that drew his audience in.

In 1953, Wilson replaced Clyde McPhatter in Billy Ward & the Dominos, one of the best and most influential pre-rock R&B acts. McPhatter had recently left the group to form the Drifters. In 1956, Wilson left the Dominos to pursue a solo career. Around the same time, a young jazz fan, Berry Gordy, was hanging out in the Detroit clubs trying to interest performers and their managers

in his songwriting. Wilson and Gordy found what they were looking for in one another, and by 1958, Wilson had notched his first Top 10 R&B hit with "To Be Loved" and his first Top 10 pop hit with "Lonely Teardrops."

After Gordy moved on to build Motown, Wilson would continue to have a string of hits, with a sound that would include more pop arrangements and veer further away from his R&B roots. He floundered for the better part of the next seven years until he scored with "Your Love Keeps Lifting Me Higher And Higher" in 1967.

A Tribute From The King

During an informal jam session with Jerry Lee Lewis and Carl Perkins in 1956, Presley told his fellow musicians the following story: "I heard this guy in Las Vegas playing with Billy Ward and his Dominoes. He tried so hard. And he got much better, boy, much better than that record of mine. He was real slender. He was a colored guy. And he sang it slower than me." Then Presley went into a sultry rendition of "Don't Be Cruel," with a completely different phrasing from Presley's biggest hit. He perfectly imitated the young Jackie Wilson's inflections. And for the last line, Presley took the song up an octave in a nod to Wilson. When Presley finished, he turned to his onlookers and said, "I went back four nights straight and heard that boy do it. He sung the hell out of that song."

JACKIE WILSON WAS A MASTER OF CONNECTING WITH AUDIENCES THROUGH HIS DYNAMIC PERFORMANCES.

NUGGET: On September 29, 1975, Jackie Wilson was performing in Dick Clark's *Rock And Roll Revue* at the Latin Casino in Cherry Hill, New Jersey. He was about to begin a rendition of "Lonely Teardrops," when he collapsed from a massive heart attack from which he never recovered. He died in 1984.

GREATEST HITS

Year	Song
1957	"Reet Petite (The Finest Girl You Ever Want to Meet)"
1958	"To Be Loved"
	"Lonely Teardrops"
1959	"That's Why (I Love You So)"
	"I'll Be Satisfied"
1960	"Night"
	"Alone at Last"
1961	"My Empty Arms"
1963	"Baby Workout"
1966	"Whispers (Getting' Louder)"
1967	"(Your Love Keeps Lifting Me) Higher and Higher"

STEVIE WONDER

MAY 13, 1950–

Stevie Wonder accepted no limitations. He refused to be limited by blindness. He refused to be denied stylistically. He refused to be confined lyrically. He refused to accept any racial or gender bias. And he lives as he sings, constantly and successfully striving for the higher ground.

Steveland Morris was born in Saginaw, Michigan, into a lower middle-class family. His family moved to Detroit in 1953. Blind at birth, Stevie devoured blues and radio programs as a boy. By age 8, he was playing bongos on the street corner with a friend who played guitar. By the time he was 11 years old, he was able to play piano, drums, and harmonica. Passing churchgoers disapproved of Stevie's street music but it delighted Gerald White, whose brother Ronald happened to be one of Smokey Robinson's Miracles. Stevie was invited to audition for Motown, where he wowed the label's founder, Berry Gordy, with his harmonica playing and charming personality.

By 1963, he was marketed as "Little Stevie Wonder, 12-year-old genius." Indeed, his first single "Fingertips" bears this out with its virtuosic chromatic harmonica and his riveting live performance. But it was two years—an eternity in Motown terms—before he would have another hit. "Uptight (Everything Is Alright)," peaked at #3. It was not insignificant that the song was about the triumph of love over class barriers; such concerns would come up again in Wonder's work. In fact, politics were clearly on his mind on his next big hit, a gospel-inflected version of Bob Dylan's "Blowin' in the Wind."

Wonder filtered nothing out. He extolled the virtues of Simon & Garfunkel as vociferously as he cited Bobby "Blue" Bland and Jimmy Reed as influences.

NUGGET: Stevie Wonder was a renowned trickster. A skillful mimic, he often called Berry Gordy's secretary and in a perfect imitation of the Motown founder's voice he would demand $500,000. Although no checks were cut, he did manage to use this scheme to con the label out of a new tape recorder for his personal use.

IN 1973, STEVIE WONDER RELEASED *INNERVISIONS*, WHICH MANY BELIEVE TO BE HIS FINEST ALBUM.

He was as inspired by *Sgt. Pepper* as he was by Sly & the Family Stone. By the time he had declared his independence from Motown at age 21, many of these influences would surface in his ambitious albums of the '70s: *Talking Book*, *Innervisions*, and *Fulfillingness' First Finale*.

Wonder began to explore different sounds and textures, using state-of-the-art synthesizers and keyboards. So while the first album of his independent years wasn't a commercial success, *Music of My Mind* demonstrated that he was adding new dimensions to his music—more complicated song structures, rhythms, and chords. The next album, *Talking Book*, exploited Wonder's potential. On one hand, Wonder mastered the pop vocabulary with the sublime "You Are the Sunshine of My Life." Sophisticated in its music but simple in its words, no pop singer could resist having a go at it, from Frank Sinatra to Liza Minnelli to Perry Como. On the other hand "Superstition," was Wonder's

Wonder Power

In 1971, Wonder turned 21, giving him the right to renegotiate his contract with Motown. After a bidding war with Clive Davis' CBS Records and Ahmet Ertegun's Atlantic Records, Wonder opted to stay with Motown on the condition that he be given complete creative control of his music, an unheard-of demand for Motown performers who until that point were essentially tools of the producers and writers. Wonder changed all that. Motown would never be the same, and neither would pop music. For Motown, the move reinforced a trend started by Marvin Gaye's *What's Going On*. While no one could dispute Motown founder Berry Gordy's golden touch, the music created by Gaye and Wonder introduced a strong social consciousness and would redefine popular music.

crowning achievement. The song was built around an incessant funky blues riff played on the clarinet. His social commentary would become more pointed later in his career, but it would never be more artful than on "Superstition."

He allied himself with progressive political causes. He thumbed his nose at invitations to the White House from President Ford. He believed in the power of racial integration and advocated for it in his '70s albums. The 1973 album *Innervisions* included "Living for the City," which described the economic

STEVIE WONDER WAS ONE OF THE MOST ARTICULATE VOICES FOR RACIAL INTEGRATION IN THE '70S.

> *"The best way to get an important and heavy message across is to wrap it up nicely. It's better to try and level out the weight of the lyrics by making the melody lighter. After all, people want to be entertained, which is all right by me."* —Stevie Wonder

reality of urban black neighborhoods, and "Higher Ground," one of the most inspirational messages of integration to hit the Top 10.

While on tour in 1973, Wonder was in a serious car accident that left him in a coma for a week and robbed him of his sense of smell. After recovering, he made his most successful record to date, *Fullfillingness' First Finale*, which included "Boogie on Reggae Woman" and "You Haven't Done Nothin'." The album collected four Grammys.

Moving from pop ballads to big band jazz to fusion workouts to classic funk, 1976's *Songs in the Key of Life* was a sprawling consolidation of all the music Wonder loved.

Wonder's next effort, *Journey Through the Secret Life of Plants*, the soundtrack to a documentary that was never released, aimed to personify plant life as an allegory for a sort of spiritual awakening. It contained some lovely jazz instrumentals and ideas for anyone who took the time and trouble to find them. But few people did, and it was Wonder's first commercial flop of the decade. *Hotter Than July*, released a year later, returned Wonder to more familiar ground. The highlight of the album was "Happy Birthday," his paean to Martin Luther King Jr. and the campaign to make his birthday a national holiday. But it effectively marked the end of Wonder's influence on the country's musical and political zeitgeist.

He continued to score hit singles through the '80s. By the '90s, they had trailed off, but his soundtrack to Spike Lee's *Jungle Fever* was a potent reminder of Stevie's

skill. It would take him 10 years to make the 2005 album *A Time to Love*, and while it didn't regain his '70s glory, it did demonstrate that 40 years into his career, he was capable of not only updating his sound but bringing new and vibrant elements to it.

NUGGET: Stevie Wonder accepted his Grammy for the 1976 album *Songs in the Key of Life* remotely from Nigeria where he was traveling. But the audio connection was poor, leading Wonder to cut out from the broadcast. Andy Williams, the host of the show, trying to gain control of the unplanned occurrence, stammered to Wonder, "If you can't hear me, can you at least see me?"

It's Good to be King

In 1976, Stevie Wonder announced his "retirement" from music, although the move was strictly a negotiating ploy to extract better contractual terms from Motown. When the label moved from Detroit to Los Angeles, much of their homegrown talent defected, leaving Stevie Wonder, by far, the most important cash generator for the label. He used this leverage to gain an unheard-of 20 percent royalty rate, at least three times as much as standard rates. He also got $13 million over seven years, a king's ransom in 1976. But then, Stevie Wonder was a king. His next album *Songs in the Key of Life* topped the charts for 14 weeks, yielded two Top 10 singles and won four Grammys.

STEVIE WONDER, PICTURED HERE IN THE '60S, SCORED HIS FIRST #1 HIT AT AGE 12.

GREATEST HITS

Year	Song
1963	"Fingertips–Pt 2"
1965	"Uptight (Everything Is Alright)"
1966	"Blowin' in the Wind"
1967	"I Was Made to Love Her"
1970	"Signed, Sealed, Delivered, I'm Yours"
1972	"Superstition"
1973	"You Are the Sunshine of My Life"
	"Higher Ground"
	"Living for the City"
1974	"You Haven't Done Nothin'"
	"Boogie on Reggae Woman"
1977	"Sir Duke"
1985	"Part Time Lover"

SELECT DISCOGRAPHY

ABBA

1973	RING RING
1974	WATERLOO
1975	ABBA
1977	ARRIVAL
1978	THE ALBUM
1979	VOULEZ-VOUS
1980	SUPER TROUPER
1981	THE VISITORS
1993	GOLD

CHRISTINA AGUILERA

1999	CHRISTINA AGUILERA
2000	MI REFLEJO
	MY KIND OF CHRISTMAS
2002	STRIPPED
2006	BACK TO BASICS

BEACH BOYS

1962	SURFIN' SAFARI
1963	SURFIN' U.S.A.
	SURFER GIRL
	LITTLE DEUCE COUPE
1964	SHUT DOWN VOL. 2
	ALL SUMMER LONG
1965	TODAY
	SUMMER DAYS (AND SUMMER NIGHTS!!)
	BEACH BOYS' PARTY
1966	PET SOUNDS
1967	SMILEY SMILE
	WILD HONEY
1970	SUNFLOWER
1971	SURF'S UP
1973	HOLLAND
1974	ENDLESS SUMMER
1976	15 BIG ONES
1977	LOVE YOU
2003	SOUNDS OF SUMMER: THE VERY BEST OF THE BEACH BOYS

BEASTIE BOYS

1986	LICENSED TO ILL
1989	PAUL'S BOUTIQUE
1992	CHECK YOUR HEAD
1994	ILL COMMUNICATION
1998	HELLO NASTY
1999	THE SOUNDS OF SCIENCE
2004	TO THE 5 BOROUGHS
2005	SOLID GOLD HITS

THE BEATLES

1963	PLEASE PLEASE ME
	WITH THE BEATLES
1964	A HARD DAY'S NIGHT
	BEATLES FOR SALE
1965	HELP!
	RUBBER SOUL
1966	REVOLVER
1967	SGT. PEPPER'S LONELY HEARTS CLUB BAND
1967	MAGICAL MYSTERY TOUR
1968	THE BEATLES
1969	YELLOW SUBMARINE
	ABBEY ROAD
1970	LET IT BE
1973	1962–1966
	1967–1970
1988	PAST MASTERS VOL. 1
	PAST MASTERS VOL. 2
1995	ANTHOLOGY 1
1996	ANTHOLOGY 2
	ANTHOLOGY 3

BEE GEES

1967	BEE GEES' 1ST
1968	HORIZONTAL
	IDEA
1969	ODESSA
1971	2 YEARS ON
	MELODY
	TRAFALGAR
1972	TO WHOM IT MAY CONCERN
1973	LIFE IN A TIN CAN
1974	MR. NATURAL
1975	MAIN COURSE
1976	CHILDREN OF THE WORLD
1977	SATURDAY NIGHT FEVER
1979	SPIRITS HAVING FLOWN
1981	LIVING EYES
1987	E.S.P.
1989	ONE
1997	STILL WATERS
2001	THIS IS WHERE I CAME IN

THEIR GREATEST HITS: THE RECORD

BEYONCE

| 2003 | DANGEROUSLY IN LOVE |
| 2006 | B'DAY |

BOBBY "BLUE" BLAND

1958	BLUES CONSOLIDATED
1961	TWO STEPS FROM THE BLUES
1963	CALL ON ME
1964	AIN'T NOTHING YOU CAN DO
1966	THE SOUL OF THE MAN
1967	TOUCH OF THE BLUES
1974	DREAMER
1976	TOGETHER AGAIN (WITH B.B. KING)
1998	GREATEST HITS VOL 1.: THE DUKE RECORDINGS
2001	THE ANTHOLOGY

MARY J. BLIGE

1992	WHAT'S THE 411
1994	MY LIFE
1997	SHARE MY WORLD
1999	MARY
2001	NO MORE DRAMA
2002	DANCE FOR ME
2003	LOVE & LIFE
2005	THE BREAKTHROUGH

MICHAEL BOLTON

1975	MICHAEL BOLTON
1976	EVERY DAY OF MY LIFE
1983	MICHAEL BOLTON
1985	EVERYBODY'S CRAZY
1987	THE HUNGER
1989	SOUL PROVIDER
1991	TIME, LOVE & TENDERNESS
1993	THE ONE THING
1997	ALL THAT MATTERS
1998	MY SECRET PASSION
2002	ONLY A WOMAN LIKE YOU
2006	BOLTON SWINGS SINATRA

Bon Jovi

1984	Bon Jovi
1985	7800 Fahrenheit
1986	Slippery When Wet
1988	New Jersey
1992	Keep the Faith
1994	Cross Road
1995	These Days
2000	Crush
2002	Bounce
2003	This Left Feels Right
2004	100,000,000 Bon Jovi Fans Can't Be Wrong
2005	Have a Nice Day

Booker T. & the MGs

1962	Green Onions
1965	Soul Dressing
1967	Hip Hug-Her
1968	Doin' Our Thing
1968	Soul Limbo
1970	McLemore Avenue
1994	The Very Best of Booker T. & The MGs

Pat Boone

1962	Pat Boone's Greatest Hits
1997	In a Metal Mood: No More Mr. Nice Guy
2000	20th Century Masters
2006	We Are Family: R&B Classics

Boyz II Men

1991	Cooleyhighharmony
1994	II
1997	Evolution
2000	Nathan Michael Shawn Wanya
2002	Full Circle
2004	Throwback
	Legacy: The Greatest Hits Collection

Garth Brooks

1989	Garth Brooks
1990	No Fences
1991	Ropin' the Wind
1992	The Chase
1993	In Pieces
1994	The Hits
1995	Fresh Horses
1997	Sevens
1999	In the Life of Chris Gaines
2001	Scarecrow

James Brown

1963	Live at the Apollo
1968	Live at the Apollo
1971	Revolution of the Mind
1984	Roots of a Revolution
1988	Motherlode
1991	20 All Time Greatest Hits
	Star Time
1992	Love Power Peace
1996	Foundations of Funk—A Brand New Bag: 1964–1969
	Funk Power 1970: A Brand New Thang
	Make It Funky—The Big Payback: 1971–1975

Jackson Browne

1972	Jackson Browne (Saturate Before Using)
1973	For Everyman
1974	Late for the Sky
1976	The Pretender
1977	Running on Empty
1980	Hold Out
1983	Lawyers in Love
1986	Lives in the Balance
1989	World in Motion
1993	I'm Alive
1996	Looking East
1997	The Next Voice You Hear: The Best of Jackson Browne
2002	The Naked Ride Home
2004	The Very Best of Jackson Browne
2005	Solo Acoustic Vol. 1

Mariah Carey

1990	Mariah Carey
1991	Emotions
1993	Music Box
1995	Daydream
1997	Butterfly
1998	#1's
1999	Rainbow
2001	Glitter
2002	Charmbracelet
2005	The Emancipation of Mimi

Carpenters

1969	Ticket to Ride
1970	Close to You
1971	Carpenters
1972	A Song for You
1973	Now & Then
1975	Horizon
1976	A Kind of Hush
1977	Passage
1981	Made in America
1983	Voice of the Heart
1985	Yesterday Once More
2000	Singles 1969–1981

Ray Charles

1957	Ray Charles
1958	Ray Charles at Newport (live)
	Soul Brothers
1959	The Genius of Ray Charles
1960	Genius + Soul = Jazz
1961	The Genius After Hours
1962	Modern Sounds in Country and Western Music
	Modern Sounds in Country and Western Music Vol. 2
1994	The Best of Ray Charles: The Atlantic Years
1997	Genius & Soul: The 50th Anniversary Collection
	The Complete Swing Time & Down Beat Recordings 1949–1952
1999	Ultimate Hits Collection
2004	Genius Loves Company

Cher

1969	3614 Jackson Highway
1971	Gypsys, Tramps & Thieves
1973	Half Breed

1987 CHER
1989 HEART OF STONE
1998 BELIEVE
2005 GOLD

CHICAGO
1969 CHICAGO TRANSIT AUTHORITY
1970 CHICAGO II
1975 CHICAGO IX: GREATEST HITS
1984 CHICAGO XVII
2002 THE VERY BEST OF CHICAGO:
     ONLY THE BEGINNING

THE COASTERS
1958 THE COASTERS
1993 THE VERY BEST OF THE COASTERS

SAM COOKE
1964 SAM COOKE AT THE COPA
1965 THE GOSPEL SOUL OF SAM COOKE
     WITH THE SOUL STIRRERS, VOL. 1
1975 THE GOSPEL SOUL OF SAM COOKE
     WITH THE SOUL STIRRERS, VOL. 2
1986 THE MAN AND HIS MUSIC
1995 THE RHYTHM & THE BLUES
2000 THE MAN WHO INVENTED SOUL
2003 PORTRAIT OF A LEGEND
2005 ONE NIGHT STAND: SAM COOKE
     LIVE AT THE HARLEM SQUARE
     CLUB, 1963

CULTURE CLUB
1982 KISSING TO BE CLEVER
1983 COLOUR BY NUMBERS
1984 WAKING UP WITH THE HOUSE
     ON FIRE
1986 FROM LUXURY TO HEARTACHE
1987 THIS TIME: THE FIRST FOUR YEARS

BOBBY DARIN
1959 THAT'S ALL
1991 SPLISH SPLASH
1991 MACK THE KNIFE

DESTINY'S CHILD
1998 DESTINY'S CHILD
1999 THE WRITING'S ON THE WALL

2001 SURVIVOR
2004 DESTINY FULFILLED
2005 #1's

NEIL DIAMOND
1970 TAP ROOT MANUSCRIPT
1971 STONES
1972 HOT AUGUST NIGHT
1973 JONATHAN LIVINGSTON SEAGULL
1976 BEAUTIFUL NOISE
1978 YOU DON'T BRING ME FLOWERS
1979 SEPTEMBER MORN
1980 THE JAZZ SINGER
1982 HEARTLIGHT
2005 12 SONGS

DION
1962 LOVERS WHO WANDER
1978 RETURN OF THE WANDERER
1989 YO FRANKIE
2000 KING OF THE NEW YORK STREETS
2005 BRONX IN BLUE

CELINE DION
1990 UNISON
1992 CELINE DION
1993 THE COLOUR OF MY LOVE
1995 POWER OF LOVE
     THE FRENCH ALBUM
1996 FALLING INTO YOU
1997 LET'S TALK ABOUT LOVE
1998 THESE ARE SPECIAL TIMES
1999 ALL THE WAY: A DECADE OF SONG
2002 A NEW DAY HAS COME
2005 ON NE CHANGE PAS

DIXIE CHICKS
1998 WIDE OPEN SPACES
1999 FLY
2002 HOME
2006 TAKING THE LONG WAY

DR. DRE
1992 THE CHRONIC
1996 DR. DRE PRESENTS . . . THE
     AFTERMATH
1999 2001

2002 CHRONICLE: BEST OF THE WORKS

FATS DOMINO
1991 THEY CALL ME THE FAT MAN: THE
     LEGENDARY IMPERIAL RECORDINGS
2002 FATS DOMINO JUKEBOX: 20
     GREATEST HITS
     WALKING TO NEW ORLEANS
2003 ESSENTIAL FATS DOMINO

THE DRIFTERS
1968 DRIFTERS' GOLDEN HITS
1988 ALL-TIME GREATEST HITS & MORE
     1959–1965
     LET THE BOOGIE WOOGIE ROLL:
     GREATEST HITS 1953–1958
1993 THE VERY BEST OF THE DRIFTERS
1996 ROCKIN' & DRIFTIN': THE DRIFTERS
     BOX

DURAN DURAN
1981 DURAN DURAN
1982 RIO
1983 SEVEN AND THE RAGGED TIGER
1986 NOTORIOUS
1988 BIG THING
1995 THANK YOU
1998 GREATEST
2004 ASTRONAUT

EAGLES
1972 EAGLES
1973 DESPERADO
1974 ON THE BORDER
1975 ONE OF THESE NIGHTS
1976 THEIR GREATEST HITS
     HOTEL CALIFORNIA
1979 THE LONG RUN
1994 HELL FREEZES OVER
2003 THE VERY BEST OF THE EAGLES

EARTH, WIND & FIRE
1971 EARTH, WIND & FIRE
     THE NEED OF LOVE
1972 LAST DAYS AND TIME
1973 HEAD TO THE SKY
1974 OPEN OUR EYES

1975	THAT'S THE WAY OF THE WORLD
	GRATITUDE
1976	SPIRIT
1977	ALL 'N ALL
1978	THE BEST OF EARTH, WIND & FIRE,
	VOL. 1
1979	I AM
1980	FACES
1981	RAISE!
1983	POWERLIGHT
1988	THE BEST OF EARTH, WIND & FIRE,
	VOL. 2
1998	GREATEST HITS

ELECTRIC LIGHT ORCHESTRA

1971	ELECTRIC LIGHT ORCHESTRA
1972	ELO II
1973	ON THE THIRD DAY
1974	ELDORADO
1975	FACE THE MUSIC
1976	A NEW WORLD RECORD
1977	OUT OF THE BLUE
1979	DISCOVERY
1981	TIME
1983	SECRET MESSAGES
1986	BALANCE OF POWER
1990	AFTERGLOW
1995	STRANGE MAGIC
2001	ZOOM

MISSY ELLIOTT

1997	SUPA DUPA FLY
1999	DA REAL WORLD
2001	MISS E . . . SO ADDICTIVE
2002	UNDER CONSTRUCTION
2003	THIS IS NOT A TEST!
2005	THE COOKBOOK

EMINEM

1999	THE SLIM SHADY LP
2000	THE MARSHALL MATHERS LP
2002	THE EMINEM SHOW
2004	ENCORE
2005	CURTAIN CALL: THE HITS
2006	EMINEM PRESENTS: THE RE-UP

EN VOGUE

1990	BORN TO SING
1992	FUNKY DIVAS
1997	EV3
2001	THE VERY BEST OF EN VOGUE

EURYTHMICS

1983	SWEET DREAMS (ARE MADE
	OF THIS)
	TOUCH
1984	1984 (FOR THE LOVE OF BIG
	BROTHER)
1985	BE YOURSELF TONIGHT
1986	REVENGE
1987	SAVAGE
1989	WE TOO ARE ONE
1999	PEACE
2005	THE ULTIMATE COLLECTION

EVERLY BROTHERS

1958	SONGS OUR DADDY TAUGHT US
	THE EVERLY BROTHERS
1960	IT'S EVERLY TIME
	THE FABULOUS STYLE OF THE
	EVERLY BROTHERS
1963	EVERLY BROTHERS SING GREAT
	COUNTRY HITS
1965	ROCK 'N SOUL
	BEAT & SOUL
1966	IN OUR IMAGE
1984	THE REUNION CONCERT
	EB 84
1986	CADENCE CLASSICS: THEIR 20
	GREATEST HITS
1999	ALL-TIME ORIGINAL HITS

FLEETWOOD MAC

1968	PETER GREEN'S FLEETWOOD MAC
1969	ENGLISH ROSE
	PIOUS BIRD OF GOOD OMEN
	THEN PLAY ON
1970	KILM HOUSE
1971	FUTURE GAMES
1972	BARE TREES
1973	PENGUIN
	MYSTERY TO ME
1974	HEROES ARE HARD TO FIND

1975	FLEETWOOD MAC
1977	RUMOURS
1979	TUSK
1982	MIRAGE
1987	TANGO IN THE NIGHT
1990	BEHIND THE MASK
1997	THE DANCE
2006	GREATEST HITS

THE FOUR SEASONS

1962	SHERRY & 11 OTHERS
1963	BIG GIRLS DON'T CRY AND
	TWELVE OTHERS
1964	DAWN (GO WAY) AND 11 OTHER
	GREAT SONGS
	RAG DOLL
1988	ANTHOLOGY: FRANKIE VALLI & THE
	FOUR SEASONS
2003	THE VERY BEST OF FRANKIE VALLI
	& THE FOUR SEASONS
2006	THE DEFINITIVE POP COLLECTION

ARETHA FRANKLIN

1967	I NEVER LOVED A MAN THE WAY I
	LOVE YOU
1968	LADY SOUL
	ARETHA NOW
1969	SOUL '69
1970	SPIRIT IN THE DARK
1971	YOUNG GIFTED AND BLACK
1972	AMAZING GRACE
1980	ARETHA SINGS THE BLUES
1985	WHO'S ZOOMIN' WHO
	30 GREATEST HITS
1992	QUEEN OF SOUL: THE ATLANTIC
	RECORDINGS

MARVIN GAYE

1971	WHAT'S GOING ON
1973	LET'S GET IT ON
1974	ANTHOLOGY
1976	I WANT YOU
1978	HERE MY DEAR
1981	IN OUR LIFETIME
1982	MIDNIGHT LOVE
1995	THE MASTER 1961–1984

Genesis

1969	From Genesis to Revelation
1970	Trespass
1971	Nursery Cryme
1972	Foxtrot
1973	Selling England by the Pound
1974	The Lamb Lies Down on Broadway
1976	Trick of the Tail
	Wind and Wuthering
1978	. . .And Then There Were Three
1980	Duke
1981	Abacab
1983	Genesis
1986	Invisible Touch
1991	We Can't Dance
1999	Turn It on Again: The Hits

Goo Goo Dolls

1987	Goo Goo Dolls
1989	Jed
1990	Hold Me Up
1993	Superstar Car Wash
1995	A Boy Named Goo
1998	Dizzy Up the Girl
2001	Ego, Opinion, Art & Commerce
2002	Gutterflower
2006	Let Love In

Green Day

1991	1,039/Smoothed Out Slappy Hours
1992	Kerplunk
1994	Dookie
1995	Insomniac
1997	Nimrod
2000	Warning
2001	International Superhits
2004	American Idiot

Al Green

1967	Back Up Train
1970	Green Is Blues
1971	Al Green Gets Next to You
1972	Let's Stay Together
	I'm Still in Love with You
1973	Call Me
1973	Livin' for You
1974	Al Green Explores Your Mind
1975	Al Green's Greatest Hits
	Al Green Is Love
1976	Full of Fire
	Have a Good Time
1977	The Belle Album
1982	Precious Lord
1983	I'll Rise Again
1985	He Is the Light
1993	Don't Look Back
2003	I Can't Stop
2005	Everything's OK

Hall & Oates

1972	Whole Oates
1973	Abandoned Luncheonette
1974	War Babies
1976	Bigger than the Both of Us
1980	Voices
1981	Private Eyes
1982	H2O
1983	Rock 'N Soul: Greatest Hits Pt 1
1984	Big Bam Boom
1988	Ooh Yeah

Whitney Houston

1985	Whitney Houston
1987	Whitney
1990	I'm Your Baby Tonight
1992	The Bodyguard
1998	My Love Is Your Love
2000	The Greatest Hits
2002	Just Whitney

The Impressions

1989	The Definitive Impressions
1992	The Anthology 1961–1977
1997	The Very Best of the Impressions
2001	Ultimate Collection

Janet Jackson

1982	Janet Jackson
1984	Dream Street
1986	Control
1989	Rhythm Nation 1814
1993	Janet
1995	Design of a Decade: 1986–1996
1997	The Velvet Rope
2001	All for You
2004	Damita Jo
2006	20 Y.O.

Michael Jackson

1972	Ben
1979	Off the Wall
1982	Thriller
1987	Bad
1992	Dangerous
1995	HIStory
1997	Blood On the Dance Floor
2001	Invincible

The Jam

1977	In the City
	This Is the Modern World
1978	All Mod Cons
1979	Setting Sons
1980	Sound Effects
1982	The Gift
1983	Snap

Jay-Z

1996	Reasonable Doubt
1997	In My Lifetime, Vol. 1
1998	Vol. 2: Hard Knock Life
1999	Vol. 3: Life and Times of S. Carter
2001	The Blueprint
2003	The Black Album
2006	Kingdom Come

Billy Joel

1971	Cold Spring Harbor
1973	Piano Man
1974	Streetlight Serenade
1976	Turnstiles
1977	The Stranger
1978	52nd Street
1980	Glass Houses

1982	The Nylon Curtain
1983	An Innocent Man
1986	The Bridge
1989	Storm Front
1993	River of Dreams
2001	The Essential Billy Joel

Elton John

1969	Empty Sky
1970	Elton John
1971	Madman Across the Water
	Tumbleweed Connection
1972	Honky Chateau
1973	Don't Shoot Me, I'm Only the
	Piano Player
	Goodbye Yellow Brick Road
1974	Caribou
1975	Captain Fantastic and the
	Brown Dirt Cowboy
	Rock of the Westies
1976	Blue Moves
1979	Victim of Love
1980	21 at 33
1983	Too Low for Zero
1986	Leather Jackets
1988	Reg Strikes Back
2001	Songs From the West Coast
2002	Greatest Hits 1970–2002
2006	The Captain and the Kid

Carole King

1970	Writer
1971	Tapestry
	Music
1972	Rhymes & Reasons
1973	Fantasy
1974	Wrap Around Joy
1975	Really Rosie
1976	Thoroughbred
1982	One to One
1989	City Streets

Madonna

1983	Madonna
1984	Like a Virgin
1986	True Blue
1987	Who's that Girl
1989	Like a Prayer
1990	I'm Breathless
1990	Immaculate Collection
1992	Erotica
1994	Bedtime Stories
1995	Something to Remember
1997	Evita
1998	Ray of Light
2000	Music
2001	GHV2
2003	American Life
2005	Confessions on a Dance Floor

Barry Manilow

1973	Barry Manilow
1974	Barry Manilow II
1975	Tryin' to Get the Feeling
1976	This One's for You
1977	Live
1978	Even Now
1979	One Voice
1981	If I Should Love Again
1987	Swing Street
2005	The Essential Barry Manilow
2006	The Greatest Songs of the
	Fifties
	The Greatest Songs of the
	Sixties

Paul McCartney

1970	McCartney
1971	Ram
	Wild Life
1973	Red Rose Speedway
	Band on the Run
1975	Venus and Mars
1976	Wings at the Speed of Sound
	Wings Over America
1978	London Town
	Wings Greatest
1979	Back to the Egg
1982	Tug of War
1988	Choba B CCCP
1993	Off the Ground
1997	Flaming Pie
1999	Run Devil Run
2001	Wingspan

George Michael

1987	Faith
1990	Listen Without Prejudice, Vol. 1
1996	Older
2004	Patience

Moby

1992	Moby
1993	Ambient
1995	Everything Is Wrong
1996	Animal Rights
1999	Play
2002	18
2005	Hotel

The Monkees

1966	The Monkees
1967	More Of The Monkees
	Headquarters
	Pisces, Aquarius, Capricorn &
	Jones Ltd.
1968	The Birds, the Bees & the
	Monkees
	Head
1986	Pool It!
1996	Justus
2003	The Best of the Monkees

Rick Nelson

| 1990 | Legendary Masters |
| 2005 | Greatest Hits |

No Doubt

1992	No Doubt
1995	Beacon Street Collection
	Tragic Kingdom
2000	Return to Saturn
2001	Rock Steady
2003	The Singles 1992–2003

Olivia Newton-John

1971	If Not for You
1973	Let Me Be There
1974	If You Love Me, Let Me Know
1975	Have You Never Been Mellow
1978	Totally Hot
1981	Physical

2005   GOLD

*NSYNC
1998   *NSYNC
2000   NO STRINGS ATTACHED
2001   CELEBRITY
2005   GREATEST HITS

OASIS
1994   DEFINITELY MAYBE
1995   (WHAT'S THE STORY) MORNING
         GLORY
1997   BE HERE NOW
1998   THE MASTERPLAN
2000   STANDING ON THE SHOULDERS OF
         GIANTS
2002   HEATHEN CHEMISTRY
2005   DON'T BELIEVE THE TRUTH
2006   STOP THE CLOCKS

THE O'JAYS
1969   THE O'JAYS IN PHILADELPHIA
1972   BACK STABBERS
1973   SHIP AHOY
1991   EMOTIONALLY YOURS
2001   THE ULTIMATE O'JAYS

P. DIDDY
1997   NO WAY OUT
1999   FOREVER
2001   THE SAGA CONTINUES
2006   PRESS PLAY

PET SHOP BOYS
1986   PLEASE
1987   ACTUALLY
1988   INTROSPECTIVE
1990   BEHAVIOR
1991   DISCOGRAPHY
1993   VERY
1996   BILINGUAL
1999   NIGHTLIFE
2002   RELEASE
2003   POP ART
2006   FUNDAMENTAL

WILSON PICKETT
1965   IN THE MIDNIGHT HOUR
1966   THE WICKED PICKETT
1967   THE SOUND OF WILSON PICKETT
1992   A MAN AND A HALF
1993   THE VERY BEST OF WILSON PICKETT

THE PLATTERS
1991   THE MAGIC TOUCH: AN
         ANTHOLOGY
1998   ENCHANTED: THE BEST OF THE
         PLATTERS

ELVIS PRESLEY
1956   ELVIS PRESLEY
         ELVIS
1957   LOVING YOU
1958   KING CREOLE
1959   50,000,000 ELVIS FANS CAN'T
         BE WRONG
1960   ELVIS IS BACK!
1961   BLUE HAWAII
1967   HOW GREAT THOU ART
1969   FROM ELVIS IN MEMPHIS
1970   ELVIS IN PERSON AT THE
         INTERNATIONAL HOTEL, LAS VEGAS
1974   A LEGENDARY PERFORMER VOL. 1
1987   THE COMPLETE SUN SESSIONS
1991   NBC-TV SPECIAL
1992   THE KING OF ROCK 'N' ROLL: THE
         COMPLETE 50S MASTERS
1993   FROM NASHVILLE TO MEMPHIS:
         THE ESSENTIAL 60S MASTERS
1995   COMMAND PERFORMANCES: THE
         ESSENTIAL 60S MASTERS II
         WALK A MILE IN MY SHOES: THE
         ESSENTIAL 70S MASTERS
1999   ARTIST OF THE CENTURY
2002   1'S
2006   THE COMPLETE MILLION DOLLAR
         QUARTET

PRINCE
1978   FOR YOU
1979   PRINCE
1980   DIRTY MIND
1981   CONTROVERSY

1983   1999
1984   PURPLE RAIN
1985   AROUND THE WORLD IN A DAY
1986   PARADE
1987   SIGN O THE TIMES
         THE BLACK ALBUM
1988   LOVESEXY
1991   DIAMONDS AND PEARLS
1992   LOVE SYMBOL
1993   HITS/THE B-SIDES
1994   COME
1995   THE GOLD EXPERIENCE
1996   EMANCIPATION
1998   CRYSTAL BALL
2004   MUSICOLOGY
2006   3121

BONNIE RAITT
1971   BONNIE RAITT
1972   GIVE IT UP
1973   TAKIN' MY TIME
1974   STREETLIGHTS
1975   HOME PLATE
1977   SWEET FORGIVENESS
1979   THE GLOW
1982   GREEN LIGHT
1986   NINE LIVES
1989   NICK OF TIME
1990   THE BONNIE RAITT COLLECTION
1991   LUCK OF THE DRAW
1994   LONGING IN THEIR HEARTS
1998   FUNDAMENTAL
2002   SILVER LINING
2003   THE BEST OF BONNIE RAITT ON
         CAPITOL 1989–2003

CLIFF RICHARD
1959   CLIFF
2002   SINGLES COLLECTION
2003   30 YEARS OF HITS

LIONEL RICHIE
1982   LIONEL RICHIE
1983   CAN'T SLOW DOWN
1986   DANCING ON THE CEILING
1996   LOUDER THAN WORDS
1998   TIME

2001	Renaissance
2003	The Definitive Collection
2004	Just for You
2006	Coming Home

Linda Ronstadt

1969	Hand Sown . . . Home Grown
1970	Silk Purse
1971	Linda Ronstadt
1973	Don't Cry Now
1974	Heart Like a Wheel
1975	Prisoner In Disguise
1976	Hasten Down the Wind
1977	Simple Dreams
1978	Living In the USA
1980	Mad Love
1982	Get Closer
1983	What's New
1984	Lush Life
1986	For Sentimental Reasons
1987	Canciones de Mi Padre
1989	Cry Like A Rainstorm—Howl Like The Wind
1990	Mas Canciones
1994	Winter Light
1995	Feels Like Home
2002	The Very Best of Linda Ronstadt

Run-DMC

1984	Run-DMC
1985	King of Rock
1986	Raising Hell
1988	Tougher Than Leather
1990	Back from Hell
1993	Down With the King
1999	Crown Royal
2002	Greatest Hits

Frank Sinatra

1955	In the Wee Small Hours
1956	Songs for Swingin' Lovers
1957	Come Fly with Me
	A Swingin' Affair
1958	Only the Lonely
1959	Come Dance with Me!
1960	Ring-A-Ding-Ding

1960	Nice 'N' Easy
1962	Sinatra & Strings
1965	September of My Years
1966	Strangers in the Night
	Sinatra at the Sands
1967	Francis Albert Sinatra & Antonio Carlos Jobim
1973	Ol' Blue Eyes Is Back
1984	L.A.Is My Lady
1990	The Capitol Years
1991	Sinatra Reprise: The Very Good Years
1996	Swing And Dance With Frank Sinatra
1997	Portrait of Sinatra: Columbia Classics
2005	The Essential Frank Sinatra with the Tommy Dorsey Orchestra

Sly & the Family Stone

1967	A Whole New Thing
1968	Dance to the Music
	Life
1969	Stand!
1970	Greatest Hits
1971	There's a Riot Goin' on
1973	Fresh
1974	Small Talk
1975	High On You
1976	Heard Ya Missed Me, Well I'm Back
1979	Back on the Right Track
1983	Ain't But the One Way

Britney Spears

1999	Baby One More Time
2000	Oops . . . I Did It Again
2001	Britney
2003	In the Zone
2004	Greatest Hits: My Prerogative

Phil Spector

| 1963 | A Christmas Gift for You |
| 1991 | Back to Mono (1958–1969) |

Spice Girls

1996	Spice
1997	Spiceworld
2000	Forever

The Spinners

1970	2nd Time Around
1972	Spinners
1974	Mighty Love
	New And Improved
1975	Pick of the Litter
1993	The Very Best of the Spinners

Dusty Springfield

1964	A Girl Called Dusty
	Stay Awhile—I Only Want to Be with You
1965	Ev'rything's Coming Up Dusty
1966	You Don't Have to Say You Love Me
1967	The Look of Love
1969	Dusty In Memphis
1970	A Brand New Me
1998	The Very Best of Dusty Springfield
2001	Ultimate Collection

Gwen Stefani

| 2004 | Love.Angel.Music.Baby |
| 2006 | The Sweet Escape |

Rod Stewart

1969	The Rod Stewart Album
1970	Gasoline Alley
1971	Every Picture Tells a Story
1972	Never a Dull Moment
1975	Atlantic Crossing
1977	Foot Loose and Fancy Free
1978	Blondes Have More Fun
1980	Foolish Behaviour
1981	Tonight I'm Yours
1989	Storyteller: the Complete Anthology
1996	Handbags & Gladrags
2002	It Had to Be You: the Great American Songbook

2003 As Time Goes By: the Great American Songbook Vol. 2
2004 Stardust: the Great American Songbook Vol. 3
2005 Thanks For The Memory: the Great American Songbook Vol. 4
2006 Still The Same: Great Rock Classics Of Our Time

Barbra Streisand

1963 The Barbra Streisand Album
     The Second Barbra Streisand Album
1964 The Third Album
     People
1965 My Name Is Barbra
1970 Greatest Hits
1971 Stoney End
     Barbra Joan Streisand
1974 The Way We Were
1978 Songbird
     Barbra Streisand's Greatest Hits Vol. 2
1980 Guilty
1985 The Broadway Album
2002 The Essential Barbra Streisand

Donna Summer

1975 Love To Love You Baby
1978 Live And More
1979 Bad Girls
     On the Radio
1980 The Wanderer
1983 She Walks Hard for the Money
1994 Endless Summer

The Supremes

1964 Where Did Our Love Go
1966 I Hear A Symphony
2005 Gold

James Taylor

1968 James Taylor
1970 Sweet Baby James

1971 Mud Slide Slim & the Blue Horizon
1972 One Man Dog
1974 Walking Man
1975 Gorilla
1976 In the Pocket
     Greatest Hits
1977 JT
1979 Flag
1981 Dad Loves His Work
1985 That's Why I'm Here
1988 Never Die Young
1991 New Moon Shine
1993 Live
1997 Hourglass
2002 October Road

Justin Timberlake

2002 Justified
2006 FutureSex/LoveSounds

TLC

1992 Ooooooohhh . . . On the TLC Tip
1994 CrazySexyCool
1999 FanMail
2002 3D
2004 Now and Forever: the Hits

Shania Twain

1993 Shania Twain
1995 The Woman in Me
1997 Come on Over
2002 Up!
2004 Greatest Hits

Dionne Warwick

1964 Anyone Who Had a Heart
1965 Here I Am
1967 The Windows of the World
1989 The Dionne Warwick Collection: All-Time Greatest Hits

Jackie Wilson

1992 Mr. Excitement
1993 The Very Best of Jackie Wilson

Stevie Wonder

1962 The Jazz Soul of Little Stevie
1963 The 12 Year Old Genius
1971 Where I'm Coming From
1972 Music of My Mind
     Talking Book
1973 Innervisions
1974 Fulfillingness' First Finale
1976 Songs In the Key of Life
1977 Looking Back
1979 Journey Through the Secret Life of Plants
1980 Hotter than July
1982 Original Musicquarium I
1985 In Square Circle
1987 Characters
1991 Jungle Fever
1995 Conversation Peace
     Natural Wonder
2002 Definitive Collection
2005 A Time to Love

BIBLIOGRAPHY

Books

BOWMAN, ROB. *SOULSVILLE USA: THE STORY OF STAX RECORDS*. NEW YORK: SCHIRMER BOOKS, 1997.

BROWN, JAMES AND BRUCE TUCKER. *JAMES BROWN: THE GODFATHER OF SOUL*. NEW YORK: THUNDER'S MOUTH PRESS, 1997.

CARLIN, PETER AMES. *CATCH A WAVE: THE RISE FALL AND REDEMPTION OF THE BEACH BOYS' BRIAN WILSON*. EMMAUS, PA.: RODALE BOOKS, 2006.

CHARLES, RAY AND DAVID RITZ. *BROTHER RAY*. CAMBRIDGE, MASS.: DA CAPO PRESS, 2004.

DIORIO, AL. *BOBBY DARIN, THE INCREDIBLE STORY OF AN AMAZING LIFE*. PHILADELPHIA: RUNNING PRESS, 2004.

DOBKIN, MATT. *I NEVER LOVED A MAN THE WAY I LOVE YOU: ARETHA FRANKLIN*. NEW YORK: ST. MARTIN'S PRESS, 2004.

ELLIOTT, BRAD. *SURF'S UP! THE BEACH BOYS ON RECORD 1961–1981*. N.P.: SURF'S UP BOOKS, 2003.

FONG-TORRES, BEN. "RAY CHARLES, 1973." IN *THE ROLLING STONE INTERVIEWS 1967-1980*, EDITED BY PETER HERBST, 258–271. NEW YORK: ST. MARTIN'S PRESS, 1981.

FONG-TORRES, BEN. "STEVIE WONDER, 1973." IN *THE ROLLING STONE INTERVIEWS 1967-1980*, EDITED BY PETER HERBST, 280–287. NEW YORK: ST. MARTIN'S PRESS, 1981.

FONG-TORRES, BEN. *THE MOTOWN ALBUM*. NEW YORK: ST. MARTIN'S PRESS, 1990.

GAMBACCINI, PAUL. "ELTON JOHN, 1973." IN *THE ROLLING STONE INTERVIEWS 1967–1980*, EDITED BY PETER HERBST, 288–299. NEW YORK: ST. MARTIN'S PRESS, 1981.

GEORGE, NELSON. *THE DEATH OF RHYTHM & BLUES*. NEW YORK: E.P. DUTTON, 1989.

GEORGE, NELSON. *WHERE DID OUR LOVE GO?* LONDON: OMNIBUS PRESS, 2003.

GILLETT, CHARLIE. *THE SOUND OF THE CITY*. CAMBRIDGE, MASS.: DA CAPO PRESS, 1996.

GOODMAN, FRED. *MANSION ON THE HILL*. NEW YORK: VINTAGE BOOKS, 1998.

GRAY, MICHAEL. *THE BOB DYLAN ENCYCLOPEDIA*. NEW YORK: THE CONTINUUM INTERNATIONAL PUBLISHING GROUP, 2006.

GURALNICK, PETER. *DREAM BOOGIE: THE TRIUMPH OF SAM COOKE*. NEW YORK: LITTLE, BROWN & CO., 2005.

GURALNICK, PETER. *CARELESS LOVE*. NEW YORK: LITTLE, BROWN & CO., 1999.

GURALNICK, PETER. *LAST TRAIN TO MEMPHIS*. BOSTON: BACK BAY BOOKS, 1994.

GURALNICK, PETER. *LOST HIGHWAY*. NEW YORK: HARPER & ROW, 1989.

GURALNICK, PETER. *SWEET SOUL MUSIC*. NEW YORK: HARPER & ROW, 1986.

HANNUSCH, JEFF. *I HEAR YOU KNOCKIN'*. VILLE PLATTE, LA.: SWALLOW PUBLICATIONS, 2005.

HANSEN, BARRY. "DOO-WOP." IN *THE ROLLING STONE ILLUSTRATED HISTORY OF ROCK & ROLL*, EDITED BY JIM MILLER, 83–91. NEW YORK: RANDOM HOUSE, 1980.

HANSEN, BARRY. "RHYTHM AND GOSPEL." IN *THE ROLLING STONE ILLUSTRATED HISTORY OF ROCK & ROLL*, EDITED BY JIM MILLER, 15–18. NEW YORK: RANDOM HOUSE, 1980.

HARRIS, JOHN. *BRITPOP!: COOL BRITANNIA AND THE SPECTACULAR DEMISE OF ENGLISH ROCK*. CAMBRIDGE, MASS.: DA CAPO PRESS, 2004.

LEFCOWITZ, ERIC. *THE MONKEES TALE*. N.P.: LAST GASP, 1989.

LENNON, JOHN ET.AL. *THE BEATLES ANTHOLOGY*. SAN FRANCISCO: CHRONICLE BOOKS, 2000.

MARCUS, GREIL. *MYSTERY TRAIN*. NEW YORK: DUTTON, 1990.

MARSH, DAVE. *THE HEART OF ROCK N SOUL*. NEW YORK: PLUME BOOKS, 1989.

McDonough, Jimmy. *Shakey: Neil Young's Biography*. New York: Anchor Books, 2003.

McEwan, Joe. "Jackie Wilson." In *The Rolling Stone Illustrated History of Rock & Roll*, edited by Jim Miller, 117–119. New York: Random House, 1980.

McEwan, Joe. "The Sound Of Chicago." In *The Rolling Stone Illustrated History of Rock & Roll*, edited by Jim Miller, 143–147. New York: Random House, 1980.

Rachlis, Kit. "The Everly Brothers." In *The Rolling Stone Illustrated History of Rock & Roll*, edited by Jim Miller, 72–76. New York: Random House, 1980.

Reynolds, Simon. *Rip It Up and Start Again*. New York: Penguin Books, 2006.

Ribowski, Mark. *He's A Rebel: Phil Spector: Rock & Roll's Legendary Producer*. Cambridge, Mass: Da Capo Press, 2007.

Ritz, David. *Divided Soul: The Life of Marvin Gaye*. Cambridge, Mass.: Da Capo Press, 1991.

Roberts, David, ed. *British Hit Singles & Albums*. N.P: Guinness World Records, 2006.

Shaw, Greg. "Brill Building Pop." In *The Rolling Stone Illustrated History of Rock & Roll*, edited by Jim Miller, 120–128. New York: Random House, 1980.

Ward, Ed et al. *Rock of Ages*. New York: Rolling Stone Press, 1986.

Wenner, Jann. "Phil Spector, 1969." In *The Rolling Stone Interviews 1967–1980*, edited by Peter Herbst, 60–75. New York: St. Martin's Press, 1981.

Werbin, Stuart. "James Taylor and Carly Simon, 1973." In *The Rolling Stone Interviews 1967–1980*, edited by Peter Herbst, 246–257. New York: St. Martin's Press, 1981.

Werner, Craig. *Higher Ground: Stevie Wonder, Aretha Franklin, Curtis Mayfield and the Rise and Fall of American Soul*. New York: Crown Publishers, 2004.

Wexler, Jerry and David Ritz. *The Rhythm and the Blues*. New York: Alfred A. Knopf, 1993.

Whitburn, Joel. *Top Pop Singles 1955–2002*. Menomonee Falls, Wis.: Record Research Inc. 2003.

Whitburn, Joel. *Top R&B Singles 1942-1988*. Menomonee Falls, Wis.: Record Research Inc. 1988.

White, Adam and Fred Bronson, *The Billboard Book of #1 R&B Hits*. New York: Billboard Books, 1993.

White, Timothy. "Billy Joel, 1980." In *The Rolling Stone Interviews 1967–1980*, edited by Peter Herbst, 414–423. New York: St. Martin's Press, 1981.

White, Timothy. *Rock Lives*. New York: Henry Holt, 1990.

Winner, Langdon. "The Sound Of New Orleans." In *The Rolling Stone Illustrated History of Rock & Roll*, edited by Jim Miller, 35–44. New York: Random House, 1980.

Wolfe, Tom. "The First Tycoon of Teen." In *The Kandy-Kolored Tangerine-Flake Streamline Baby*. New York: Bantam, 1999.

NEWSPAPER ARTICLES

Anderman, Joan. "Accidental Rock Star? Moby's Mix Plays Well." *Boston Globe*, October 19, 2000, Arts Section, Third Edition.

Bakker, Tiffany. "Christina Aguilera—Has the Dirty Girl Cleaned Up Her Act?" *Sunday Telegraph Magazine*, August 6, 2006.

Bledsoe, Wayne. "Volumes of Success; Olivia Newton-John Wrote the Book on Pop Music." *Knoxville News-Sentinel*, September 15, 2002, Showtime Section, Final Edition.

Boehm, Mike. "No Doubt Given Room to Grow." *Los Angeles Times*, April 2, 1992, Entertainment Desk, Orange County Edition.

Boehm, Mike. "Orange, Blond, Platinum." *Los Angeles Times*, February 16, 1997. Calendar Desk, Home Edition.

Boehm, Mike. "The Certainty of No Doubt." *Los Angeles Times*, March 16, 1996, Entertainment Desk, Orange County Edition.

Boucher, Geoff and Randy Lewis. "Ahmet Ertegun: 1923–2006; His Atlantic Records Shaped Pop Music." *Los Angeles Times*, December 15, 2006, Metro Desk, Home Edition.

Boyar, Jay. "Streisand on Streisand." *Orlando Sentinel*, December 22, 1991, Arts & Entertainment Section, 3 Star Edition.

Brady, Emma. "The Saturday Interview—Living Legend Just Keeps on Movin'." *Birmingham Post*, June 19, 2004.

Bream, Jon and Chris Riemenschneider. "Prince: An Oral History." *Star-Tribune* (Minneapolis), March 14, 2004, Metro Edition.

"Britney Spears: Teen Pop's Reigning Princess." *BPI Entertainment News Wire*, March 3, 1999.

Broder, John. "Michael Jackson Is Booked on Molesting Charges That He Calls Lies." *New York Times*, November 21, 2003, National Desk, Late Edition—Final.

Brown, Joe. "Moby: Sailing Beneath the Raves." *The Washington Post*, October 29, 1993, Weekend Section, Final Edition.

Clarke, Norm. "Henley Says Eagles Working on Album." *Las Vegas Review Journal*, January 30, 2007.

Cromelin, Richard. "Felice Bryant, 77; Songwriter Penned Pop Hits of 1950s." *Los Angeles Times*, April 23, 2003, Metro Desk, Home Edition.

Di Nunzio, Miriam. "Rock's Golden Boy: Jon Bon Jovi Still Rollin' Out the Hits." *Chicago Sun-Times*, July 21, 2006, Weekend Section, Final Edition.

Di Nunzio, Miriam. "Singing Songs She Loves So Easy for Ronstadt." *Chicago Sun-Times*, June 11, 2004, Weekend Plus Section, North City Zone Edition.

D'Silva, Beverley. "Grease Is Still the Word." *Sunday Times*, June 28, 1998.

Eckstein, Sandra. "Lopes Pleads Guilty to Arson In Blaze at Rison's House." *Atlanta Journal*, December 29, 1994, Local News Section.

Emerson, Bo. "O'Jays Doing OK . . . Again Back on the Charts, 29 Years (And A Musical Generation) Later." *Atlanta Journal and Constitution*, December 26, 1987, Leisure Guide Section.

Farhi, Paul. "Settling an Old Score? Singer Michael Bolton Lost a Plagiarism Fight, But He Could Win R&B Legend Ronald Isley's Fortune." *The Washington Post*, February 22, 2000, Style Section, Final Edition.

Finn, Timothy. "Elements of Success: Great Music, Great Shows Earth, Wind & Fire Nears Three Decades of Soul, Jazz & Pop." *Kansas City Star*, September 18, 1998, Metropolitan Edition.

"Five Go Wild In Hotpants." *Scotland on Sunday*, December 22, 1996.

Franks, Alan. "Let Him Be (Interview with Paul McCartney)." *The Times* (London), November 6, 2004, Magazine Section.

Gould, Phil. "Profile—Sir Cliff Richard—Bachelor Boy Hits the Big 60." *Belfast News Letter*, October 10, 2000.

Graham, Jefferson. "Wilburys, a.k.a. Super Rockers." *USA Today*, October 17, 1988, Life Section, Final Edition.

Greene, Bob. "Jackie Wilson: May He Rest In Peace." *Chicago Tribune*, June 30, 1987, Tempo Section, Sports Final Edition.

Gross, Joe. "Singer's Remarks Stir Up Country." *Austin American-Statesman*, March 15, 2003.

Gunderson, Edna. "Rick Rubin, Music's Rock." *USA Today*, July 7, 2006, Life Section, Final Edition.

Hand, Lise. "Summer of Wham!" *Sunday Tribune* (Ireland), June 29, 2003.

Harrington, Richard. "Bonnie Raitt, Dry and High; The Singer's Long Road to Sobriety and a Hit Album." *The Washington Post*, June 13, 1989, Style Section, Final Edition.

Harrington, Richard. "Jay-Z's Rhymes of Passion; The Master Rapper, Putting the Heart of Ghetto Life Into His Hard-Core Tracks." *The Washington Post*, January 2, 2000, Sunday Arts Section, Final Edition.

Harrington, Richard. "Lionel Richie: He Writes the Songs." *The Washington Post*, May 27. 1984.

Harrington, Richard. "Run-DMC and the Rap Flap For a Hot Trio, Violence & Criticism on the Concert Trail." *The Washington Post*, August 29, 1986.

Harris, Beth. "Whitney's Tribute to Mentor Marred by Odd Behavior." *Associated Press*, April 12, 2000.

Hilburn, Robert. "Clive Davis; Hands On, Hands Off." *Los Angeles Times*, January 14, 2007, Calendar Desk, Home Edition.

Hilburn, Robert. "Does He Still Have the Rx?" *Los Angeles Times*, October 24, 1999, Calendar Desk, Home Edition.

Hilburn, Robert. "Eurythmics Use Tension to Bring Emotions to Their Music." *Los Angeles Times*, August 10, 1986.

Hoerburger, Rob. "The Power of Love." *New York Times*, June 20, 1993, Magazine Desk, Late Edition—Final.

Holden, Stephen. "Frank Sinatra Dies at 82; Matchless Stylist of Pop." *New York Times*, May 16, 1998, Cultural Desk.

Holden, Stephen. "Madonna Goes Heavy on Heart." *New York Times*, June 26, 1986, Arts and Leisure Desk, Late City Final Edition.

Holden, Stephen. "Sammy Cahn, Word Weaver of Tin Pan Alley, Dies at 79." *New York Times*, January 16, 1993, Cultural Desk, Late Edition—Final.

Holden, Stephen. "The Pop Life (Interview with Mariah Carey)." *New York Times*, June 13, 1990, Cultural Desk, Late Edition—Final.

Hunt, Dennis. "Pet Shop Boys Try to Keep a Low Profile." *Los Angeles Times*, May 29, 1988, Calendar Desk, Home Edition.

Hunt, Dennis. "Celine Dion: Canadian Singer Branches Out—to Danceable Pop and a U.S. Audience." *Los Angeles Times*, April 14, 1991, Calendar Desk, Home Edition.

Jones, Jack. "Rick Nelson Killed in Plane Crash." *Los Angeles Times*, January 1, 1986, National Desk, Home Edition.

Kim, Jae-Ha. "Boys Named Goo—Wheel of Fortune Lands on Dolls After Nine Years." *Chicago Sun Times*, April 30, 1995, Showcase Section, Late Sports Final Edition.

Law, Cally. "Genesis of a Band." *The Times* (London), July 24, 2004, Features Section, Home Edition.

Leeds, Jeff. "Virgin Records Bets Big on Carey's $80-Million Deal." *Los Angeles Times*, April 4, 2001, Financial Desk, Home Edition.

Lewis, Randy. "Gwen: Solo. Bolder. Wiser." *Los Angeles Times*, November 7, 2004, Calendar Desk, Home Edition.

Marshall, Scott. "Singer Lopes Free After Bond Is Cut On Arson Charge." *Atlanta Constitution*, June 11, 1994. Local News Section.

Matsumoto, Jon. "Wilson Pickett Plans to Pick Up Where He Left Off." *Los Angeles Times*, September 22, 1995, Entertainment Desk, Orange County Edition.

McAllister, Sue. "Pop Singer George Michael Arrested in Restroom of Beverly Hills Park Courts." *Los Angeles Times*, April 9, 1998, Metro Desk, Home Edition.

McDaniel, Mike. "'Tis Garth Brooks—What's a Phenomenon Like Him Doing in an Interview Like This?" *Houston Chronicle*, March 1, 1998, Features Section, 2-Star Edition.

McLeese, Don. "Houston Label Made 45s With A .45." *Austin American-Statesman*, January 7, 1993, Onward Section, Final Edition.

McFadden, Robert D. "Stampede at City College." *New York Times*, December 30, 1991, Metropolitan Desk, Late Edition—Final.

McMillan, Penelope. "Nelson Riddle, Composer and Arranger for Top Stars, Dies." *Los Angeles Times*, October 7, 1985, Metro Desk, Home Edition.

McNair, James. "She's Still Standing." *The Independent*, October 19, 2006, The Independent, Features Section.

Mervis, Scott. "The Spinners: How Motown Outcasts Became Stars." *Pittsburgh Post-Gazette*, July 4, 2003, Arts & Entertainment Section.

"Monkee Shines Decades Later, Group's Bassist Is Still a Believer." *Arizona Republic*, April 5, 2001, The Rep Section, Final Chaser Edition.

Morast, Robert. "20 Years of Madonna." *Argus Leader*, July 20, 2003, Life Section.

Morrow, Terry. "Dionne; 'I Am Not A Diva,' She Declares." *The Knoxville News-Sentinel*, January 7, 2000, Final Edition.

Morse, Steve. "Rod Stewart Digs Into His Past." *Boston Globe*, May 5, 1993, Living Section, City Edition.

Morse, Steve. "The Diamond Touch 30 Years Later." *Boston Globe*, August 28, 1992, Arts & Film Section, City Edition.

Morse, Steve. "Traveling Wilburys Look Familiar." *Boston Globe*, August 26, 1988, Arts and Film Section, Third Edition.

Neister, Alan. "Queen of Pop Takes Common Approach (Stevie Nicks interview)." *The Globe and Mail* (Toronto), May 12 2001, Weekend Review Section, Metro Edition.

Nixon, Chris. "Can He Get A Witness? (Al Green Interview)." *San Diego Union Tribune*, June 19, 2003. Entertainment Section.

Palmer, Robert. "Jackson Browne Belts It Out." *New York Times*. July 31, 1983, Arts and Leisure Desk, Late City Final Edition.

Palmer, Robert. "Marvin Gaye Is Shot And Killed." *New York Times*, April 2, 1984.

Pareles, Jon. "James Brown, the Godfather of Soul, Dies at 73." *The New York Times*, December 26, 2006, Cultural/Arts Section, Late Edition—Final.

Pareles, Jon. "Lisa Lopes, Rapper, Dies in Honduras Crash at 30." *New York Times*. April 27, 2002, National Desk.

Patterson, Bryan. "King Is Queen of Charts." *Sunday Herald Sun* (Australia), August 20, 2006, First Edition.

Perkins, Ken Parish. "Talent Drives This Music Machine." *The Dallas Morning News*, December 4, 1990, Today Section, Home Final Edition.

Perusse, Bernard. "'Midwife' To Rock 'N' Roll: Singer Pat Boone Says He Helped Turn Whites on to R&B." *Montreal Gazette*, January 5, 2005, Arts & Life Section. Final Edition.

Philips, Chuck, "Bad Bay II Man Sean "Puffy" Combs has Ambition to Match his Talent and Ego." *Los Angeles Times*, May 25, 1997, Calendar Desk, Home Edition.

Philips, Chuck. "John, Taupin To Ink $39-Million Publishing Pact Pop Music." *Los Angeles Times*, November 4, 1992, Entertainment Desk, Home Edition.

Purcell, Andrew. "I Saw the Devil Himself (Interview with Dion)." *The Guardian*, December 15 2006, Film & Music Section.

Raihala, Ross. "Now, It's Time for Al Green's Fans to Keep the Faith." *St. Paul Pioneer Press*, May 19, 2005, Weekend Life Section, St. Paul Edition.

Riemenschneider, Chris. "Jackson Will Re-Record 'Care' Lyrics Pop Music." *Los Angeles Times*, June 23, 1995, Entertainment Desk, Home Edition.

"Rev C.L. Franklin, 69 (Obituary)." *The Washington Post*, July 29, 1984.

Ross, Barbara and Bill Hutchinson. "Pick Trash or Jail, Boy George Told." *New York Daily News*, June 27, 2006, News Section, City Final Edition.

Ross, Barbara et al. "Puffy Hit With 2 Gun Raps Weapons Charges in Club Shooting." *New York Daily News*, January 14, 2000, News Section, Final Edition.

Schoemer, Karen. "Bobby (Blue) Bland, Honored at Last." *New York Times*, November 22, 1991, Weekend Desk, Late Edition—Final.

SELVIN, JOEL. "OPEN SEASONS." SAN FRANCISCO CHRONICLE, DECEMBER 3, 2006, SUNDAY DATEBOOK SECTION, FINAL EDITION.

SHERMAN, MARK AND SCOTT MARSHALL. "FIRE GUTS HOME OF FALCONS' RISON." ATLANTA JOURNAL, JUNE 9, 1994, LOCAL NEWS SECTION.

SIEGAL, BUDDY. "HARLEY CRASH JUST A TEMPORARY SETBACK AS EX-CHICAGO SINGER PETER CETERA HITS THE ROAD TO TOUT LATEST CD." LOS ANGELES TIMES, NOVEMBER 14, 1995, ENTERTAINMENT DESK, ORANGE COUNTY EDITION.

SMITH, ANDREW. "I ALWAYS THOUGHT BEING FAMOUS . . . " (INTERVIEW WITH JUSTINE FRISCHMANN) THE OBSERVER, MARCH 10, 2002.

STANLEY, BOB. "THE BROTHERS WIN, THEN THE BROTHERS GRIM." THE TIMES (LONDON), OCTOBER 21, 2005. FEATURES SECTION.

"STEFANI EXCITED AT MAKING NO DOUBT'S 'GREATEST RECORD.'" WORLD ENTERTAINMENT NEWS NETWORK, MARCH 23, 2007.

STEINER, SUSIE. "FANS PROTEST AT EVANS BAN ON CLIFF RICHARD." THE TIMES (LONDON), OCTOBER 20, 1998.

STEVENSON, RICHARD W. "GEORGE MICHAEL LOSES LAWSUIT AGAINST SONY." NEW YORK TIMES, JUNE 22, 1994, CULTURAL DESK, LATE EDITION—FINAL.

STEWART, LAURA. "FAME IS NICE, BUT FOR '70S STAR LINDA RONSTADT, THE SONG'S THE THING." CHICAGO DAILY HERALD, MARCH 24, 2006, TIME OUT SECTION.

SWIFT, JACQUI. "I WOULD LOVE TO BE RESPECTED LIKE THE ARTISTS THAT HAVE INSPIRED ME (INTERVIEW WITH BEYONCE KNOWLES)." THE SUN. SEPTEMBER 1, 2006, FEATURES SECTION.

TIMMS, ED. "NELSON INQUIRY FOCUSES ON PLANE HEATER." THE DALLAS MORNING NEWS, JANUARY 15, 1986, NEWS DESK, HOME FINAL EDITION.

VAN MATRE, LYNN. "WITH DIONNE, CISSY AND ARETHA IN THE FAMILY, HOW CAN WHITNEY HOUSTON FAIL?" CHICAGO TRIBUNE, SEPTEMBER 29, 1985, ARTS SECTION, FINAL EDITION.

VAZIRI, AIDIN. "GREEN DAY PULLS THE PLUG ON ICONIC BERKELEY INDIE LABEL LOOKOUT OVER UNPAID ROYALTIES." SAN FRANCISCO CHRONI-CLE, AUGUST 6, 2005, DAILY DATEBOOK SECTION, FINAL EDITION.

WAZIR, BURHAN. "NEVER MIND THE AGE GAP (INTERVIEW WITH GREEN DAY)." THE TIMES (LONDON), JULY 2, 2005, MAGAZINE SECTION.

WEATHERFORD, MIKE. "BUCK RAM PROTECTED PLATTERS NAME UNTIL THE END." THE LAS VEGAS REVIEW-JOURNAL, JANUARY 4, 1991.

WEINGARTEN, MIKE. "ALL MADE UP, READY TO GO THERE'S NO STOPPING MISSY 'MISDEMEANOR' ELLIOTT AS SHE SHAKES UP THE MALE-DOMINATED HIP-HOP WORLD." LOS ANGELES TIMES, FEBRUARY 1, 1998, CALENDAR DESK, HOME EDITION.

"WHO KILLED TUPAC SHAKUR?" LOS ANGELES TIMES, SEPTEMBER 7, 2002, BUSINESS DESK, HOME EDITION.

WILLIAMSON, NIGEL. "NAUGHTY LITTLE SISTER—INTERVIEW—JANET JACKSON." THE TIMES (LONDON), MAY 12, 2001.

ZIMMERMAN, DAVID. "TWAIN MEETS COUNTRY: THE CANADIAN ARTIST CLICKS IN NASHVILLE." USA TODAY, JUNE 19, 1995, LIFE SECTION, FINAL EDITION.

"ZOLA TAYLOR, 69, R&B SINGER, IS DEAD." ASSOCIATED PRESS, MAY 1, 2007.

MAGAZINE ARTICLES

"BEATING A BAD RAP; COMBS ON J. LO, FAME AND TRYING TO CLEAR HIS NAME." NEWSWEEK, MAY 20, 2002.

BIRD, MARYANN. "THE SPICE INVADERS." TIME, FEBRUARY 3, 1997.

CROUSE, TIMOTHY. "THE STRUGGLE FOR SLY'S SOUL AT THE GARDEN." ROLLING STONE, OCTOBER 14, 1971.

FONG-TORRES, BEN. "THE TRAVELS OF SYLVESTER STEWART." ROLLING STONE, MARCH 21, 1970.

GOLDMAN, LEA. "CAPITALIST RAP." FORBES, JULY 3, 2006.

GREGORY, SEAN. "DASHING DIVERSIFICATION." TIME, DECEMBER 8, 2003.

Helligar, Jeremy et al. "Against All Odds: Overcoming a Past Filled With Poverty and Sudden Tragedy, Shania Twain Emerges as a Happily Married Pop Superstar." *People*, June 14, 1999.

Hewitt, Paulo. "The Punk and The Godfather." *Melody Maker*, October 11, 1980.

Johnson, Pamela. "Mary J's Moment of Peace." *Essence*, July 1, 1999.

Kenon, Marci. "An Interview With The Boyz." *Billboard*, November 3, 2001.

Kiersh, Edward. "Sly Stone's Heart Of Darkness." *Spin*, December 1985.

"Lionel Richie Survives Three 'Devastating' Events and Returns to his Love of Music." *Jet*, May 20, 1996.

Mitchell, Gail. "Quincy Jones: From Bebop to Hip-Hop." *Billboard*. November 26, 2005.

Paoletta, Michael. "Setting Mimi free: Mariah 'Digs Deep' on upcoming album." *Billboard*, March 28, 2005.

Rosen, Craig. "On Nashville, Christmas, Barbra and Image-breaking (Interview with Donna Summer)." *Billboard*, September 3, 1994.

Sutherland, Mark. "Genesis Revs Back Up with Collins for Stadium Tour." *Billboard*, November 7, 2006.

Taylor, Chuck. "Jive's Britney Spears Sets Top 40 Abuzz With Rhythm-Leaning 'Baby One More Time.'" *Billboard*, October 24, 1998.

Tyrangiel, Josh. "Shania Reigns; Shania Twain Aims To Sell More Records Than Anyone In History—And She Just May." *Time*, December 9, 2002.

Wallwork, Rebecca. "Justin Timberlake: Pop's Biggest Pinup Said Bye Bye Bye to the Pack Life, and Hello to Himself and Respect." *Interview*, February 1, 2003

White, Timothy. "This Is Where We Came In." *Billboard*, March 24, 2001.

Television Shows

Jackson Browne: Going Home. August 1994. Dir. Janice Engel, Disney Channel.

Whitney Houston. *Primetime*. December 4, 2002. Presenter: Diane Sawyer. ABC.

Film

Dixie Chicks. 2006. *Shut Up And Sing*. Produced and directed by Barbara Kopple and Cecilia Peck. New York: The Weinstein Co. DVD.

ACKNOWLEDGMENTS

Tony Sachs read every word of this manuscript, offered suggestions, corrected key errors, and generally raised the quality of the discourse throughout the duration. Even if he weren't my best friend, I would still call him a great editor. Quite simply the book wouldn't exist without his help.

Sylke Jackson was at various times my sparring partner, an astute critic, my confidante, my advocate, my sounding board, and the bane of my existence. In other words, she's an awesome editor.

Nycdonline.blogspot.online provided much needed entertainment and inspiration. Robert MacMillian and David Edelman talked me down from the ledge at key moments and probably don't even realize how important they were to the process. David Schweitzer and Franklin Paul were a big help in the early going.

I'd like to thank my Mom and Dad for making me possible. I'd also like say a special thank you to my grandfather Sam Caney, who is the fount from which all of my musical interest springs.

All U.S. chart positions come from Billboard via Joel Whitburn's Record Research. All U.K. chart positions come from the Official U.K. Charts via Guinness World Records. All information on the Grammys comes from the Recording Academy and grammy.com. The Songwriters Hall of Fame was a fabulous resource of biographical information. Of course, allmusic.com is a Godsend. And Ralph's Pizzeria on Franklin Avenue provided great meatball subs.

Finally, I dedicate this book and everything I will ever write to Deborah Caney and our children Zoe and Jacob. Daddy's coming upstairs now.

PICTURE CREDITS